Consuming Experience

This book is directly linked to the contemporary trend on experiential consumption and marketing. It highlights the idea that an experience is not something that can be readily managed by firms and is not limited to the market: an individual's daily life is made up of consuming experiences that can occur with or without a market relation.

This exciting new text offers an overview of the consumption experience. It outlines a continuum of experiences of consuming that consumers go through:

- Experiences that are mainly constructed by consumers around small items that constitute their daily life, such as organic products and non-profit or local associations.
- Experiences that have been co-developed by companies and consumers. Tourism or adventure projects, rock concerts, and cultural events are part of this approach.
- Experiences that have been largely developed by the companies where consumers are immersed in a hyper-real context such as fashion, sports brands, edutainment, and retail.

Broad and comprehensive, this book provides a challenging vision of the consumption experience.

Antonella Carù is Professor of Marketing at Bocconi University, Milan, Italy.

Bernard Cova is Professor of Marketing at Euromed Marseilles, School of Management, France and Visiting Professor at Bocconi University, Milan, Italy.

Consuming Experience

16510

Edited by

Antonella Carù and Bernard Cova

Routledge
Taylor & Francis Group

LONDON AND NEW YORK

First published 2007
by Routledge
2 Park Square, Milton Park, Abingdon, Oxon OX14 4RN

Simultaneously published in the USA and Canada
by Routledge
270 Madison Ave, New York, NY 10016

Routledge is an imprint of the Taylor & Francis Group

© 2007 Antonella Carù and Bernard Cova for editorial selection and
material; individual contributors, their own contribution

Typeset in Perpetua and Bell Gothic by
Prepress Projects Ltd, Perth, UK
Printed and bound in Great Britain by
Antony Rowe Ltd, Chippenham, Wiltshire

British Library Cataloguing in Publication Data
A catalogue record for this book is available from the British Library

Library of Congress Cataloging in Publication Data
Consuming experience/edited by Antonella Carù and Bernard Cova.
p. cm.
   Includes bibliographical references and index.
   1. Consumer behavior – Social aspects. 2. Identity (Psychology) 3.
Consumption (Economics) – Psychological aspects. 4. Consumers –
Psychology. I. Carù, Antonella. II. Cova, Bernard.
HF5415.32.C6595 2006
658.8′342–dc22
                                    2006014545

ISBN10: 0-415-38243-2 (hbk)
ISBN10: 0-415-38244-0 (pbk)

ISBN13: 978-0-415-38243-4 (hbk)
ISBN13: 978-0-415-38244-1 (pbk)

Contents

CONTENTS

Figures

Tables

Case vignettes

Notes on contributors

Michela Addis is Assistant Professor of Marketing at Universitá Bocconi, Milan. She also teaches at the Marketing Department, SDA Bocconi School of Management. Her research interests refer to postmodernism and consumption experience from both consumers' and companies' perspectives. She has published on these topics in the *Journal of Consumer Behavior* and the *European Journal of Marketing*. Recently, she has also published a marketing book on consumption experience.

Eric J. Arnould is PETSMART Distinguished Professor, Norton School of Family and Consumer Sciences, University of Arizona. Previously, he was the E.J. Faulkner College Professor of Agribusiness and Marketing and Director of CBA Agribusiness Programs at the University of Nebraska-Lincoln. His research on consumer culture theory, services marketing, and African marketing channels appears in the major US marketing journals and other social science periodicals and books. He serves on the review boards of several marketing journals and is active in applied research as well. Dr. Arnould holds a PhD in social anthropology from the University of Arizona.

Olivier Badot is Full Professor at ESCP-EAP Paris, senior researcher at the University of Caen-Basse Normandie (IAE), and Visiting Professor at the School of Management of the University of Ottawa. His research focuses on retailing: he has developed a specific semio-ethnological approach to analyze the roles played by retailers in their environment and to audit their strategies and mix consistency. Professor Badot has published around twenty (individual or collective) books, and many scientific articles and reports, and has given numerous lectures and speeches in French, English, or Spanish. He holds two PhDs: one in industrial economics (ENST Paris) and one in ethnology (La Sorbonne).

Stefania Borghini is Assistant Professor of Marketing at Universitá Bocconi and SDA Bocconi School of Management, Milan. Her research interests are related to organizational creativity, consumer culture theory, symbolic consumption in b2c as well as b2b contexts where she has adopted a postmodern and multiple perspective. She has presented her papers to several academic conferences and published her articles in the *Journal of Knowledge Management* and Italian journals.

Antonella Carù is Professor of Marketing at Universitá Bocconi and SDA Bocconi School of Management, Milan. Her research interests focus on services marketing, arts and cultural marketing, and the experiential perspective on consumption and marketing. She has published on these topics in various national and international journals (*International Journal of Arts Management*, *International Journal of Services Industry Management* and *Marketing Theory*) and books. She is Managing Editor of *Finanza, Marketing e Produzione*, a leading management journal in Italy.

Vanni Codeluppi is Professor of Sociology at IULM University, Milan. He has long studied theories and communicative aspects of consumption, advertising, fashion, shopping centers, and new stores. He has published many articles and books on this topic.

Bernard Cova is Professor of Marketing at Euromed Marseilles – School of Management and Visiting Professor at Universitá Bocconi, Milan. Ever since his first papers in the early 1990s, he has taken part in postmodern trends in consumer research and marketing, while emphasizing a Latin approach (e.g., tribal marketing). He has published on this topic in the *International Journal of Research in Marketing*, the *European Journal of Marketing*, *Marketing Theory*, and the *Journal of Business Research*. He is also known as a researcher in b2b marketing, especially in the field of project marketing.

Véronique Cova (ex. Véronique Aubert-Gamet) is Associate Professor of Services Marketing at the Paul Cézanne University of Aix-Marseille III. Her research interests focus on consumer culture, servicescapes design, and postmodern consumption. She specializes in services design and the way consumers reappropriate the offering through diversion tactics. She has published in various French and international journals (*International Journal of Service Industry Management*, *European Journal of Marketing*, *Journal of Business Research*) and books.

Daniele Dalli is Full Professor of Marketing at the University of Pisa in Italy. His main area of research is consumer behavior, with a special focus on consumer–brand relationships. He has published in journals such as the *Journal of Business Research* and other Italian journals. He is the co-author of a consumer behavior textbook for undergraduate and master's courses. He is a member of the editorial board of leading Italian journals and acts as a reviewer for international journals and conferences.

Marc Filser is Professor of Marketing at the University of Burgundy in Dijon (France). He has been conducting extensive research in the areas of consumer behavior and retailing for the last twenty years. He has explored the diversity of the functions of retailing for the consumer beside the traditional vision of a place to simply purchase goods. He has co-authored *Distribution. Organisation et Stratégie* and published the results of his research in *Retail, Distribution and Consumer Research*, *European Retail Digest*, and *Décisions Marketing*.

Benoît Heilbrunn is Assistant Professor of Marketing at ESCP-EAP Paris. Trained as a philosopher and semiologist, his areas of interest and investigation include material culture, design management, and branding. He has co-edited *European Perspectives on Consumer Behaviour* and written books such as *Le logo* and *La consommation et ses sociologies*.

Patrick Hetzel is Chaired Professor of Marketing at Université Panthéon-Assas Paris II, where he is in charge of the research center for management studies (LARGEPA), and Visiting Professor at the University of Innsbruck (Austria). His publications focus on consumer behavior, channel management, design management, relational marketing, and semiotics. He has published more than fifty papers on these topics in various journals in France and abroad. He is the former editor of *Décisions Marketing*, a managerial journal of AFM (the association of marketing academics in France).

Robert V. Kozinets is an Associate Professor of Marketing at York University's Schulich School of Business. An anthropologist by training, he has consulted with hundreds of companies and published articles in journals such as the *Journal of Marketing*, the *Journal of Consumer Research*, and the *Journal of Marketing Research*.

Richard Ladwein is Professor of Marketing at the University of Lille (IAE), France. He has published many research papers and written a book on consumer behavior. His research investigates both ordinary and extraordinary consumption experiences (e.g., video games, tourism, Christmas ritual, ordinary materialism). He has developed a website devoted to his research: www.culture-materielle.com.

Stefano Podestà is Full Professor at Universitá Bocconi, Milan, where he is also the Dean of the Institute of Corporate Economics and Management. He is the editor of the *Finanza Marketing e Produzione*, one of the leading management journals in Italy. His research interests are competition and its evolution, as well as consumer behavior. He is also involved in the postmodern debate about the new challenges of marketing. On this specific topic, he has published in the *European Journal of Marketing*.

Eric Rémy is Professor of Marketing at Rouen University, France, where he organized the consumption society's conferences. His research deals with consumption behavior and, more specifically, social links as well as regional and social consumers' identities. His works belong to the postmodern trend of research and focus on the theatricality of the offering and the societal dimension of the value.

Simona Romani is Associate Professor in Marketing at the University of Sassari in Italy. Her main research interests are in the field of consumer behavior, advertising, and branding. She has published on this topic in *Advances of Consumer Research*, the *Journal of Product and Brand Management*, and in the proceedings of several international conferences.

Chiara Santoro graduated in 2003 in Economics for the Arts, Culture, and Communication at Universitá Bocconi, Milan. She focused her studies on marketing. Her dissertation thesis, supervised by Professor Gabriele Troilo, analyzed live experience at rock concerts using semiotics and experiential marketing theories. She currently works as communication and press officer for Kiver, a music marketing company based in Milan.

John F. Sherry, Jr joined the Notre Dame Marketing faculty in 2005 as the Herrick Professor of Marketing and Chairman of the Department, after twenty years at Northwestern. He is an anthropologist (PhD from the University of Illinois in 1983) who studies both the sociocultural and symbolic dimensions of consumption and the cultural ecology of marketing. He has researched, taught, and lectured around the globe. He is a fellow of the American Anthropological Association as well as of the Society for Applied Anthropology. Sherry is a past president of the Association for Consumer Research and a former associate editor of the *Journal of Consumer Research*.

Gabriele Troilo is Associate Professor of Marketing at Universitá Bocconi, Milan, and SDA Bocconi School of Management, Milan. He is Visiting Professor at Universidad Autonoma de Barcelona and at ESCP-EAP Paris in 2006. He teaches Marketing the Arts and Cultural Products, and his present research areas are esthetic consumption and consumers' perceptions of beauty. He is Vice President of the European Marketing Academy.

Preface

Marketing theory and practice have been marked since the early 2000s by the rise of so-called experiential approaches, whose roots go back more than 20 years. These approaches have provided a timely response to the major changes affecting consumption in our western societies and forced companies in turn to revisit their marketing efforts. In reaction to this evolution, some observers have started to espouse the idea of a new marketing panacea that they call experiential marketing, or the marketing of experiences. Unfortunately, and as has far too often been the case in the field of marketing, this new panacea tends to reduce the notion of experience to something that is simple and can be readily managed by firms. This is because it focuses more on the modalities by which companies create experiences, and less on trying to understand the complex nature of consumers' actual consumption experiences and/or how they interact with the corporate product offers generating such experiences.

Faced with this state of affairs and bolstered by a whole group of Euro-Mediterranean researchers who all share the same critical analysis (one based on a postmodern approach to consumption and marketing), we have designed a book project offering an overview of the consumption experience. This vision is broader and more comprehensive than the one conveyed by experiential marketing, without neglecting the marketing dimensions involved. In other words, this is neither a book about consumers' experiential behavior nor a manual on experiential marketing, but a work that tries to embrace all of the modulations that can exist between a consumer and a company during the production of a consumption experience. In short, this book is written in such a way as to be accessible and didactic without falling prey to a "how to do" approach.

Since the very beginning of this project, we have tried to promote research involving French and Italian institutions. Studies in these fields have rarely been translated into English, despite their important contribution to knowledge about the consumption experiences. To mention only a few of the most prolific institutions in consumption experience research: in France, IAE in Dijon (tied to the University of Burgundy), ESCP-EAP (Paris), and Euromed (Marseilles); and in Italy, Bocconi University (Milan) and the University of Pisa's Economics Department. Nine of the authors are Italian, and eight are French. This should not be construed as meaning that the book is trying to push, come what may, some sort of Euro-Mediterranean consumption experience model in opposition to a North American one. Three of its authors, and fairly significant ones at that, come from North America (one from the University of Notre Dame in Indiana, one from the Schulich School of Business in Toronto, and one from the Norton School of Family and Consumer Sciences in Tucson, Arizona). Moreover, the chapter bibliographies are largely filled with Anglo-American contributions to this subject.

Lastly, this project could never have taken shape without the very constructive input received from Routledge's Francesca Heslop; the help of our translators Mike Hammersley, Alan Sitkin, and Elizabeth Cook; and the kind support of our colleagues, notably the ESRC Seminar Series on Critical Marketing's six founding members (Miriam Catterall, Christina Goulding, Pauline Maclaran, Richard Elliott, Mike Saren, and Avi Shankar), plus Annamma Joy and Michael Gibbert, to whom we extend our most heartfelt thanks.

Part I

Setting up the scene of the consumer experience

Chapter 1

Consuming experiences
An introduction
Antonella Carù and Bernard Cova

KEY POINTS

■ It is through consumption that people build up and reinforce their identities.

■ Today consumers seek to experience immersion into thematic settings rather than merely to encounter finished products.

■ The production of a consuming experience includes staging, active customer participation, and a narrative.

■ Experiential marketing aims at creating extraordinary experiences for consumers.

■ People's daily life is made up of consuming experiences that can occur with or without a market relation.

After the marketing mid-life crisis during the 1980s, many marketers were hoping that the 1990s would involve a refocusing on relationship marketing and customer relationship management (CRM), a solid and innovative concept that highlights the relational sphere and its derivatives. Fifteen years on, this approach appears unfortunately to have gone as far as it can, largely due to marketing's excessive rationalizing of the relationship between firms and consumers. As a result, the discipline is now placing its hopes on the concept of "Experience," a notion that first arose in consumption and marketing studies in a seminal article written by Holbrook and Hirschman (1982): "The Experiential Aspects of Consumption: Consumer Fantasy, Feelings and Fun." Twenty years later, experience has evolved to become a key element in the understanding of hedonistic consumer behavior. It has also become the main foundation for an experience economy (Pine and Gilmore, 1999), recently followed by the advent of experiential marketing (Schmitt, 1999, 2003), an area that tends to highlight immersion in consuming experiences as opposed to the mere purchasing of simple products or services. This type of marketing is supposed to offer a response to the existential desires of today's consumers.

AN EXPERIENTIAL VIEW OF CONSUMPTION

Since the 1960s and 1970s, consumption has progressively disengaged from its essentially utilitarian conception, one that was based on products' and services' use value. Consumption has become an activity that involves a production of meaning, as well as a field of symbolic exchanges. Consumers do not consume products or services. Quite the contrary, they consume the products' meanings and images, and take it for granted that an object will fulfill certain functions. It is the object's image that makes the difference. Although it may seem surprising to talk about meanings and symbols in those areas that have tended to be dominated by marketing and commercial objectives, it is despite and beyond such objectivism that a product can turn into a vector of esthetics. Latently and manifestly, the 1980s were an era when the estheticization of everyday life (and its corollary, hedonism) infiltrated the field of consumption. Consumers became progressively perceived as emotional beings seeking sensorial experiences that they could derive from their interactions with the products and services found in the market system. What this entails is an embodiment of meanings in the form of experiences. Individuals are put on stage in a way that emphasizes sensuality and the significance of the experiences they live through. Consuming experiences have been theorized as personal and subjective experiences that people go through, ones that are often laden with emotionality for the consumer (Holbrook and Hirschman, 1982).

Since then, consumer behavior researchers (Addis and Holbrook, 2001) have tried to rebalance the functional and utilitarian vision of consumption by applying a so-called experiential perspective that focuses on hedonistic values and individual subjectivity (Figure 1.1). Heir to a tradition that is both microeconomic and psychological (whether behaviorist or cognitivist) in nature, the customary utilitarian vision of consumption highlights the search

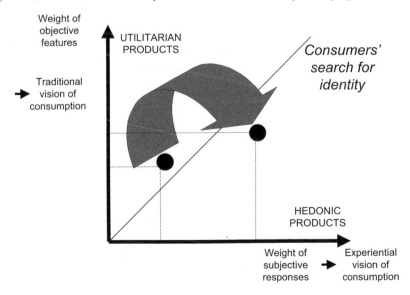

Figure 1.1 The experiential vision of consumption (adapted from Addis and Holbrook, 2001).

for information and the multiattribute processing of mechanisms of influence – the aim being to optimize transactions undertaken by isolated individuals. Inversely, in an experiential perspective, consumers are less interested in maximizing their benefits and more focused on hedonistic gratification within a given social context. Consumption here provokes sensations and emotions that do much more than merely respond to an individual's own needs, as they also touch upon the consumer's search for an identity. In the view of many sociologists, the vehicle for an individual's construction of his/her identity is no longer work (in other words, productive activity), but consumption. On the other hand, philosophers, poets, and moralists who study the culture have questioned whether people work to live or whether they live to work. The dilemma that has come to preoccupy our contemporaries can usually be formulated thus: should we consume to live or should we live to consume? Today, people consume mainly to exist (identity) and not only to live (needs). It is through consumption that people build up and reinforce their identities, which are increasingly eroded by factors such as unemployment, divorce, the break-up of a family, mobility, etc. We no longer simply "run a few errands" – we now "live experiences," usually ones that are embodied as they call upon all of our senses.

THE CONSUMING EXPERIENCE

The origin of the concept of experience can be found in the romantic currents of the eighteenth century, that is in a way of life that emphasized change, diversity, and imagination (Holbrook, 1997). The goal here was the development of an interesting life in which an individual could feel fulfilled and complete. Romanticism associated the search for intensive pleasure with states of extreme emotional excitement, contrasting them with the lukewarm mediocrity of daily life. Combined with western society's quest for an identity, this led to a search for experiences. The more individuals focused on their own life, the more they demanded that the trivialities of their daily existence be imbued with meaning. Living experiences became the only thing of any interest. This turned the consumer into a romantic hero, the romance here being his/her daily life.

The salient attributes of experiential consumption are as follows:

- consumers are not only consumers;
- consumers act within situations;
- consumers seek meaning;
- consumption involves more than mere purchasing.

In the experiential perspective, the consumption experience is no longer limited to pre-purchase activities (stimulation of a need, search for information, assessment, etc.) or to postpurchase activities (assessment of satisfaction), but includes a series of other activities that influence consumers' decisions and future actions. As such, consuming experiences are spread over a period of time that can be divided into four major stages (Arnould *et al.*, 2002):

- the preconsumption experience, which involves searching for, planning, day-dreaming about, and foreseeing or imagining the experience;
- the purchasing experience, which involves choosing the item, payment, packaging, and the encounter with the service and the environment;
- the core consumption experience, which involves sensation, satiety, satisfaction/ dissatisfaction, irritation/flow, and transformation;
- the remembered consumption experience and the nostalgia experience, in which photographs are used to relive a past experience based on narratives and arguments with friends about the past, something that tends toward the classification of memories.

As a result, the consuming experience is more than a mere shopping experience, e.g., an individual's experience at a point-of-sale (also called a service encounter in services research). This concept of a shopping experience has, since the 1970s, been based on a series of studies that have looked at purchasing behavior at the point-of-sale and tried to supersede the hypothesis of consumer rationality. What was first revealed was a so-called recreative type of consumer. Broader studies that were conducted subsequently highlighted hedonistic behavior in most consumers, diverting attention away from the utilitarian to the hedonistic value of shopping. In these studies, the consumer is seen as an individual who is emotionally involved in a shopping process in which multisensory, imaginary, and emotive aspects are specifically sought after and appreciated. Retailing research converged here with sociological studies that focused on the same issues (Falk and Campbell, 1997), the assumption being that the enjoyment derived from shopping does not stem from buying, wanting, or desiring products, but that shopping is a socioeconomic means of socializing and enjoying oneself and the company of others while making purchases. Hedonistic and utilitarian motivations thus become so closely intertwined that it would seem wrong to countermand them. Examples of shopping experiences range from cultural consumption in a museum to spectacular consumption at Nike Town, Chicago.

Although shopping was initially deemed to constitute the main field of experiential consumption, today, it would appear that the explosion of subjectivity has generalized throughout western society, thereby extending the experiential domain to all sectors of consumption. Some would even characterize modern consumption as something akin to the pleasure of being immersed in McDisneyfied banalities. Having said that, there is little agreement as to the source and level of pleasure that consumers derive from such experiences. For some observers (particularly for specialists in what has been called "retail re-enchantment"), pleasure stems from a McDonald's-type experiential shaping of daily banalities. They say that the re-enchantment of our daily lives entails a whole succession of micropleasures, recurring affordable microtreats that derive from in-store consuming experiences. Through a number of polysensorial stimulations, consumption here is transformed into an entertainment opportunity and into a hedonic experience. For other analysts, notably the proponents of postmodern marketing (Firat and Dholakia, 1998), what pleasure offers is a total immersion in an original experience. Here, the emphasis is on modern consumers' growing quest for immersion in varied experiences, their aim being to explore the multiplicity of new meanings they can inject into their lives. The idea is that a consumer comes to market to produce his/her identity, so that s/he is in fact seeking the experience of being immersed in a thematized framework rather than a mere encounter with some finished product. These immersions in enclavized and secure contexts contrast with the stress of people's daily lives, and sometimes go as far as to help them to live other persons' experiences. This immersion in a consuming experience is tantamount to diving into a framework that has been totally thematized, enclavized, and made secure. One notable example of this is Rainforest Café.

Whether at the level of a simple experiential shaping or at the deeper level of a total immersion in a thematized framework, experiential consumption (construed as a staging in which individuals find themselves surrounded by a vast symbolic system) appears to be indistinguishable from the advent of simulations and virtuality. One of the main dimensions of today's consumption is what the sociologist Baudrillard (1988) once termed hyper-reality. We increasingly satisfy ourselves with a reality composed of images, accepting copies as a substitute for anything else. Our secret is that we no longer want originality with its harsh reality, preferring sweetened artifices instead. We find copies to be truer than the reality they are supposed to represent. Even more poignantly, today reality seems to have disappeared – all we have left are images, illusions, and simulations, i.e., copies of real things, manifestations without any origins or intrinsic reality. Images have become incapable of imagining reality, because that is what they themselves have become (Baudrillard, 1988). Most postmodern examples of hyper-reality involve the consumption of leisure-oriented simulations. Without even mentioning Disney World (which is no more or less than one gigantic simulation), Aquaboulevard and other facilities such as Center Parcs offer interesting examples of simulated beaches and parks that some consumers prefer to real beaches and parks. All in all, today we can clearly observe consumers' tendency to prefer simulated experiences to reality. Moreover, these simulated experiences have become increasingly spectacular and extravagant (Ritzer, 1999).

THE PRODUCTION OF EXPERIENCES

Although it is widely accepted within an experiential perspective that consumers are not passive agents reacting to stimuli but, instead, the actors and the producers of their own consuming experiences (however hyper-real these may be), firms have nevertheless worked hard to facilitate the production of such experiences. The methods advanced to enable firms to (co)-produce experiences on consumers' behalf have one point in common – they try to create a theater and a stage for both the consumer and what the company is offering. This is achieved through in-depth work on the decor, i.e., on the environmental design and on the atmosphere at the point-of-sale. When a firm or a brand delivers only products and not services, it is advisable that it create its own premises (theaters of consumption) so that the consumer can experience its products without the intrusion of any competing influences. This is what happens in Nike Towns or in other concept or flagship stores. Further examples include Nutella (hazelnut spread) restaurants or Nespresso cafés. The commercial premises' design must be managed in a completely coherent manner, all the way down to the smallest detail, if the firm wants to air the brand's theme accurately and stimulate all five senses of the individual for whose benefit this staging is taking place. Where opinions differ is with regard to which elements can be used to complete this staging. Some pundits stress a necessarily active participation by the customer, as well as the importance of offering a "memorabilia mix." Others twin this notion of active customer participation with the staging actions being undertaken by the facilitators (which can involve the presence of specific types of contact personnel or customers who can be used to guide the consumer through the experience). Other analysts emphasize the product's narrative, i.e., the intrigue or the story that the corporate offer and the consumer will be enacting.

All in all, the production of experiences can be deemed to include three main facets:

- decor, design, staging, with special attention being paid to multisensorial stimulation;
- active participation by the consumer, helped by all sorts of facilitators who specify each party's role in all of the rituals being set up in the orbit of what the company is offering (see case vignette 1.1);
- the narrative, story, and intrigues that are created, the most important of which is the creation of memories, usually in the form of derivative products (see case vignette 1.1).

CASE VIGNETTE 1.1: "EVERY GUINNESS IS A UNIQUE EXPERIENCE"

"Every Guinness is a unique experience" is the title of this famous Irish beer maker's latest advertising campaign in France (spring 2003). To help consumers have this experience, Guinness proactively explained to consumers which rituals and role should be part of their interaction with its product if they wanted to feel the same pleasure with a new can of Draught Guinness as they do when they go to a pub.

> In Ireland and across the world, people go to pubs to celebrate Draught Guinness as a ritual. They admire the bartender's talent when pouring the beer into pint glasses and watch its creamy head rise slowly. They know how to be patient. Draught Guinness now also comes in cans, enabling you to experience this ritual at home.

This excerpt from a newspaper advertisement for Draught Guinness tries to highlight certain typically ritualistic and non-functional dimensions of the Guinness consumption experience in a pub — namely, those aspects that make it unique: the need to take one's time ("be patient") and the human touch ("the bartender's talent"). These dimensions are also recapped in a box that explains to the consumer how s/he can use Draught Guinness to complete this ritual (actual participation) and "enjoy authentic Guinness at home." By so doing, people can both extend their memory of their experience in the pub and reproduce it at home in what becomes "an uncompromising ritual."

Step 1: Leave the Guinness at least three hours at the bottom of your refrigerator. Take a can of Guinness and find a 33-cl glass. Open the can and listen while the gas escapes. Wait until the head starts to rise.

Step 2: Carefully pour the beer against the side of your glass. Pour the entire contents of the can out in one fell swoop.

Step 3: Take your time to observe the creamy head that will rise to the top of your glass. Your Guinness is ready to be tasted.

This advertising does not replace the ritualized experience of the pub with the immediacy of a functional consumption at home. Quite the contrary, it stresses the exact steps in the process that the consumer must fastidiously adhere to so as to create an experience at home that is similar to the one s/he has at the pub ("leave," "listen," "wait," "take your time").

FROM THE PRODUCTION OF EXPERIENCES TO EXPERIENTIAL MARKETING

Toward the late 1990s, a specific marketing school of thought returned to these incipient approaches to the production of experiences and turned them into the basis of a complete managerial approach, one in which the experiential perspective was entirely reversed. In experiential marketing, experience has become a new type of company offer alongside commodities, products, and services (Pine and Gilmore, 1999). It is a fourth category, and one that is particularly well adapted to the needs of the postmodern consumer.

In this vision, a good experience must be unforgettable, if not extraordinary. Reintegrating the idea of immersion (Firat and Dholakia, 1998), experiential marketing then suggested that consumption be turned into a series of extraordinary immersions for the consumer who could then engage in the unforgettable processes that constitute the experience or, even better, be transformed because of these experiences. Experiential marketing experts believe that the shift from a commodity to a transformation increases the economic value of a company's offer (Pine and Gilmore, 1999). By so doing, this school of thought appropriates experience studies by the famous psychologist Csikszentmihalyi (1997), in which the best experience is considered to be a flow one, i.e., an exceptional moment during which what we feel, desire, and think are in total harmony. Only a small fraction of consumer experiences can be classified as flow activities. However, flow activities are pivotal for marketing because they represent peak experiences (Arnould et al., 2002). As such, it is indeed this specific flow vision of the consumption experience that has become the foundation of the entire experiential approach in marketing (see case vignette 1.2). To achieve this type of flow experience, marketing has recycled and implemented Baudrillard's notion of hyper-reality: an experience becomes extraordinary thanks to increasingly spectacular and surprising decors and due to the ever greater scope of the extravagances and simulations in which the consumer will be immersed.

CASE VIGNETTE 1.2: ARGUMENTS USED BY EXPERTS IN EXPERIENTIAL MARKETING

Increasingly, marketers understand that consumers are living human beings with experiential needs: consumers want to be stimulated, entertained, educated, and challenged. They are looking for brands that provide meaningful experiences and thus become part of their lives . . . Experiences are personal events that occur in response to some stimulations (e.g., as provided by marketing efforts before and after purchase). An experience involves the entire living being and can be infused into a product, used to enhance a service, or created as an entity into itself. Experiences provide consumers a way to engage physically, mentally, emotionally, socially, and spiritually in the consumption of the product or service making the interaction meaningfully real.

Momentum Experiential Marketing (McCann-Erickson) website.
http://www.mccann.com/aboutus/mem.html

The achievement of these extraordinary experiences has been the main area of discussion for various experts (Pine and Gilmore, 1999; Schmitt, 1999, 2003; LaSalle and Britton, 2003) who developed different experiential marketing approaches. The main point is that experiences must be memorable and must involve the individual's personal sphere: experts answered the question on how to create this kind of experiences in different ways, always trying to codify a sequence of steps or activities useful to reach that goal. According to Pine and Gilmore (1999), the staging is the core of extraordinary experiences' creation, as the production and the supply are the core of goods and services production respectively. They identify some specific actions for the experience "staging": the first one is the preparation of the stage, which varies according to the different areas of the experience (entertainment, education, desire to escape, and esthetic experience) and to the different opportunities offered by each area; the second one is turning experience into a show, by giving it a specific theme; for this purpose, they identify a list of possible functional themes. Again, it is necessary to personalize the experience, to search for a sole value for the customer, which is based on the ability to surprise him/her. In this extraordinary experience creation process, the metaphor evoked is the one of theater, which, in its various forms, represents the model. In the title of his first book, *Experiential Marketing: How to Get Customers to Sense, Feel, Think, Act and Relate to Your Company and Brands*, Schmitt (1999) makes clear the idea that the goal of experiences' creation is to introduce specific customer behaviors and reactions. Thus, customer experience management (CEM) (Schmitt, 2003) is the process of strategically managing a customer's entire experience with a product or a company, a process that has five basic steps: analyzing the experiential world of the customer; building the experiential platform; designing the brand experience; structuring the customer interface; and engaging in continuous innovation. LaSalle and Britton (2003) shift the attention to the customer's decisional process in order to spot the actions to be undertaken by the company in each phase. The consumer's decisional process is made up of five stages – discover, evaluate, acquire, integrate, and extend – through which the consumer moves during consumption. By examining these stages, a business can see rewards and sacrifices through its customers' eyes, thus uncovering the real value of an offering.

RESISTANCE TO EXPERIENTIAL MARKETING

Whereas research in consumer behavior has tended to adopt a conceptualization that views experience as a subjective episode in an individual's construction/transformation (stressing emotional and sensorial dimensions to the detriment of a cognitive dimension), experiential marketing has imbued experience with a more objective meaning, focusing on the company's planning and implementation of what it is offering, while accentuating the idea that the outcome should be something that is very significant and unforgettable for the consumer living through this experience. In just a few years, experiential marketing has changed the status of consuming experiences, displacing them from what consumers have personally gone through to participation in a consumption festival dominated by excess, extravagance, magic, spectacularity, and simulation.

Having said that, there has been a great deal of criticism of the limited and planned nature of these consuming experiences, which are very manipulative and predetermined and therefore meet with resistance from some consumers. Indeed, such experiences leave the consumer very little room to really participate in their conception and construction. Consumers become actors only insofar as they are allowed to do this, i.e., when they fulfill their role as a consumer overwhelmed by the experience's context. Yet, consumers seemingly not only want to be immersed in their experiences but also seek to design and actively produce them. For many consumers, an experience is more than the simple acceptance of a prepackaged offer revolving around a theme that has been chosen by the firm (thematization of the experience) – some of it must also be left unorganized so that it can become appropriable. A good example of the appropriation of experience in the daily life of our hypermodern contemporaries is the consumption of holidays. Seventy percent of all Europeans produce their own holidays. This is a way for them to appropriate their vacations.

To an experience that has been organized and planned by the firm, the consumer can oppose a creation of experiences that is very different in nature, one that can be described as the art of living as it is characterized by the art of diverting commercial experiences (de Certeau, 1984). The consumer, acting alone or in a group, diverts the product, service, and especially the preplanned experience away from its original intention (as determined by the existing market system) in an attempt to reappropriate it in accordance with his/her own rules. By so doing, s/he prepares a new prism for analyzing the event, one that can be non-commercial and even anticommercial in tone. This also means getting involved on a local scale in a system whose imposition the consumer refuses to accept. There are many examples of such diversions today. Relatively organized and dominated by a protest attitude, they seek to create an opposition to the omnipotence of certain world companies, with recent examples including McDonald's and "Pigeon McNuggets" actions or Danone and the famous "I boycott Danone" website. Along these same lines, we also find pub destroyers and other "adbusters," not to mention England's "Reclaim The Streets" movement. All of these groups signify our contemporaries' crucial need to reappropriate their daily experiences. At the same time, many collective experiences have tended to reappropriate products and services found in the market system without this being part of a conscious protest. Examples include fan associations that dig up and pamper yesterday's products such as the old Mini car or Apple Newton pad. The meanings and usages that these groups are associating with such products differ from what was originally intended. Moreover, this building of meaning through experience and shared emotion constitutes a daily episode in the creation, consolidation, and preservation of a communitarian sentiment within such groups. What all of these actions have in common is that they constitute experiences that help the product or service to evolve beyond its simple status as a merchandise, thereby enabling consumers to have an experience that is not totally commercial in nature while continuing to function within a commercial framework, i.e., one that is defined by the interactions that brands and companies have initiated.

A CONTINUUM OF CONSUMING EXPERIENCES

Moving on to consider consuming experiences, it is essential to go beyond a view of experience that is totally dependent on what the market system offers. The sociology of consumption (Edgell *et al.*, 1997) has highlighted four types of consumption experience as a function of the mode of provision, which is not just a market question. These are: family experiences resulting from family ties; friendship experiences resulting from reciprocal relations within a community; citizenship experiences linked to relations with the state; and consumer experiences connected to exchanges with the market (Table 1.1).

This indicates that an individual's daily life is made up of consuming experiences that can occur with or without a market relation. Each experience is not, therefore, necessarily a market consumption experience or consumer experience. The consuming experience of a meal at a friend's house is linked to a sphere outside the market, even if products from the market may be consumed. In the same way, the communal consumption of a self-produced show is outside the notion of a consumer experience. Thus, for the sociologists of consumption, social relations shape the experience of consuming (Edgell *et al.*, 1997). Moreover, experiential marketing is interested only in the specific social context of the market, in which the individual is a consumer living experiences with the supplier and with other consumers.

All in all, we can outline a continuum of consuming experiences that consumers go through:

Table 1.1 *The conditions of consuming experiences*

Mode of provision	Access conditions/ social relations	Manner of delivery	Social context
Market	Price/exchange	Managerial	Consumer with other consumers
State	Need/right	Professional	Citizens/users with other citizens
Household	Family/obligation	Family	Members of the family with other members
Communal	Network/reciprocity	Volunteer	Friends or neighbors with other friends or neighbors

Adapted from Edgell *et al.* (1997).

■ At one extreme are experiences that are mainly constructed by the consumers and which can involve company-provided products or services. Here, the firm is pursuing a traditional product or service marketing approach, and it is the consumer who organizes his/her own experience. Traditional products such as pasta, the small items that constitute our daily life, and most particularly organic products and non-profit or local associations are prime examples here.

■ In the middle, we find experiences that have been co-developed by companies and consumers (see case vignette 1.3). Here, the firm provides an experiential platform base on which the consumer can develop his/her own experience. The firm imbues the experience with a potential, turning it into a veritable raw material composed of certain diffuse elements that the consumer can mold, and which will therefore assume the shape of his/her own experience. Sports tourism or adventure packages, rock concerts, and cultural events are part of this approach.

■ At the other extreme, we find experiences that have largely been developed by companies and in which consumers are immersed in a context that is frequently hyper-real in nature. Here, the firm is pursuing a total experiential marketing approach and plans all details of the experience on the consumers' behalf. Nowadays, fashion and sports brands, as well as toys and other forms of entertainment, specialize in this approach.

CASE VIGNETTE 1.3: RED BULL CO-CREATED EXPERIENCES

The market research results were devastating. The thin color of the new drink was totally unappetizing, the sticky mouth feel and taste were deemed "disgusting." And the concept of "stimulates mind and body" was – at best – rated irrelevant. The verdict by the research firm: "No other new product has ever failed this convincingly." But Dietrich Mateschitz was past the point of no return. He had exited the corporate world exactly three years prior to the new product development (NPD) research to import a new type of energy drink he discovered in Asia called Red Bull. And it was not just the destructive consumer reactions to his drink that would make his entrepreneurial career initially miserable.

What Mateschitz learned from the NPD research was how important context was to the success of Red Bull. No wonder the concept had failed in the sterile environment of a research studio. Red Bull needed to be experienced. Just like Gatorade worked in taste testing only when participants were dehydrated and the Gatorade ice cold, Red Bull will not score highly in a laboratory situation. It Is at its core a functional drink, intended to provide a boost of energy. But on top, to survive in a category where image rules, Red Bull needed to establish an attitude (vs. an image), and not just be sold as an over-the-counter nutraceutical, if it wanted to reach significant scale. The bulk of Red Bull's marketing has been (what conventional marketers would call) below-the-line. Red Bull needs to be experienced within the right context, in terms of both functional needs and appropriate ambience. Hence, the bulk of the brand's marketing is spent on extensive sampling and event sponsorship.

Red Bull isn't a distant and aspirational marketer (e.g., "Look how cool we are. Don't you wish you could be one of us? Well, buy ____!"). Its marketing takes place on the street. With the people. The favorite anecdote of Alex Wipperfürth (2005), a researcher in the US leading consulting boutique, Plan B in San Francisco:

> *A sampling team got wind that I threw World Cup parties every night last summer at my place for about 20 or so soccer fanatics. They surprised us at 4 am during the Germany vs. USA quarterfinals match, with their hot and fun sampling team providing just the right startling energy boost all of us needed at that moment. Of course, as soccer goes, the Germans won in the end, but the game will be more readily forgotten than the Red Bull team for all of us crazed supporters. We became participants in the event, ready to tell our friends not only how cool it was for them to come by, but more importantly how Red Bull really helped keep us awake and alert.*

A convincing, entertaining, and memorable event that no broadcast campaign could ever duplicate. Red Bull furthermore ensures that consumers do not feel pressured to drink Red Bull in a certain way. During their sampling, they always provide a full and closed can, so that consumers can decide when and how much to try. "We don't try to control how people use Red Bull," explains North American spokeswoman Emma Cortes. There is no right way to use Red Bull, no code of conduct (for consumers). Consumers are asked to use their imagination in fitting Red Bull into their lives. It helps get them deeper into the Red Bull experience and truly understand its role. This is hands-on absorption of a breakthrough product, rather than processing an abstract communication effort. Creative participation keeps the brand relevant as it encourages consumers to continuously reinterpret Red Bull for themselves. And it underlines the often overlooked message that it stimulates the mind (not just the body).

Based on information included in Wipperfürth (2005)

The continuum of consumption experiences serves to structure this whole book. Its introduction is followed by two chapters commenting on the role that the consumer/company interaction plays in the construction of an experience. This is done from two perspectives: one focusing on how consumers interact with an experiential context's varying dimensions; the other revolving around the different ways in which firms facilitate consumer immersion in an experience. Mobilizing three previously identified positions concerning the continuum of consumption experiences, the chapters that follow offer theoretical and practical input grounded in an analysis of specific experiential contexts. For experiences that are mainly constructed by consumers themselves, the book first studies the sort of experiences that people might have in a non-profit context, goes on to look at a traditional food product, and concludes with typical day-to-day objects. For co-constructed experiences, the book begins with trekking-related experiences, moves on to rock concerts, and concludes with fashion wear. Lastly, for experiences that are mainly company constructed, the book starts with a look at people's experiences in an edutainment context, turns to sports brands, and ends with the mass retail sector.

DISCUSSION QUESTIONS

- What are the major drivers of experiential consumption?
- Why are consuming experiences rooted in romanticism?
- How should a consuming experience be staged?
- Why do experiential marketing approaches provoke consumer resistance?
- Why develop active consumer participation in the production of experiences?

REFERENCES

Addis, M. and Holbrook, M.B. (2001) "On the Conceptual Link between Mass Customisation and Experiential Consumption: An Explosion of Subjectivity." *Journal of Consumer Behaviour* 1(1): 50–66.

Arnould, E., Price, L. and Zinkhan, G. (2002) *Consumers*. New York: McGraw-Hill.

Baudrillard, J. (1988) *Selected Writings*. Stanford, CA: Stanford University Press.

de Certeau, M. (1984) *The Practice of Everyday Life*. Berkeley, CA: University of California Press.

Csikszentmihalyi, M. (1997) *Finding Flow. The Psychology of Engagement with Everyday Life*. New York: Basic Books.

Edgell, S., Hetherington, K. and Warde, A. (eds) (1997) *Consumption Matters: The Production and Experience of Consumption*. Oxford: Blackwell.

Falk, P. and Campbell, C. (eds) (1997) *The Shopping Experience*. London: Routledge.

Firat, A.F. and Dholakia, N. (1998) *Consuming People: From Political Economy to Theaters of Consumption*. London: Routledge.

Holbrook, M.B. (1997) "Romanticism, Introspection and the Roots of Experiential Consumption: Morris the Epicurean." *Consumption, Market and Culture* 1(2): 97–164.

Holbrook, M.B. and Hirschman, E.C. (1982) "The Experiential Aspects of Consumption: Consumer Fantasy, Feelings and Fun." *Journal of Consumer Research* 9(2): 132–140.

LaSalle, D. and Britton T.A. (2003) *Priceless: Turning Ordinary Products into Extraordinary Experiences*. Boston: Harvard Business School Press.

Pine, B.J. and Gilmore, J. (1999) *The Experience Economy: Work is Theatre and Every Business a Stage*. Boston: Harvard Business School Press.

Ritzer, G. (1999) *Enchanting a Disenchanted World*. Thousand Oaks, CA: Pine Forge Press.

Schmitt, B.H. (1999) *Experiential Marketing: How to Get Customers to SENSE, FEEL, THINK, ACT and RELATE to Your Company and Brands*. New York: The Free Press.

Schmitt, B.H. (2003) *Customer Experience Management*. Hoboken, NJ: John Wiley & Sons.

Wipperfürth, A. (2005) *Brand Hijack: Marketing without Marketing*. New York: Portfolio.

Chapter 2

Agents in paradise

Experiential co-creation through emplacement, ritualization, and community

John F. Sherry, Jr, Robert V. Kozinets, and Stefania Borghini

KEY POINTS

- Consumers co-create their consumption experiences with producers.
- Consumers have powerful and personally significant experiences in themed environments.
- A form of playful consumption that we call "ludic autotely" occurs in themed environments, and smart marketers are recognizing this.
- Consumers "play along" with marketers' rules, but only to a certain extent.
- Spectacles are perhaps the ultimate form of consumer experience, and they may be changing and becoming more open to consumer co-creation.

> Did you ever fly a kite in bed?
> Did you ever walk with ten cats on your head?
> Did you ever milk this kind of cow?
> Well, we can do it.
> We know how.
> If you never did,
> you should.
> These things are fun
> and fun is good.
>
> Dr. Seuss (1960) "One Fish, Two Fish, Red Fish, Blue Fish"

Dr. Seuss' simple and beautiful poetry artfully communicates a basic truth. Human beings are not content simply to lie in bed, to walk a straight line, or to milk a regular type of cow. They constantly seek new experiences. More important than the mere provision of these experiences, however, is the role of imagination in their enactment (Sherry, 2005). The characters in Dr. Seuss' stories – as in so many other children's fables from *Peter Pan* to

Dragon Tales, *The Neverending Story* to *Where the Wild Things Are* — are actively creating their own experiences out of the raw materials at hand.

Consumers have always lived in an experience economy (Joy and Sherry, 2003). Consumers have always engaged imaginatively, creatively, and constructively with the world around them. In recent times, many marketing managers have become enamored with the concepts of experience economies (Pine and Gilmore, 1999) and entertainment economies (Wolf, 1999), which tend to be interpreted (superficially and, especially in relation to Pine and Gilmore's work, we would argue wrongly) as promising hordes of hungry, empty consumers waiting to be entertained by the vast thematic offerings of producers: theme parks leading to theme hotels, theme stores, theme restaurants, wall-sized screens in stores, museums, churches, gymnasiums, schools, and so on (see Gottdeiner, 1997). Yet, acts of consumer imagination are complex and multifaceted, embodied and erotic, often driven more by needs for authenticity and self-expansion than by the desire for entertainment.

In this short chapter, we seek to turn the page on experientiality as a provided phenomenon and reveal it as a complex lived phenomenon in consumer life. Experientiality — or materiality, in the terms of consumer culture theorists — with the material world, with objects, places, brands, and ideas occurs in major ways outside the marketer's ability to observe and ability to control. Consumers tend to be tricky wild things who find their own uses for marketed things and brands to be more interesting than those intended by marketers. Seeking authenticity and truth as well as fun and amusement, consumers bring their own conceptual and creative apparatus to the party.

To illustrate and develop these ideas, we will offer a range of examples from our ethnographic and netnographic research, carried out both individually and collectively. Through our consumption looking glass, we followed consumer experiences in place, time, theme, and imaginary, immersed ourselves in diverse marketscapes and flagship brand stores, attended media fan conventions, roamed doll stores and sports bars, and participated in traditional village fetes and mass-mediated festivals. Our investigative focus has taken us from the middle of the Nevada desert to the rural prealpine mountains of Italy, from downtown Chicago to Toronto's airport noise-drenched suburbs.[1] Seeking the elusive "passive" consumer who seeks the out-of-the-box experiences of modern marketing's experience economists, we were less than disappointed instead to find different brands of material experiencers, creative co-producers who added and enhanced their experiences. These consumers placed themselves on multiple stages, acted the parts, and became the experience.

Through their experiences, we extrapolate principles to assist our understanding of the types of powerful marketplace offerings that can bridge the distance between spectacularly mediated theme worlds and augmented authentic grassroots experience. In so doing, we try to close many gaps: between mass marketing and local meaning; between commercial constructions and communal feelings; between digital technology and meat puppet bodies. The result is co-created experience driven by marketers and consumers in which person and public presence become a part of the retail corporation's stage, energy, expression, and meaning, and where marketer authenticity can never be completely included in a brand, but only be signaled by its openness.

THE INTERPRETIVE COORDINATES OF EXPERIENCE CO-CREATION

We can extend Turner's classic metaphor that says that marketers study consumers for the reasons and in the ways that fishermen study fish, while consumer researchers study consumers for the reasons and in the ways that marine biologists study fish. Notwithstanding, for the moment, the fact that researchers and marketers are, in this metaphor, actually themselves fish as well, the implication is that good consumer research can help marketing by teaching about consumer habits, thoughts, and so forth, and thus helping marketers to better bait their hooks. We would argue that a number of scholars, thus far, have taken a view from the surface of the water. The critical scholars of spectacle (e.g., Debord, 1995) tend to see flocks of consumers being prodded and tricked into marketers' nets through the use of attractive theming-as-bait. Consumers are seen to be bombarded and overwhelmed, dazzled by design, blinded by behavioral science and frenetic engineering into evacuating first their minds, then their wallets.

On the other hand, pro-experience managerial gurus such as Wolf (1999) see schools of consumers swimming hungrily and fruitlessly through the waters of the market, looking for the right kind of lure. Writers such as Wolf argue that shopping is an outlet not only for bargains but for the satisfaction of genuine needs for lightness, fun, and the sharing of life experiences that make life worth living. In short, the one school of thought sees consumers are overwhelmed, driven by producer interests, and the other sees consumer driving the process of commercial experience creation, with producers responding to their needs and feedbacks.

Recently, a more nuanced view has emerged, treating the prior polarizations as partial propositions. Many scholars (Eric Arnould, Linda Price, Linda Scott, Lisa Penaloza, John Sherry, and Robert Kozinets) have written about the active role that consumers play in the process of experiential production–consumption. Consumers treat the complex common grounds of physical commercial playspaces in many ways as their own dropdown menus, drifting and choosing rapidly through their nearly infinite combinations in a myriad of ways (see, for example, Sherry, 1998). As explored in some depth at the sports-themed entertainment complex ESPN Zone Chicago (Kozinets et al., 2004), the interests of consumers and producers are embedded within each other in a process they call "interagency."

> Instead of a dichotomous view of agency in which two parties – consumers and producers – vie for control, our findings at *ESPN Zone Chicago* vividly illustrate another model: one of embedded consumer–producers, where consumers produce producers' products at the same time and as much as producers consume consumers' consumption.

Their argument is that "the will of consumers and producers turns out to be far more overlapping, mutual, and interdependent than commonly recognized" (Kozinets et al., 2004, p. 671).

Taking this interagency perspective as our starting point, we are beginning to explore the theoretical coordinates that lead to the promised land of deeply meaningful and significant

consumer experiences. What do consumers do with and in the freedom of movement granted them by open environments? How are they creative, and not creative? When do they
push back and resist, and when do they simply sit back and enjoy? We are finding that playing with agency is all a part of the play, that the successive taking control and surrendering
of the reins of consumer experience is, in itself, an important part of the game of marketing
(see Brown, 1995; Deighton and Grayson, 1995). Consumption is a dance of polarities.
Through this ancient ritual, self, community, and identity in a corporate consumer culture
are inculcated, reinforced, clarified, played with, and transformed.

FIRE: A COMPARISON OF GRASSROOTS RITUALS WITH THE IRRESISTIBLE LIGHT

We begin our overview of grassroots participation with a rather occult example drawn from
our fieldwork. Rob and John have been studying the Burning Man festival since first encountering it in a *Wired* magazine article in 1996. The Burning Man festival is a large, proto-
Utopian gathering centered upon the burning of a large wood and neon figure of a man,
in which community forms quickly and, through the large area of space of the Black Rock
desert, is liberated and freed up for playful, ideological, and spiritual pursuits that take place,
in some sense, outside the strictures of ordinary market and social logics (Figure 2.1). After
several months of working together, the three of us began discussing overlapping fire festival
traditions. Stefania noted similarities between the Black Rock festival and the Burning Old
Man and Woman Joy Fire of her native Italian village of Premosello Chiovenda (see case
vignette 2.1 for a general overview).

Figure 2.1 *Self-expression and creation of Sacred Space/Time at Burning Man.*

One of the key aspects of Burning Man is what has been termed in another investigation the event's "ludic autotely," which is the phenomenon through which the event's participants are largely responsible for creating and maintaining the playspace for other participants, outside of central organization, financing, or planning. It is play for play's sake, which of necessity plays havoc with formal organization. As with Burning Man's grassroots growth, participant enthusiasm, and creativity, the participants of the folklore traditions in the north of Italy and in the rest of Europe feel a strong sense of communal connection and participation through their fire rituals. As in many cases of ancient traditions drawing from pagan or religious origins, these rites involve the use of fire as propitiation, a necessary means of achieving "purification" from evil, old age, or pain, and/or to ward off death. They are sacrificial in the literal sense – fire is used to leave behind that which is undesired.

A similar neo-Pagan ritual meaning has emerged – largely unbidden by the event's organizers, it seems – by the participants in Nevada's Burning Man. Participants ask each other what they came to burn, and use the ritual fire as a lace to psychically purify their lives by seeking self-transformation through the removal of encumbrances in their lives (Figure 2.2). Often, they will burn photographs or other personal memorabilia that link them to past negative habits, people, and ways of thinking.

Figure 2.2 *The Infinite Fire at Burning Man.*

In recent years, studies of consumer behavior in a community of young people in a small village located in the mountains of northern Italy, Premosello Chiovenda, have revealed an analogous reinterpretation of this sacrificial fire (see case vignette 2.1). This ritual, called Carcavegia, involves the burning of a male and a female figure, which are ceremonially named for the oldest man and woman living in the village. The naming and burning are thought to be good luck for the elderly citizens, but very likely draw from earlier times when they, or stand-ins for them, were sacrificially burned, probably in a fertility ritual or other appeasement of supernatural forces.

In this village, a few volunteers have been given the responsibility of organizing the event for the rest of the community by the local authorities and associations responsible for organizing cultural activities. Over a period of time of six years, we repeatedly observed this group of young people. There were about a dozen young males, who strictly followed local traditions. We observed them as they organized the event as well as during the rest of the year. In the past, the event was considered by these people to be a time for participating in village social life, which they found enjoyable and rewarding. However, the new organizers have recently begun viewing the event in a special way. Rather than regarding the bonfire simply as a game or social event to occupy them for one week in the year, as was the case for their fathers and grandfathers before them, this generation seems to be treating the event more seriously. Unlike their predecessors, they spend more time on a number of activities which transcend ceremonial preparations. They invest considerable time in the forest, cutting wood, preparing the effigy, and then running through the village streets signaling the date of the approaching event. They invest significant time to prepare people socially and emotionally for the ritual experience, just as organizers did in the distant past when the ritual was not only considered traditional or entertaining, but was also rich and redolent with religious and magical meanings.

CASE VIGNETTE 2.1: CARCAVEGIA[2]

Red sparks and smoke are illuminating the darkness of a freezing night in early January, rising up over the flames consuming two human-like figures, while around the great bonfire, the dark and heavy sound of the horn mixes with a repetitive, plangent ringing of the bells.

This scene, which harkens back to faraway times and places when human sacrifices were common, unfolds in contemporary Premosello Chiovenda, a mountain village in Valle Ossola, a valley in north-east Italy about 100 km from Milan. The celebration is the "Carcavegia," a traditional ceremony that villagers have perpetuated from time immemorial, when every 5 January they meet in the middle of the village to burn *al vecc* (the old man) and *la vegia* (the old woman). The ritual begins with the building of a pyre from any combustible material available. The two human-like, stuffed figures representing the oldest persons from the village are placed on the top the pyre (Figure 2.3).

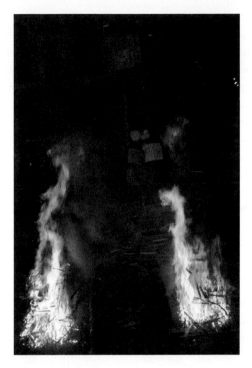

Figure 2.3 *The fire of Carcavegia.*

As for other events in various localities along the Alpine chain and in the Po valley that are comparable in terms of both period and means of celebration, the origins of Carcavegia remain as mysterious as ever. We can attribute Celtic origins to this ancient tradition; according to some local historians, this ceremony recalls the pagan feast of the dendrophors who raised a pine dedicated to Cibele and Attis. Following other interpretations, we can link these rituals to the pagan sun theory and the natural cycle of the seasons or to the purification theory. In many instances, the bonfire ritual symbolizes burning and keeping witches, and therefore evil, away.

Nowadays, the ceremony has lost its original meaning; nonetheless, it has kept a magic and spiritual allure. In the Carcavegia, the bonfire is merely the epilogue of a festival that begins on 2 January. Teenagers and young men are the ones who are in charge of staging the ceremony as part of a tourist event that combines tradition and entertainment in a folkloristic mood. Up to the evening before Epiphany, the streets are full of young people collecting combustible material for the pyre to the sound of horns and bells, while others make the stuffed figures of the *vecc* and the *vegia* with a card around their necks bearing the names and surnames. Year after year, obviously, given the longevity of the locals, the chosen persons change. At the last Carcavegia, in 2005, the man had been born in 1914. This is certainly not a sign of disrespect toward senior citizens but, rather, the continuation of a tradition based on the idea that burning the oldest two in the village can bring good luck. If the two persons cannot go out in the evening, the day before, they can even invite the young people with the *pupun* (the stuffed figures) to their home and offer drinks and sweets. Rarely are the man and woman to be burnt in effigy offended by the honor received (Figure 2.4).

In the recent past, the event in Premosello Chiovenda has begun to embody a different meaning for this community of young organizers. The performance of the bonfire ritual and its staging activities are becoming more and more a representation of their identity and the signification of their shared and distinctive social project.

The young male organizers do not view the event as a transitional period in their lives. They have invested themselves in it and made it a symbol of their lifestyle. Indirectly and unknowingly rebelling against the more liberal and secular lifestyle of their parents and fellow villagers, a trend started by the ambitious yuppies of the 1980s, their role in maintaining their grandfathers' and great-grandfathers' lifestyle involves laying claim to their group identity by way of contrast to the contemporary life of their local community. This seems very much like the generational pendulum swings between secular and religious ideologies and conservative and liberal ideologies noted by a number of historians.

During the rest of the year, these young males study, practice sports, and go to bars and

Figure 2.4 Al vecc *(the old man) and* la vegia *(the old woman) burned in 2004.*

other places of entertainment, just as most other people of their age. But their lives are spartan, based on the simple and genuine values of life in the mountains. They relish authenticity. To them, this ancient ritual is a way to strip away the modern world and its multiple levels of falsehoods and wrongs. Although they live the life of well-off adolescents and young people alongside that of peasant life, they are returning to a simpler agrarian lifestyle based upon tradition and nostalgia. They devote themselves to agriculture and animal rearing, having bought, either individually or collectively in the last two years, animals for breeding. They renovate old stables. They are supporting themselves mainly by physical labor and economic sacrifices. Their day is divided between doing things connected with their social status as high school and university students, sons, workers and so on, and performing acts connected with creating a lifestyle that more faithfully brings them into touch with a primal, older way of life that they consider to be authentic and genuine. Observing the multitasking represented by their behavior, actions, speech, and consumer styles, it is interesting to note how this form of identification and distinction from previous generations requires the performance of the fire ritual for its legitimization.

This ritual provides the stage on which they act out their chosen lives, enact their reference values. It represents the ability, strength, and energy catalyzed in the boys' daily lives, the part that other people do not see during the year and which, in the final analysis, should not be seen because it is linked to the value of simplicity. It is an enactment of local ethos more than merely a retro-touristic performance for outsiders. Mountain life does not require individuals to make their lives into a spectacle; only nature and transcendent forces are required. Bonfire time, or Carcavegia as it is called in Premosello, is a time for turning nature's life cycles into a spectacle, from birth to death, for the appearance of magic, the sense of the wonder of nature that follows its course as it always has, year after year. Nature is incorporated, embodied, and harnessed in the ritual giving local ethos a primal charge, in classic Turnerian fashion.

Given the importance of this time and the intrinsic sacredness of the ritual, the spectacle has to be magnificent. Just as with Burning Man's ever growing and ever more mass-mediated spectacle, the bonfire must be very high as it symbolizes the strength and energy of the people who have created and tended it. Competitive and masculine, the bigger the fire, the stronger and more suitable the male. The fire should be huge, frightening, and imposing, signaling a more powerful village than the neighboring village, halfway down the mountain, which is holding its own fire ritual. The bonfire glows out on the mountain, proclaiming an existential "we are here" once a year, and simultaneously symbolizing the continuity of life. The young men, far from conformists, have their own sense of right and wrong, driven by the fire's innate competitive rules. They resist the safety restrictions imposed by the local authority for the event, viewing them as antithetical to the event's competitive meanings and striving soul. They are unwilling to compromise; "their" fire must be large and frightening, not small and unimpressive. Much is at stake.

The fire's success symbolizes the abilities and legitimacy – the worthiness in the eyes of whichever gods one chooses – of this small village community. Likewise, it elevates the team of young men who, fighting against the postmodern tide of capricious and superficial demands of the ever-changing global present, are able to prove through a rite of passage that they can handle well the fire passed on to them by prior generations.

The Burning Man and Burning Old Man and Woman Joy Fire rituals have common origins and surprisingly similar themes. The deep involvement of consumers in the Burning Man festival has been documented extensively elsewhere (e.g., Kozinets, 2002; Kozinets and Sherry, 2004). However, the organization, competition, spirituality, and self-governance of these shared experiences are, we believe, no accident. They are central to our understanding of the forces that drive the communal adoption of participation in social environments (Figure 2.5).

The spectacle, the emancipatory, purifying, cleansing, and literal power of fire, is no doubt part of the ritual, but "fire" is an energetic concept that could be applied to many spectacles in our world, including concerts, celebrity, mass media appearances, religion, sports, war, and even major business spectacles such as trade shows. Each, like the bonfire, promises its own variety of transcendence as well as entertainment. Each has a fanatical following. Each has its leaders and its more passive audiences. But especially in the fire rituals we have described above, the active participation by devoted attendants, which we call a form of "ludic autotely," is crucial to belief and to psychic resonance. At Burning Man, where thousands of people build theme camps for one another, where people are constantly admonished to "radically participate" and that there are "no spectators" at the event, active co-creation is woven into the very fabric of the gathering. The grassroots result of this participation is simple, primal, and profound. When people participate – whether they be Mountain Men re-enactors, Civil War re-enactors, Renaissance Fair re-enactors, Star Trek fans, X-files convention organizers, Star Wars movie line campouts, river rafters, sky-divers, anti-Nike activists, Mac user groups, online coffee connoisseurs, massively multiplayer Halo2 gamers, or Harley-Davidson brandfest organizers – they are brought into the circle of the fire. In ludic autotely, they create for each other. They share with and care for one an-

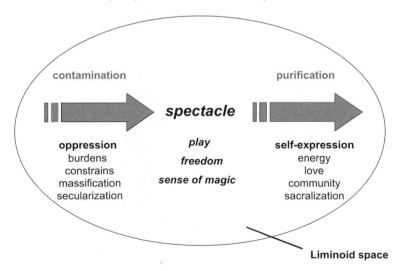

Figure 2.5 The co-creation of fire rituals.

other. They build on the creative energy of their fire. They create a separate space, away from the mundane. Through their sacrifices and gifts, they co-construct a sense of the sacred.

The liminal is a threshold quality of the second stage of ritual that involves a change to participants, often a transformation of their social status (Turner, 1974). The liminal state, when ritual actors are betwixt and between their old and new identities, is characterized by ambiguity, openness, disorientation, transition, and indeterminacy. In industrial societies, the process is called "liminoid" (Turner, 1974). The process of purification in Figure 2.5 takes place in a particular liminoid zone, with all of the liminal's sense of uncertainty and possibility, but with none of its formalized ritual status change.

IN ANOTHER FUEGO: THE COMMERCIAL PRODUCTION OF CONSUMER PARTICIPATION

We will consider a form of consumption that is related to the experiential themed environment of places such as ESPN Zone, a super-themed multifarious sports bar-based entertainment complex created by the master imaginers at the Disney Company (Figure 2.6).

In Italy, we have studied and found similar types of behavior at two major fairs for car lovers and related sports, Motor Show and My Special Car Show (see case vignette 2.2). For five days every year, fans sharing this interest meet in Bologna for a regular annual meeting to preview new cars and racing sports items, to try out new technology, to have "hands-on" experience with the cars and motorbikes of the future, to see their favorite champions racing. They gather for the pure pleasure of performing in front of enthusiasts. In this context,

Figure 2.6 The atrium of ESPN Zone, Chicago: the gateway to the world of televisual experience of sport.

27

consumers temporarily live in a world full of surprises and fun linked to their favorite sport, they build on their own identities as experts, and they gather information and enjoy the experience of living at the forefront of innovation. By trying out the new cars and new technology, visitors can not only exchange ideas about the products and develop their own brand preferences, but can also test their expertise and build their own identity as racing connoisseurs.

CASE VIGNETTE 2.2: MOTOR SHOW AND MY SPECIAL CAR SHOW

The Motor Show, held for more than thirty years in Italy, is a sector-focused exhibition dedicated to the world of motoring, cars, and motorcycles. In December, more than a million motoring enthusiasts keep an appointment for nine days, during which the most important global producers present the innovations in the sector to dealers and to the public. The exhibition covers an area of 460,000 square feet, of which 300,000 square feet is dedicated to competitions, performance exhibitions, and product tests. In this area, there are more than 400 exhibitors of cars, motorcycles, and related products and services.

The exhibition has been enriched over time. Today, alongside the presentation and testing of product innovations, competitions and product exhibitions of the highest level are held in which champions from various disciplines participate, meeting their fans in an atmosphere of entertainment and in celebration of the motor industry (Figure 2.7).

In line with the strategy of making the visitor/consumer ever more the protagonist, the organizers have held a second event alongside the exhibition, dedicated to car enthusiasts, and in particular to car tuning. Since 2004, Rimini has been the location for the "My Special Car Show" dedicated to the "celebration" of the personalized car. During this event, not only can the players in the custom and sports car sectors present their products and services, but consumers can

Figure 2.7 *New product exhibition and entertainment at the Motor Show.*

also exhibit their own personalized cars and share a common passion with the visitors. In the "My Special Club" section, clubs can hire special areas where they can show their members' cars. In this context, the exhibition space and opportunity are important occasions not only to share a passion but also to "exhibit" and to be observed, even rewarded.

Of major interest to us was the participatory aspect of the show, its own brand of ludic autotely. Because some of the consumers wish to star in the show and feature their own personal experiences, and resist the limited ways in which the marketers expect them to participate, for several years, the fair has had a section dedicated to custom cars and cars personalized by consumers. Much as with Burning Man's many art cars, theme camps, and technological innovations, ordinary people at these shows exhibit their own personalized cars, showing interested visitors the devices and innovations that they have created with their own taste and creativity.

Gradually, the section took on the role of a stage for a person's own performance, for the intermingling of individual identity project, life themes, interests, and branded products. In this situation, the consumer/builder and the visitors who share interests and curiosity contribute to the creation of an event and a phenomenon, going beyond the boundaries originally envisioned by event organizers. This transformation from trade show to star of the show seemed to make all the difference to participants. The level and degree of entertainment shifted, and the experimental area assumed the coordinates of liminal space (Turner, 1974). New layers of authenticity and meaning accreted. Over time, the phenomenon became so significant that the organizers created a special fair dedicated exclusively to this section of the main fair, which is held today in another city, Rimini, at a different time of the year. Today, therefore, car enthusiasts have their own physical space and time for an ad hoc event which ultimately ratifies their "sovereignty."

As one of the participants explained, these consumers/builders sometimes dedicate hundreds of hours of their free time to work on their cars, using their creativity and practical skills to make them unique. During the event, their "baby" comes to life in front of an audience that can appreciate and understand its value and also relate to its creators (Figure 2.8).

What is fascinating to note about these examples is the role of consumer participation in even the most industrial events. The indomitable creativity of the human spirit shines through these examples, as consumers usurp ESPN Zone's themed environment and, say, use a rifle simulation to turn into snipers preying on innocent bystanders, or to become celebrities in a pickup game of basketball on a mini-court (see Kozinets et al., 2004). In Burning Man, major degrees of freedom are fully utilized, producing an out-of-this-world artistic and experimental experience. In fact, the etymology of both the words experiment and experience are the same: the Latin root experiri, a test or a trial. Consumers are testing creatively, trying through their actions to express themselves, their individuality. This

Figure 2.8 *Exhibiting creativity at My Special Car Show.*

experimentation is found throughout all four of our example sites in varying degrees but, in each case, the results are profound and unmistakable: where consumers are given large degrees of freedom to create or co-create with organizers, they feel it as authenticity, a type of soulfulness and meaning, and they respond with enthusiasm, energy, and action. Marketers may think that their job is to provide a prepackaged total experience – but consumers must add their dreams, ideals, values, history, meanings, and personalities to these raw ingredients. In the end, it is only the consumers' experience that counts.

Play becomes a competitive activity in these environments as well, and this is another powerful force (Figure 2.9). Consumers struggle against time and each other, in rituals originally designed – and perhaps still culturally and biologically wired – as placemarkers in time and space. They contend with other elements as well, notably an *arrangement of the game* which surrounds the process. This includes the rules and order of the game, the hedonistic aspects of the game, the degrees of freedom, the types of players and referees, the creation of a game-playing community that shares the game and thus realizes it or makes it real. It also includes the *real and imaginary space* in which the game takes place, the place wherein the game's contrasts with day-to-day reality are made evident.

Playfulness in these rituals becomes not a side-benefit, but an expression of their very essence, as luminous, frightening, and powerful creative forces play with lives and human events, so too do humans play with the forces of ritual and nature. The play, the ritual, the participation, the growth, and allusions to transformation and transmutation are essential and fundamental activities in themselves, ontological constituents of human life (Fink, 1986) that, we would argue here, are fundamental to experiential marketing practice and consumption. "The play's the thing" is a bardic encapsulation of ludic autotely.

Figure 2.9 *Play at ESPN Zone.*

WALKING ACROSS THE BONFIRE: CONSUMER CREATION AND CO-CREATION

Anthropology and phenomenological geography tell us that the importance of the physical and tangible environment of a space cannot be understated and must be carefully managed. Space is transformed into place through the incorporation and acknowledgment of cultural meaning, of boundaries, rules, structures, paths, which consumers interpret and use as journey-makers to find their own ways. As marketers design experiences, it is powerful to consider what consumers will use these experiences for. Each pilgrimage may be part of a larger pyramid, each experience part of a larger journey. Experiences become the raw material of life. Place becomes a space for need fulfillment, interpreted, sculpted, modeling.

The co-creation of consumer experience by a self-aware, creative, and active consumer who is able to interpret and freely redefine rules and proposals from marketers can be based on several foundational elements that we have described in this chapter: rules, challenges, competition, community, tradition, history, enactment, and embodiment. The presence of strong culture enhances all of these elements and, in today's society, as suggested by the Italian and American fire rituals, a strong sense of tradition and nostalgia seem to signal authenticity to consumers. With their own creativity, imagination, and openness, marketers and their companies might design experiences responsive to customization by the consumer. Marketers might view even the most elaborate experiences as ingredients that consumers will use in different ways for their own differing recipes for life and happiness. Consumers become the co-authors of their own experiences, assisted and listened to by marketers, who offer an incredible profusion of images, myths, stories, and experiences.

The never-ending story of consumers as co-creative wild things will then continue, as the children's stories foretell that they will. With marketers in tow, consumers will mix and match, blending, as our opening Dr. Seuss rhyme avers, kites and their beds, and walking with a row of upright cats on their heads. The boundless creativity of the consumer is, and always was, the source of marketing experience and consumption experientiality.

DISCUSSION QUESTIONS

- What other examples can you think of that involve the strong consumer co-creation of experience?
- If consumers create their own experiences, doesn't this mean they are producers? Can you create and consume at the same time?
- Does it really make sense to call all shopping mall experiences creative or experiential? Or might these ideas just apply to certain stores or spaces?
- Which are some of the strongest forces that drive consumers' participation in these environments?
- What do you think the future holds for playful consumer experiences such as the type we described here? Will we see more or less of them? Why?

NOTES

1 Containing some original material, this chapter also summarizes and combines the findings of already published research, while both recapitulating and advancing new theory. Through citation of this larger body of work, we refer readers throughout to these other studies.

2 We are grateful to our key informants, Pierantonio and Silvano Ragozza, for their contribution in collecting data about the origins and evolution of the Carcavegia ritual.

REFERENCES

Brown, S. (1995) *Postmodern Marketing*. London: Routledge.

Debord, G. (1995) *The Society of the Spectacle*. New York: Zone.

Deighton, J. and Grayson, K. (1995) "Marketing and Seduction: Building Exchange Relationships by Managing Social Consensus." *Journal of Consumer Research* 21(March): 660–676.

Fink, E. (1986) *Oasi della Gioia. Idee per una ontologia del Gioco*. Salerno: Edizioni 10/17.

Gottdeiner, M. (1997) *The Theming of America*. Boulder, CO: Westview.

Joy, A. and Sherry, J.F., Jr (2003) "Speaking of Art as Embodied Imagination: A Multisensory Approach to Understanding Aesthetic Experience." *Journal of Consumer Research* 30(September): 259–282.

Kozinets R.V. (2002) "Can Consumers Escape the Market? Emancipatory Illuminations from Burning Man." *Journal of Consumer Research* 29(June): 20–38.

Kozinets, R.V. and Sherry, J.F., Jr (2004) "Dancing on Common Ground: Exploring the Sacred at Burning Man." In: St. John, G. (ed.) *Rave Culture and Religion*. New York: Routledge, 287–303.

Kozinets, R.V., Sherry, J.F., Jr, Storm, D., Duhachek, A., Nuttavuthisit, K. and DeBerry-Spence, B. (2004) "Ludic Agency and Retail Spectacle." *Journal of Consumer Research* 31(December): 658–672.

Pine, B.J., II and Gilmore, J.H. (1999) *The Experience Economy: Work is Theatre and Every Business a Stage*. Boston: Harvard Business School Press.

Sherry, J.F., Jr (ed.) (1998) *Servicescapes: The Concept of Place in Contemporary Markets*. Chicago: AMA.

Sherry, J.F., Jr (2005) "Brand Meaning." In: Calkins, T. and Tybout, A. (eds.) *Kellogg on Branding*. New York: John Wiley & Sons.

Turner, V. (1974) "Liminal to Liminoid in Play, Flow and Ritual: An Essay in Comparative Symbology." *Rice University Studies* 60(3), 53–92.

Wolf, M. (1999) *The Entertainment Economy: How Mega-Media Forces are Transforming our Lives*. New York: Random House.

Chapter 3

Consumer immersion in an experiential context

Antonella Carù and Bernard Cova

KEY POINTS

- Immersion is the means by which consumers access an experience.
- Firms can create and manage experiential contexts, not experiences.
- These experiential contexts can involve stores, factories, brandfests, or websites.
- A good experiential context should be enclavized, secured, and thematized.
- Support systems, collective action, and self-determination can be used to facilitate consumer immersion.

In just a few years, immersion in a consumption experience has become a major theme in consumer behavior literature. A consumption experience is understood here as the possibility of developing meaning and substance in life. Contemporary consumers supposedly prefer being immersed in consumption experiences to simply purchasing products or services. Consumption is made up of "immersion into experiential moments of enchanted, multifaceted and spectacular encounters" (Firat and Dholakia, 1998, p. 101). Experiential marketing approaches (Pine and Gilmore, 1999) and postmodern consumption rhetoric (Firat and Dholakia, 1998) make widespread use of an immersion concept that has been borrowed from more or less distant disciplines such as education, literature, psychology, or religion. The concept's utilization has accelerated along with the rise of the Internet, due to many online operators' apparent attempts to immerse consumers in a virtual experience. Without forgetting the arts, where the immersion process has long been considered key to an esthetic experience, this construct is used today by analysts interested in a whole range of activities, including tourism, leisure (concerts, festivals, etc.), and sports. To really grasp this notion, which is central to the consumption experience, the present chapter will begin by developing a consumer immersion model before going on to specify the main elements of the experiential contexts that firms can create and manage. It will then conclude by detailing the tactics that firms and other institutions can pursue to facilitate immersion in an experiential context.

IMMERSING THE CONSUMER

In the field of marketing, immersion cannot be dissociated from experience, a concept that has attracted the attention of an increasing number of researchers over the past two decades: "Life is to be produced and created, in effect, constructed through multiple experiences in which the consumer immerses" (Firat and Dholakia, 1998, p. 96). Immersion is perceived as a means of accessing a consumption experience: "Immersion produces the experience" (Firat and Dholakia, 1998, p. 97). In other words, the consumption experience would appear to be a subjective occurrence that people go through by pursuing a process of being immersed in an experiential context. It has been widely acknowledged that today's consumers seek immersion in a variety of experiences ranging from a hyper-real environment (Goulding *et al.*, 2002) to a brand-related social context (Oliver, 1999). Modern practitioners generally talk about immersion in "an activity or environment . . . in the sights, sounds and smells that surround them" (Pine and Gilmore, 1998, p. 102); thus, in an experiential context, understood here as an environment, some activities have a sensorial stimulation likely to bring on the experience. For the proponents of experiential marketing (Pine and Gilmore, 1999), consumers' total, physical, and mental immersion in the activity and/or environment underpinning the experience will help to concretize the experience for them (as will their active participation). Furthermore, although the experience may result from something, for many authors, it is nothing more than an intermediary result (Firat and Venkatesh, 1995). Consumers' ultimate goal is not the experience itself but a proliferation of experiences. Today, consumers shop to produce their identities. This offers the possibility of a multitude of experiences that "give [them] a chance to experience different lifestyles that provide excursions into production or customising of alternative selves and self-images" (Firat and Dholakia, 1998, p. 97). To summarize, what we are evolving toward is a conceptualization that views immersion as a process of accessing an experience, an intermediary objective that comes on top of people's other experiences, to produce a result that is final but never finished: the consumer's ongoing identity project (Arnould and Thompson, 2005).

> In marketing, the immersion concept suffers from the sentiment of immediacy that is best conveyed by the often associated image of a consumer diving into something, a vision that tends to see immersion as nothing more than a model of instantaneous emotional induction insofar as it seems to suffice that one 'be there' to cause an immersion.
>
> (Carù and Cova, 2003, p. 48)

Indeed, the immersion concept literally implies an embodied experience, transmitting the idea of a total elimination of the distance between the consumer and the situation. A question does remain, however, as to whether immersion in a consumption experience is always a fast and quasi-instantaneous phenomenon (diving into an experiential context) or whether it involves a slower and therefore more progressive approach (Ladwein, 2003). Moreover, is immersion in a consumption experience necessarily all-encompassing, or can it be partial? In short, there are two very distinct ways of envisioning the process of being immersed in an experience, and the experiential context:

- either as something total and immediate, such as diving into water;
- or as something partial and progressive, such as a group of so-called appropriation operations.

CASE VIGNETTE 3.1: IMMERSION IN THE CONTEXT OF A CLASSICAL MUSIC CONCERT

Analysis of introspective narratives reporting on neophyte spectators' experiences during a classical music concert (Carù and Cova, 2003) highlights the fact that the consumption experience is composed of a succession of intense but short moments of Immersion, frequently interrupted by moments of much lesser intensity. As such, it is nothing like a single, instantaneous, and full-scale dive by the consumer into the deep end of the pool. It is more of a repetition of paddling or dipping one's toes into the water (to maintain the metaphor). Moreover, the consumer lives these intense moments of immersion through a complex combination of nesting, investigating, and stamping operations in which s/he conjures up all of his/her competencies and knowledge.

> When the Maestro was talking, I was able to see the images inside of myself . . . Whenever that happened I was at one with the experience.
>
> (D)

> It's beautiful! I really like the music, it's truly magical. I don't know what I'm thinking because I can't control my thoughts . . . I can't even feel my backache anymore. Physically, I feel very relaxed. I have ABSOLUTELY no interest anymore in the place or the people . . . (three lines lower). I've been thinking about work and losing concentration. The experience has been ruined.
>
> (SB)

In all of their reports, consumers identified brief moments of immersion leading to a feeling of well-being, growth, and gratification, which some described as "small victories."

> I finally understand something about music! Music can have a meaning!!! Understanding this has made me feel really happy, I now get it that when someone says that classical music is beautiful it's because they basically understand what it means.
>
> (M)

Similarly, the lack or infrequency of these short moments of immersion during the experience led to sentiments of frustration, or to a lack of appreciation for the experience.

> I just want to say that compared with what I had imagined I found it harder than expected. Probably I was thinking, maybe wrongly, that more would be "unveiled" to me.
>
> (SG)

Do consumers want to be immersed in a consumption experience, or do they want to be the ones immersing themselves? The first formulation views consumers as relatively passive and potentially manipulated by the firm, while the second sees consumers as people who are relatively active and who are able to immerse themselves in the experience. Whereas the proponents of experiential marketing (Pine and Gilmore, 1999) mainly opt for the image of immersed consumers, others (Filser, 2002) emphasize the role that consumers play as the (co)-producers of their experience, thereby supporting the notion that consumers immerse themselves. Indeed, "this recognition of consumers' (experience) production role is one of the new theoretical orientations being shared by several autonomous analytical frameworks" (Filser, 2002, p. 14). This can be connected to the idea of appropriation (Ladwein, 2003), to counterbalance the figure of an "inert" consumer who dives into an experiential context. The diving image implies that immersion is tantamount to consumers jumping into a hyper-reality that has largely been introduced by the firm itself, which means that they lose their freedom of choice due to pressure from their own emotions and sensations. The idea of appropriation, on the other hand, suggests that immersion should be thought of as a whole set of operations that consumers carry out to produce the experience by manipulating to their own advantage whatever is being done to manipulate them. Toward this end, consumers will use the tools, competencies, and aptitudes that they have developed during the course of the experience (Ladwein, 2003). Indeed, it is by acting thus that they will produce their own identity via their consumption.

> For the postmodern consumer, consumption is not a mere act of devouring, destroying, or using things. It is also not the end process of the (central) economic cycle, but an act of production of experiences and selves or self-images.
>
> (Firat and Dholakia, 1998, p. 96)

These considerations allow us to offer a consumer immersion model (Figure 3.1) in which the consumer is immersed in an experiential context either immediately and totally by diving into it, or else progressively and partially via appropriation. In this way, cumulative subjective experiences, facilitated by immersion in commercial or non-commercial contexts, help consumers to construct their own identities.

EXPERIENTIAL CONTEXTS

What is paramount for any firm that has turned to experiential marketing is to devise experiential contexts that are likely to encourage consumers' immersion, so as to render their

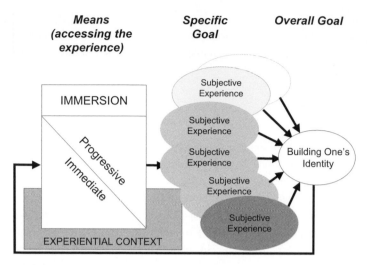

Figure 3.1 The consumer immersion model.

subjective experiences more agreeable and, where possible, unforgettable. Contrary to what the "experience economy" school asserts (Pine and Gilmore, 1999), firms do not actually offer experiences. An experience is a subjective episode that customers live through when they interact with a firm's product or service offer. A firm can therefore offer experiential contexts that consumers each mobilize in order to immerse themselves and thus to (co)-produce their own experiences. A cuisine with special recipes or ingredients plus the presence of friends – and suddenly what one has is a context that lends itself to the production of a culinary experience. Our lives are full of experiential contexts: specially fitted coaches on modern fast trains, sidewalk cafes where friends can meet for cocktails, family picnics on the beach, etc. Contexts of this kind have always been around. What is novel is the fact that companies are now taking over the production and management of such contexts – which explains their proliferation in our daily landscape.

Having understood individuals' current need for repeated immersions in contexts of this kind, retailers have been trying since the 1980s to transform their points-of-sale into environments conducive to the advent of so-called shopping experiences (Filser, 2002). A great deal of work has been done on shopping environments, including the way sales spaces are designed, to try and re-enchant customers (Firat and Ventakesh, 1995). These efforts have taken a very specific turn since the late 1990s, on account of producers' desire to give consumers brand experiences that will immerse them in "branded" experiential contexts. The creation and management of experiential contexts has become one of brand management's main activities. The aim here is to facilitate consumers' immersion in an enchanted environment. Of course, consumers can experience a brand outside of such contexts, for example at home using the brand's products, but for the company, the key experiential contexts are the ones that will allow it to closely control and guide the processes by which people access the experience, as well as the experience itself. Four major types of brand experience contexts have been identified:

- Brand stores such as Apple stores, Nike Town, and Audi Forum, which lead to highly "branded" shopping experiences. In so-called brand flagship stores (Kozinets *et al.*, 2002, p. 20), consumers find the kind of "lavish decor, sleek finishes and attention to the smallest details" that will likely respond to Pine and Gilmore's (1999) injunctions concerning the need to promote shopping experiences that are increasingly fun and can be assimilated with the type of experiences people have at theme parks such as Disney World.

- Brand plants such as Volkswagen's Autostadt in Wolfsburg, the Crayola Factory in Two Rivers Landing (Pennsylvania), the Guinness Brewery in Dublin, or the Heineken Experience in Amsterdam, where people can have a factory experience. Today, the border between a tourist attraction and a plant is less and less clear-cut, to the extent that people often have to pay to visit a brand plant, including the brand museum that is so often part of a plant or adjacent to it. The borders can also be very blurry in the case of theme parks; one example is the Legoland chain. The idea here is to have a complex that immerses the consumer, for longer periods of time than would be the case with a brand store, in the history and production processes of a brand's products.

- Brandfests, with examples including the various celebrations and outings that Harley-Davidson or Ducati (case vignette 3.2) have organized to encourage a festival experience. These brand-related events are opportunities for consumers to have an embodied experience of the brand by entertaining a direct contact with it (McAlexander and Schouten, 1998). Here, immersion is facilitated by the fact that participants are offered the possibility of developing and/or reinforcing physical contacts with staff or products. The experiential context is ephemeral and constantly changing in such instances, much like people's experiences at live shows (Puhl *et al.*, 2005).

- Brand websites (i.e., the Mini and Nutella websites) are now being designed to give people a virtual experience. Most texts on consumption experiences are implicitly grounded in real contexts, whether natural or artificial (Kozinets *et al.*, 2002), but the Internet's rise has made people accept the possibility that the context of their experience will be virtual in nature, driven by advances in so-called immersion technologies, notably when applied to online games.

CASE VIGNETTE 3.2: THE EXPERIENTIAL CONTEXTS OF THE DUCATI BRAND

The epitome of a legendary brand, Ducati is seen as the Ferrari of the motorcycle world, due to its history, products, and even the fact that it is located in Bologna (only 30 km from Modena). Having been taken over nine years ago by Federico Minoli, this Italian brand has benefited from some major *brand management* efforts that have been notably translated into the development of a coherent system of experiential contexts that all play strongly on the emotional dimension of what has been identified as the Ducati experience.

Ducati stores

There are 140 Ducati stores in the world, including fifty in Italy. Unlike brand dealerships, Ducati stores offer not only motorcycles but also alternative product ranges such as Ducati Corsa clothes lines, all in an atmosphere that is likely to be very enticing to brand fanatics. Each of these stores has an architecture adapted to its specific location and country, while also including certain indispensable elements that define Ducati, particularly the omnipresence of red and white, the colors of staff uniforms, for example. Such stores are totally dedicated to the brand.

The Ducati plant and its museum

Ducati's top fans can visit its factory close to Bologna, where everything is open to them except for the secret Ducati competition corner (people are offered a porthole so they can glimpse what is going on inside). The factory has been transformed into a veritable church. In Federico Minoli's words:

> When I took over the company, there were leaks in the plant roof. The first thing I did was to build a museum, however. This immediately led to a strike by workers but also showed what direction we wanted to take. After all, Ducati was no longer in a position to use technological advances to differentiate itself from the competition. The Japanese have much greater possibilities in this domain than we do. To justify our high price strategy, for a same level of technology, we have to leverage other strengths like the Ducati myth, our originality and our history.

Ducati festivals

Ducati organizes not one single annual event but a series of regional, national, and international happenings, all of which are occasions to celebrate the brand and create greater proximity with consumers' daily lives. Events include consumer meets at tracks, as on 25 and 26 June 2005 at Rossa Corsa II in Croix en Ternois, where 150–200 confirmed Ducatists used the course to put on demonstrations and help everyone discover the joys of racing in an unpressured environment. There are also collective outings such as the Centopassi, organized over 21–24 July 2005 to allow bikers to test their driving capabilities and endurance on extremely demanding mountain roads and over awe-inspiring summits. Most of these events are enclavized (i.e., no other brands are present) and closely watched over by Ducati personnel.

Ducati websites
Every major country has its own Ducati website. These sites are generally organized into five sections (racing, history, community, products, and stores) that
clearly translate the priority given to living with the brand as opposed to the
actual purchasing act. They also refer to other contexts, often details on Ducati
stores, maps, and opening hours for the Bologna factory plus announcements
about (and, above all, photo reports on) Ducati festivals. Under the heading "I
was there, were you?" in the "Photo Gallery" section, there are pictures of consumers sharing emotions during such events.

Regardless of the type of experiential context in question (whether it involves a brand
or not), a company has to ensure that the context is simultaneously enclavized, secure, and
thematized. Indeed, these are the three qualities that will constitute the context's underlying foundations (Firat and Dholakia, 1998), making it easier for consumers to focus their
attention, and thus to be immersed:

■ The context must be enclavized with specific boundaries as this lets consumers break
with (and step outside of) their daily lives, bringing them into a separate world of
enchantment where all of the usual worries and hardships that they face in their
ordinary lives disappear. Furthermore, "the enclave limits the intrusion of elements
that do not belong to the theme and, thereby, enhances the intensity of the experience"
(Firat and Dholakia, 1998, p. 107). Flagship stores are typically the sorts of enclaves
where people can focus on everything a brand is offering without any intrusion from
external elements, i.e., from another brand (Kozinets *et al.*, 2002).

■ The context must be secure and closely monitored as this eliminates the need to pay
attention to oneself or to one's children or things – all concerns that people have
in their daily lives. "The immersion of self in this hyperreal but secure environment
contrasts sharply with the pressures often faced in everyday life" (Goulding *et al.*, 2002,
p. 281). Consumers would rather not have to deal with the hard reality, preferring
environments and activities that are more watered down and controlled, and which
minimize the risks they take.

■ The context must be thematized. A great deal of attention has been paid at the point-
of-sale to the need to thematize the experiential context (Pine and Gilmore, 1999).
This acts as a symbolic packaging of the context, notably by ascribing meaning to the
act of consumption. A theme can be an activity, era, region, population, or combination
of these elements, and must be very distinctive. In any event, a firm must make efforts
to enunciate and materialize this theme.

Some criticize the underlying foundations of company-created and -managed experiential contexts (Cova and Cova, 2001) as being totalitarian in nature, hence conceivably

leading to rejection by certain consumers. Questions can be raised as to how efficient it is to seek this kind of coherence if it implies conditions that are almost "prison-like." The customary response by the proponents of thematization (Pine and Gilmore, 1999) lies in the idea of the consumer's concentration. In this view, consumers cannot access an experience if their attention disperses.

The company must then work to enunciate and materialize the theme. This involves creating theater effects and *staging* the company's product or service offer, and putting the consumer *on stage*, through major efforts impacting the décor, such as environmental design and locational atmospherics (Pine and Gilmore, 1999). These efforts revolve around sensorial and imaginary devices that serve to overstimulate consumers' senses and imagination, thereby accentuating their ability to concentrate, which in turn accelerates their immersion:

- The overstimulation of the five senses is achieved through a polysensorial layering of consumers' senses of sight, hearing, smell, taste, and touch (Schmitt, 1999).
- The overstimulation of imagination involves a constantly renewed introduction of narratives (Filser, 2002), stories, intrigues, and images as part of a playful approach known in retail circles as shoptainment (Kozinets et al., 2002).

Once the context has been enclavized, secured, and thematized, and after the theme has been dressed in theater effects and staged, the consumer is supposed to be able to dive seamlessly into the context, thereby accessing the experience. It is here that the theories of experiential marketing and consumption re-enchantment encounter their limits. Some consumers will be able to access an experience, but not everyone. There is nothing straightforward or systematic about this access, which requires competencies or aptitudes that consumers do not necessarily have at their disposal (Ladwein, 2003). In fact, this is a construct that mainly applies to consumers who are already "experts" in a theme and/or context and can therefore dive straight into it – not to "novice" consumers who feel distant from a theme and/or its staging, a sentiment that impedes their immersion, thus killing off the experience. Spectacular staging such as enclavization can even create threshold effects for consumers in this situation. As a result, the immersion of people who are new to a brand and/or a context much more frequently assumes the sequence of nesting, exploration, and stamping, rather than a dive into something (Carù and Cova, 2003). It is not enough that a company simply creates a good experiential context – it must also and, above all, develop the means to facilitate people's immersion in this context.

HOW TO FACILITATE IMMERSION IN AN EXPERIENTIAL CONTEXT?

When working on a consumption experience, companies tend to categorize consumers by their level of expertise in a given field, whether the arts, culture, sports, or something else. For example, gardening companies, notably plant specialists, consider that, when faced with the immensity of the world of flora, only a small minority of consumers possess sufficient competencies to become immediately immersed. After all, the urbanization of our societies has led to a loss of the expertise that used to be transmitted from one generation to the next – even though, for example, 80 percent of all French households still have at least some garden space adjacent to their main residences (source: *Promojardin*, 2003). This is why firms in this sector use a typology categorizing consumers by their competencies, organized around fifteen main gardening tasks (source: *Protocoles*, 2001, covering 600 French consumers): 11 percent are "experts," capable of doing all fifteen tasks; 36 percent are "advanced," capable of doing at least thirteen tasks; 25 percent are "average," capable of doing ten tasks; and 28 percent are "novices" who can do at most six tasks. Whereas experts and many advanced gardeners can dive straight into the sorts of experiential contexts that have been created by firms such as Botanic, Jardiland, and Truffaut (thus quickly accessing the experience), average and especially novice gardeners rarely or never succeed without outside help. As a result, gardening companies, like firms in many other sectors, have developed a range of tactics to facilitate average or novice consumers' immersion into an experiential context: support systems, collective action, and self-determination. These three tactics tend to reduce the mental and/or physical distance that can exist between the consumer and the context of the experience.

Support systems

Using guides and referents are good ways of providing support. The very idea of having a facilitator who is there to ease consumer immersion into an experiential context is quite pervasive in experiential marketing nowadays (Price *et al.*, 1995).

Some evoke a *guide's* figure to express the subtle role that should be played by the particular staff member who will be present during the course of the immersion operation. Interactive vehicles can also play this consumer guidance role, however, when the immersion operation involves an experiential context, for example. Moreover, a novice's immersion depends strongly on the "guide's" ability to act as a quasi-friend, even going as far as to share some intimacy, thereby exceeding consumers' expectations of this type of service (Price *et al.*, 1995). This argues in favor of the development of contact personnel (Puhl *et al.*, 2005) to facilitate novices' immersion. The notion of perceived authenticity is very important here. Immersion will be all the easier when staff members appear to be genuine, i.e., when consumers believe that staff members are doing what they do because they are passionate or feel a sense of vocation, not just because they want to make money. In addition, contact staff members increasingly experience the brands and products that they are promoting in a similarly frenetic manner nowadays. These "passionate salespersons" are in a better position to respond to customer demands and, above all, to facilitate immersion by replacing the traditional sales talk (attributes/advantages/benefits) by an emotional discourse anchored in their own experiences with the brand (Cova and Cova, 2001). The more a guide gives of him- or herself, the more s/he extracts the experience from the confines of a purely commercial exchange, which reassures the novice consumer. In short, contact staff members play a guide's role, but this should not be confused with the role of a simple master of ceremonies ensuring that the show goes on.

The role of the *referents* can be implemented in an experiential context by means of a whole range of vehicles that contact staff members express overtly. It refers to what we find today in other fields, such as the cinema, which is very self-referential and where immersion is facilitated by the recycling and reutilization of referents taken from past films, sometimes involving the total remake or pastiche of a movie (Carù and Cova, 2003). What can be recycled are all the signs and symbols relating to a brand or a company, its past, products, key moments, and leading personalities – all of which the consumer recognizes easily. Depending on the consumer's own history, which provides him/her with a grid to analyze referents that are being revealed in a particular context, s/he will engage in *picking* behavior and progressively appropriate the perimeter of the context. This implies that a firm should also mobilize elements derived from other contexts. For example, within the framework of an initiation to classical music, what will be used are images and names coming from more widely known areas such as pop or film music so that the novice consumer has something to hold on to. This utilization of external elements softens the excessive thematization of the context, thus substantiating the views of those who advocate a moderate usage of thematization.

Collective action

Collective action involves the development and preservation of communitarian-flavored connections within an experiential context, thereby allowing for mutual learning and shared emotions. It also means supporting an understanding of (and participation in) the collective microrituals that structure all activities. Firms that think in terms of one consumer's behavior often neglect the collective dimension of an experience. And yet, the consumption experience needs to be made explicit, explained, and shared if it is to really exist. This is because the attribution of meaning to an individual experience calls for the creation of a narrative that is itself inseparable from the power to say something. An experience is never really complete if it has not been expressed, i.e., as long as it is not been communicated in linguistic or other forms. Whether one has the experience at home or elsewhere, it cannot be separated from ideas such as sharing and collective enjoyment.

Companies have therefore recently started to work on immersion's collective dimension by using group interactions to facilitate it. Many firms have understood the power of *communities* or tribes in the novice consumer's immersion (Muniz and O'Guinn, 2001), trying to develop get-togethers where expert, advanced, average, or novice consumers join forces to enable the latter, reassured by the collective atmosphere, to "test the waters." The ideas applied here include mutual learning (with the more educated training everyone else) and imitation (with novices copying experts' gestures). Certain brands such as Ducati or Harley-Davidson focus specifically on creating and preserving brand communities in which novices are taken under the wing of experts, because of the moral obligation of mutual assistance that is de rigueur in such communities (Muniz and O'Guinn, 2001). In other words, experiential contexts should be thought of as places where connections and meetings occur (Kozinets *et al.*, 2002), meaning that they cannot be characterized by smooth and transparent forms, as is the case with supermarkets that overexpose individuals and restrict their ability to meet one another. Quite the contrary, they should be bumpy and discontinuous, full of private areas and quiet corners that facilitate discrete immersions and small groups of people sharing their emotions.

Even more recently, companies have rediscovered the power of *rituals*, despite the fact that consumer behavior research has for twenty years now been emphasizing the importance of rites for consumers' individual (and especially collective) experiences. This has given us a new vision of consumption, examining it from the standpoint of participation in rituals in which individuals act jointly in a symbolic manner. It remains that rituals in an experiential context do appear to have a relatively ambivalent impact on immersion (Carù and Cova, 2003). For example, many of the applause rituals in a classical music concert constitute a real headache for novices, who do not know whether to applaud at the end of a piece. Rituals are (positive or negative) vectors of immersion, and consumers will immerse themselves in a context only if its rituals help them to advance, instead of increasing their sense of distance because they do not understand the rituals.

Self-determination

Self-determination refers both to training actions (workshops, internships, seminars) that enhance consumers' competencies and to consumers' agency once they are given the means to apply their own specific competencies. Self-determination is rooted in a vision that equates consumers with protagonists, who are traditionally considered to be operating in reaction to something. The idea here is that consumers are trying to be less passive and injecting a personal touch into their consumption experiences. Self-determination is based on the idea of consumers' active participation in an experience (Pine and Gilmore, 1999) in their attempts to broadly transcend it. This is quite straightforward for expert consumers who are capable of surmounting any participation proposal that a firm may organize, but it can also be a significant modus operandi for novices, who can use a trial and error type of process to immerse themselves more deeply.

Training is the path that is traditionally implemented by companies that rely on consumers' self-determination to facilitate their immersion (c.f., the concept of *edutainment*, see Chapter 10 in this book). By so doing, these firms are trying to improve the competencies of consumers, who will then be free to implement these attributes in their own way so as to become increasingly immersed in the experience. The issue here no longer involves guiding consumers but instead empowering them so that they can achieve their immersion all by themselves. Hence, the company-driven proliferation of work experiences, workshops, seminars, and distance learning mechanisms to give consumers the wherewithal they need. Many specialized stores even offer veritable classrooms where experts (who can be either company representatives or expert consumers) come to teach novices.

Nevertheless, it appears that the best way forward for any company that wants to incorporate an element of consumer self-determination is to offer the potential for immersion, which is a veritable smorgasbord composed of diffuse elements that consumers shape through their own immersions. The purpose of this kind of approach is not to offer customers an experience that has been predetermined and structured as part of a scrupulously organized and planned context, but instead to give them an opportunity to achieve *autonomy* by playing a full role in the design and construction of their own experience, something that goes well beyond merely participating in a planned process. In other words, a company's vision must transcend simple global program management approaches that envision experience on a point-by-point basis. Instead, it should pursue the more moderate marketing approach that consists of a unifying platform based on which a process, replete with yardsticks and marked here and there by points of reference and readjustment, can unfold in step with the consumer and his/her competencies (Cova and Cova, 2001). In short, consumer self-determination forces companies to clear up some free space within their experiential contexts and not to organize them in their entirety. "This is the clearly expressed positioning of street festivals, and of most secondary festivals, that give spectators the freedom to choose their own shows and schedules" (Puhl *et al.*, 2005, p. 64).

Companies that decide to go down an experiential marketing path should understand that they generally cannot create an experience per se. What they can do, however, is to help consumers access an experience. To achieve this, they might devise enclavized, thematized, and secured experiential contexts (such as *brands stores*, *brand plants*, *brandfests* or *brand websites*) in which consumers can immerse themselves. To facilitate such an immersion, companies should refocus on what the consumer is actually experiencing, and modulate the assistance they offer to reflect his/her levels of competency and expertise. The overall aim of this kind of approach is to generate an increased number of experiential possibilities for the consumer, who can use such occasions to build and consolidate his/her own identity.

DISCUSSION QUESTIONS

- Why isn't a consumer's immersion always immediate and total?
- What helps consumers to concentrate in an experiential context?
- What are the limitations of a context's thematization?
- Why is a consumer's immersion facilitated by the implementation of a community approach?
- What difference is there between consumer participation and self-determination?

REFERENCES

Arnould, E.J. and Thompson, C.J. (2005) "Consumer Culture Theory (CCT): Twenty Years of Research." *Journal of Consumer Research* 31(March): 868–882.

Carù, A. and Cova, B. (2003) "Approche empirique de l'immersion dans l'expérience de consommation: les opérations d'appropriation." *Recherche et Applications en Marketing* 18(2): 47–65.

Cova, V. and Cova, B. (2001) *Alternatives Marketing*. Paris: Dunod.

Filser, M. (2002) "Le marketing de production d'expériences: statut théorique et implications managériales." *Décisions Marketing* 28(Oct–Dec): 13–22.

Firat, A.F. and Dholakia, N. (1998) *Consuming People: From Political Economy to Theaters of Consumption*. London: Routledge.

Firat, A.F. and Venkatesh, A. (1995) "Liberatory Postmodernism and the Reenchantment of Consumption." *Journal of Consumer Research* 22(December): 239–267.

Goulding, C., Shankar, A. and Elliott, R. (2002) "Working Weeks, Rave Weekends: Identity Fragmentation and the Emergence of New Communities." *Consumption, Markets and Culture* 5(4): 261–284.

Kozinets, R.V., Sherry, J.F., Deberry-Spence, B., Duhachek, A., Nuttavuthisit, K. and Storm, D. (2002) "Themed Flagship Brand Stores in the New Millennium: Theory, Practice, Prospects." *Journal of Retailing* 78(1): 17–29.

Ladwein, R. (2003) "Les méthodes de l'appropriation de l'expérience de consommation: le cas du tourisme urbain." In: Rémy, E., Garubuau-Moussaoui, I., Desjeux, D. and Filser, M. (eds) *Société, Consommation et Consommateurs*. Paris: L'Harmattan, 85–98.

McAlexander, J.H. and Schouten, J.W. (1998) "Brandfests: Servicescapes for the Cultivation of Brand Equity." In: Sherry, J.F. (ed.) *Servicescapes: The Concept of Place in Contemporary Markets*. Lincolnwood, IL: NTC Business Books, 377–401.

Muniz, A. M., Jr and O'Guinn, T.C. (2001) "Brand Community." *Journal of Consumer Research* 27(March): 412–432.

Oliver, R. (1999) "Whence Customer Loyalty?" *Journal of Marketing* 63(January): 33–44.

Pine, B.J. and Gilmore, J.H. (1999) *The Experience Economy: Work is Theatre and Every Business a Stage*. Boston: Harvard Business School Press.

Price, L.L., Arnould, E.J. and Tierney, P. (1995) "Going to Extremes: Managing Service Encounters and Assessing Provider Performance." *Journal of Marketing* 59(April): 83–97.

Pulh, M., Bourgeon-Renault, D. and Bouchet, P. (2005) "Spectacles vivants, logiques de consommation et construction d'expériences: Le paradoxe d'une offre à la fois unique et plurielle." *Décisions Marketing* 37(Jan–Mar): 57–66.

Schmitt, B.H. (1999) *Experiential Marketing: How to Get Customers to SENSE, FEEL, THINK, ACT and RELATE to Your Company and Brands*. New York: The Free Press.

Part II

Consumer-driven experiences

Chapter 4

I feel good – who needs the market?

Struggling and having fun with consumer-driven experiences

Véronique Cova and Eric Rémy

KEY POINTS

- The decline in traditional non-commercial sectors and places in our postmodern consumer society has not led to a total hegemony of commercialism.
- The purpose of a consumer-driven experience is to resist the market or struggle with it, to flee from it, and even to play around with it.
- To understand consumer-driven experiences' non-commercial side, analysis must be conducted at the consumer intention level.
- When consumption experiences express the struggle against commercialization, we talk about anticommercialization experiences.
- When consumption experiences involve an interaction with commercialization, we talk about intercommercialization experiences.

At a time when, from Seattle to Porto Alegre, antiglobalization movements from across the planet are denouncing the consumer society, and when social movements are lamenting and decrying the world's commercialization, does it make any sense for us to continue to talk about (and highlight) non-commercial consumption experiences?

An initial macrosocial investigation reveals that the current form of commercial hegemony should be analyzed as the culmination of Marxian pessimistic theses postulating a hyperconsumption society's total domination over individual consumers who have been enslaved and reduced to their consumerist compulsions. This stance advances Bourdieu's, Baudrillard's, and Barthes' standard theses and tends to substantiate Marcuse (1964), who predicted the advent of a form of alienation that would spread because people had interiorized it. Instead of liberating people, technology and science, trapped in the cogs of an unstoppable growth machine, would annihilate humankind and all critical thinking. With this elimination of the critical mindset, society would become nothing more than a *unidimensional* space. All orders of discourse would become the expression of a single ideology that would serve to justify society as it is today. The alienated subject would then be absorbed into an alienated existence.

To be perfectly clear, this pessimistic view is not the one that the present chapter will be conveying. It is true that, because of their omnipresence, economics and consumption have become the new invisible forces that organize our social living with its beliefs, myths, utopias, temples, and rituals (Belk and Coon, 1993). But instead of hypothesizing alienation or that the consumer society has killed off all that is non-commercial, we prefer talking about a displacement of the traditional borders between the commercial and social spheres, even envisioning a porosity between the two. Much as the degeneration of traditional religious institutions does not in and of itself signify the end of religion, what has occurred in traditional (social, political, cultural) non-commercial spheres and locales does not per se intimate the death of non-commercialism. The microsocial level that the present analysis uses will call for greater optimism in this respect.

It is noteworthy, for example, that, despite a certain commercialization of human relationships resulting from the commercial sphere's extension into the social domain (i.e., the increased professionalism of associations and non-government organizations, or volunteer work's greater institutionalization and focus on the profitability of its actions), in another sense, we are also witnessing the opposite process, namely the decommercialization of the commercial sphere (i.e., fair trade or sustainable development policies). Emerging from this double upheaval are new forms and figures, featuring consumers who are less passive and prone to manipulation than they seem, and who in their daily lives pilot their own consumption experiences in an autonomous and personalized manner to a surprising extent. More provocatively, we could say that, if modern (and traditional) non-commercialism is dead, long live postmodern non-commercialism!

The present chapter will try to show how, for many individuals, the inexorable quest for a better world now entails a new relationship with consumer society. This will involve an analysis of consumer-driven experiences that, albeit linked to the commercial sphere, are also entwined with non-commercialism. In other words, we will be focusing on the experiences of *prosumers* who take it upon themselves to weave realities that are more human, genuine, and political, but also less commercial, in nature. And what should we do with (and say about) those factors that push organizations toward increased ethical involvement, toward actions with a higher calling, a fairer discourse, and ambitions characterized by a greater sense of citizenship?

Our vision lies somewhere in the middle of the radical dichotomy that divides this discussion into the 100 percent commercial and the 100 percent non-commercial. We will be mixing these two spheres, using as our point of reference a microsocial level that combines commercially oriented actors who want to be less commercial with socially oriented actors who want to encompass commercial logic. It is in this no man's land that consumption assumes a political meaning and individuals seek *bubbles of humanness*. It is here that consumer-driven experiences (hereafter written CDEs) are designed.

LOOKING FOR CDES

Contrary to received wisdom in this domain, focusing on CDEs signifies neither an ultimate (and at best priestly) pilgrimage to the land of the non-commercial, nor a posthumous eulogy for a dying species, nor an idealistic crusade for the good of future generations. Focusing on CDEs means discovering that entire swathes of our social lives have escaped the commercial sphere, and affirming that, in a sort of reaction to the social connection's collapse in our modern societies, what we are witnessing is the implementation of societal innovations whose purpose is to develop non-commercial spaces that have not been co-opted.

Between commercial and non-commercial experiences

One way to represent society is in terms of two very disconnected spheres. The commercial world can be considered part of the economic domain, and the non-commercial world is rooted in the social sphere. The former refers to relations between things (based on value or price and including general laws of circulation and flows), the second to relations between people (based on thoughts or emotions and including general principles of sociology). The idea here is that a very clear dichotomy exists between the economic (i.e., the market) and the social.

CASE VIGNETTE 4.1: THE FESTIVAL OF BUILDINGS, OR THE PURITY OF THE SOCIAL DOMAIN

The Rue du Printemps is a quiet street with relatively little through traffic located in Paris's seventeenth *arrondissement*. It has about twenty buildings that are each six stories high and five or six windows wide, offering solid doors with well-polished copper knockers. The street has almost no businesses, just a restaurant and a chemist at one end and a floral decoration shop at the other.

Neighbors rarely used to visit one another in the Rue du Printemps. The few times they ran into each other, they would offer a quick smile and move on. Rarely did people stop to chat. In other words, the building supervisor who decided to organize the Rue du Printemps festival for the last Tuesday in May was being very audacious indeed, dropping invitations into people's letterboxes.

The first time around it was very pleasant outside, after the sun had set and people had come home from work. Local youths tied lines of multicolored balloons between balconies. People parked their cars elsewhere to make room for a few tables perched on trestles and covered by simple tablecloths. Everyone brought cold dishes, quiches, pizza, different types of salad, cheese and fruit, fresh bread, and bottles of wine or fruit juice, sharing everything with their neighbors. A few grandmothers were carried downstairs in their wheelchairs;

---

others were happy to sit on a folding chair or sofa. Groups of people came together to chat before disbanding. Conversations covered the past and discussed the present. Children ran from one table to another, looking for a pastry or a sandwich. Grown-ups adroitly juggled cardboard plates filled with salad or some *taboulé* made by the Moroccan grocer from one street over. No one was shocked that people drank out of disposable cups.

Over the past four years, the Festival of Buildings has turned into a real tradition that no longer requires municipal authorization. The success of an action of this ilk would appear to be strongly tied to a form of spontaneity that is resolutely non-institutional in nature. The whole street gets together. Whereas smaller festivities (cocktail parties with one's neighbors or friends) bring together groups that are socially more homogeneous, neighborhood feasts assemble people from a broader range of generational, socioeconomic, or ethnic backgrounds. In this kind of atmosphere, the symbolism of exchanging food is essential. "The dishes you bring are a way of introducing and talking about yourself."

What is important is that local inhabitants can share things, deepen their relationships, and spend some time together chatting and joking. Ever since the first festival, people in the street have been greeting one another in a friendlier manner, toasting each other's good health, paying attention to neighbors, and sharing their lives: "Where are you from? Have you been here for a long time? What do you like to get up to?"

(based on information included in *Les Pères Blancs*;
www.peres-blancs.cef.fr)

The aforementioned criticism of the commercialization of the social sphere implies that a company or institution might co-opt the Festival of Buildings for its own commercial or political purposes. The main purpose of this initiative would then become economic or political, and it would target efficiency, profitability, and self-interest. The festival would lose its charm as something disinterested, spontaneous, and free, and would be seen as a commercial support system, market space, and opportunity to ask neighbors to make less noise, to negotiate urban plans, and to advertise one's business. The consumption experience concept moves away from this notion of a dichotomy between the commercial and social spheres and focuses on another form of relationship, one between people and things. This creates mixed relational forms that are no longer entirely non-commercial (social), but not yet entirely commercial.

In actual fact, the incursion (or absorption) of the commercial into the non-commercial, and vice versa, describes hybrid experiential contexts that can lead to a host of societal innovations: self-managed parental crèches, which are between having relatives or a (professionalized) crèche care for one's children; house exchange associations, which are between spending family holidays at your parents' house or renting accommodation; local exchange trading systems (LETS; www.lets-linkup.com), which are between helping friends to move and picking up their mail or purchasing whatever commercial services are offered in this area; and municipal or mobile libraries (such as www.bookcrossing.com), which are between borrowing a book from a friend or buying it. Underlying each of these innovations is an intention, a desire to live through a non-commercial experience that will interact with a commercial one. LETS exemplify how hard it is to ascertain the commercial or non-commercial nature of consumption experiences that are rooted in the mixing of these two different spheres. For example, from a commercial perspective, LETS can be viewed as a new way of commercializing relations based on mutual assistance amongst neighbors, i.e., as a form of barter, with a services market materializing where there used only to be the favors that friends would do for one another. From a non-commercial perspective, this is reminiscent of the many different forms of communitarian utopia that have tried to recreate social connections via a monetarized exchange of goods and services, the ultimate aim being the disappearance of money so that the connection alone remains. Divergent views on this subject intimate that it constitutes a new form of socialization, somewhere between a society and a community. Our hesitation is more than just theoretical, as for the moment public authorities either opt for the first vision, postulating that this system indirectly constitutes a kind of black market and that LETS should therefore be taxed or else prohibited (as craftsmen often view them as unfair competition), or, inversely, as some municipalities do, encourage their development, because they are construed as networks imbued with social and communitarian practices.

These societal innovations show that a material and political culture can make people aware of the different ways they can co-opt the (commercial and political) systems in which they find themselves. This demonstrates that the distinction between the commercial and non-commercial spheres is no longer very clear-cut and constitutes more of a question of one's own personal perspective, vision, and stance.

Intention as a key in understanding CDEs

An experience occurs when a subject encounters a reality, keeping said subject informed as to the two meanings of the term, i.e., it informs him/her as to the reality itself ("doing the experience") but also trains him/her in this reality ("having the experience"). However, this does not teach us whether the subject of an experience is in fact passive or active. Nor does etymology help us to answer this question, as the Latin verb *experiri* means both "feeling" (passive) and "trying" (active). The irreducibly passive component of an experience is what lies at the heart of the company-driven experience – the mind comes into contact with an external circumstance that it has neither invented or built, and which shapes its experience. However, the experience acquires meaning only through an interpretative activity of the mind. This always implies a certain logic, theory (albeit one that may be false or full of preconceptions), or belief – in short, an *intention.*

Intention (from the Latin *intendere*, "to tend toward") is a tension-based concept (Anscombe, 2000). In an intention, the subject is projected toward something. This is an act of awareness, whose involvement lies in its tie to the objective action being projected, and to

55

which said awareness has ascribed a meaning. Without intention, an act would be no more than a kneejerk reaction. An intention always has a praxeological dimension and is oriented toward an act. It is in the "intention to" do, suggest, and live something non-commercial that CDEs are found. A CDE is only a CDE for the particular awareness that has postulated it because it is the object of an intention.

A customer's *"intention to"* should be distinguished from the notion of motivation that is so often used in marketing. Motivation is linked to the individual so that a new equilibrium can be found wherever needs are unsatisfied – whereas intention is linked to an act under the egis of an identity-laden logic, the purpose being to offer meaning (Table 4.1).

This narrows the spectrum and casts the spotlight on the consumer. For example, certain company product or service offers can be construed as uncharted territories, spaces where a CDE might be able to take root – even if this never happens. The consumer still has the initiative and maintains free choice. Sometimes, these territories remain infertile and uncultivated because the consumer does not grasp their experiential context. On the other hand, CDEs can also crop up without having laid any roots, i.e., without the company having manifested an intention. Rather than an association between company-driven experiences and commercially motivated consumption, on the one hand, or between CDEs and commercially motivated consumption, on the other, we think that it is more accurate to envision the consumption experience's more or less company- or customer-driven orientation in terms of an intention concept. For example, CDEs can and do exist in both commercially and non-commercially motivated experiences. It is the consumer's intention that will make the difference and categorize the experience (Desmond *et al.*, 2000).

Two intentional stances can be distinguished:

- When the consumption expresses a struggle against commercialization, we talk about anticommercialization CDEs.
- When the consumption involves an interaction with commercialization, we talk about intercommercialization CDEs.

Table 4.1 *A new vision of CDEs*

Modern analytical vision	Postmodern analytical vision

At the individual level
  Motivation
  Needs
  Equilibrium
  Physical
	At the individual level
	  Intention
	  Action
	  Identity
	  Semiotics

Macro vision replete with predefined commercial and non-commercial spheres	Relatively micro vision presupposing a mixture of constructed spheres
The non-commercial aspect is defined from the outside by the researcher's objective point of view (researcher as discoverer)	The non-commercial aspect translates what the consumer has gone through plus his/her narrative (researcher as witness)

CDES AS THE OBJECT OF A STRUGGLE: ANTICOMMERCIALIZATION

The main idea here is how to regain power when one is faced with commercial domination. Consumers produce their own experiences in the form of non-commercial counterpowers (Penaloza and Price, 1993). This struggle can assume different aspects, famously starting with extraordinary political struggles, but also including less well-known ordinary ones.

CDEs as extraordinary anticommercial experiences

Whereas young people found their political outlets in the 1960s in Maoism, Trotskyism, Situationism, or (for the more conservative of them) Communism or Socialism, today's rebel youths are antiglobalization and all called Robert Johnson. Their basic discourse is congruent with an anticonsumption CDE, given that it makes references to other protest movements such as Adbusters, Robert Johnson Corporate, Guerriglia Marketing, etc. The foundations and the very existence of such movements refer endlessly to the commercial sphere and also to a consumer society whose boundaries they want to define and whose development they want to hinder (Zavestoski, 2002). In this struggle, such movements have organized themselves into fluid structures in which the search for a non-market and communitarian experience can constitute a fundamental connection.

At a basic level, a CDE is a kind of militant protest. Unlike militants, activists do not work for a political or social organization that aims to run society. They do not want to change the world – just their own world. They no longer believe in revolutionary utopia. They may be committed, but they also want to preserve their freedom of choice and rebel against any and all institutionalized entities. Theirs is not a structured ideology. They appear to be divorced from all forms of power. Activists do not seek a model. What they want instead are alternatives. To messianic visions, they prefer daily practices that can be invented indeterminately on a daily basis (Kozinets and Handelman, 2004). This activism is not without consequences for the form of the action. Activists operate alone or in small groups that are constituted whenever members meet up physically or virtually in the name of one cause or the other. Commitment is mainly based on groups that have affinities with ad hoc objectives that arise in varied and often experimental forms. Activists prefer self-organization. Their investment is ephemeral and cyclical, and it is at this level that it can assume the form of an experience. In fact, some of their forms of action differ from normal expressions of protest, and their staged and mediatized interventions can assume spectacular dimensions. Their acts will be spontaneous, targeted, and festive. The modern protester prefers many small meals to one large one.

In this sort of framework, CDEs are specifically characterized by:

■ Their hedonistic nature, the search for pleasure in action and in humor. The point here is to show one's dissatisfaction by feeling pleasure in action and by living an intense experience of transgression and collective jubilation (i.e., the San Precario appeal in Milan or collective vomiting in San Francisco).

■ Their spectacular nature, which should be conveyed by the press and therefore portrayed in the best possible light. CDEs often involve an occupation of symbolic spaces. This is in line with the desire to reappropriate public spaces when everything has been privatized (i.e., the Paris Metro or Platane Insoumis environmental actions; http://lesecocitoyens.fr.st/).

CDEs as ordinary anticommercial experiences

The end of metanarratives, and notably of the communist alternative, ultimately led to an internalization of the criticism of (and the protest against) the capitalist model (Klein, 2000). The capitalist system has co-opted the various elements of the criticism that used to be aimed at it, with commercial spaces now having canonized Gandhi, Marx, and Che Guevara. Utopia is no longer external (part of another model), nor is it ascribed to an idealized future. Today, it has a place even within the system and has become a utopia found on one's street corner, in day-to-day lives. The struggle is one of ordinary resistance (Gabriel and Lang, 1995).

How should a CDE be experienced ordinarily in a system that people criticize openly? How can people escape the laws and constraints of the marketplace, or of its fiendish ally – consumption? A whole range of tactics have been designed. Consumers will avoid looking at advertising, to the point of tearing them out of magazines. They will boycott brands and chains, take off labels, and buy organic or fair trade products. In sum, they will revisit their entire consumption behavior. Take the example of the French magazine *Decroissance* (http://www.decroissance.org/), the equivalent of Adbuster, which introduced us to Agnès, a young woman who voluntarily follows a very simple lifestyle. Agnès renovates and decorates her flat with recycled materials (using a partition she tore down as a new wall). She buys only organic materials such as Fermacell (http://www.fermacell.co.uk/), a natural dry lining board for walls, ceilings, and floors. She owns a wooden cereal mill so that she can grind organic grains (wheat, barley, red or whole rice, quinoa, millet, buckwheat, rye, etc.) that she keeps in recycled bottles. She purchases washable nappies for her eighteen-month-old child because plastic disposable ones contain toxic substances. She doesn't have a car and, when she wants to get some fresh air on weekends, she takes the train to her communal allotment. Yet she also has to compromise with the system: "I'm a translator, which is why I have a computer, it's a tool I need to work. The same applies to the washing machine, I'm forced to compromise. But I don't have a TV or a car . . . People have to compromise sometimes. For example, when I go shopping I occasionally buy biscuits or even ravioli when I'm in a rush. We even got a fridge-freezer that consumes more energy but allows me to freeze my organic vegetables if they all come in at the same time . . . I'm not a fanatic and sometimes go off track by buying bananas and tangerines. But I try to only buy what's in season and produced locally. Let's say that this is an ideal I work towards."

Ordinary anticommercial CDEs are less formal and less institutionalized in their organization of day-to-day life. They materialize at a more infraordinary level than their predecessors did. Consumption tactics, when weak parties act ingeniously to take advantage of stronger parties, lead to a politicization of daily practices (de Certeau, 1984). These types of experiences are manifested in acts of displaced consumption. All such daily acts of appropriation are born out of microstruggles, which are ad hoc solutions enabling David consumers to defeat the consumption Goliaths that are trying to dominate them. Highlighting these miniature battles calls for specific methodological approaches, such as life histories (Shankar *et al.*, 2001).

CASE VIGNETTE 4.2: SHOPPING AND THE NARRATIVE OF A LESS COMMERCIAL EXPERIENCE

A recent study on ordinary consumption experiences reveals some of the non-commercial tactics that people use when running errands. Like other housewives we interviewed, Jocelyne tells us below how and why her shopping experiences have become less commercial in nature.

Jocelyne is a thirty-eight-year-old woman who lives in a village of 1,500 inhabitants located in the southern half of France's Eure Country. She works at Center Parcs, a holiday complex for urban dwellers who miss the countryside and seek a bucolic experience, offering them chimneys, lakes, forests, exotic swimming pools, etc. One day, she noticed that she was losing half a day (including transportation time) going shopping at a hypermarket 15 km from her home. She also realized that she was not able to control herself when faced with the overflowing product displays in outlets "that make me buy things I don't need and have to store in the cupboard." She therefore decided to use the Internet and organize a home delivery service. After three months, her online merchant told her that, as she was the only customer in her part of the county, it could no longer justify servicing her. "It was when I got turned out, fired by this company, that I realized that something was wrong in the world . . . ."

Everything changed when Jocelyne decided to start going to a small grocery store in her village. "It was totally different, family-run, close to me, I was supporting our local village, it was a totally different dimension . . . Now that the grocer knows that I go shopping every Saturday, she orders things for me that she didn't offer before . . . I'm actually gaining time and money and am no longer tempted to buy more than I need, besides I couldn't, even if I wanted to . . . Compared with those huge, cold commercial structures, it is much more human, less commercial and also I've made social contacts in my village . . . It's only a bother when the grocer goes away on holidays since then I have to go back to the hypermarket . . . I did that last year and bought a bunch of stuff I didn't need, plus the parking and caddie were a huge hassle . . . it's just one big machine down there . . . ."

In ordinary anticommercial CDEs, usage or meaning is created by the consumer, who constructs the consumption experience by him/herself. This is a sort of antiprogram (Fournier, 1998), whose purpose is to achieve a local deconstruction and reconstruction of the commercial products and services' meaning and uses by means of one's daily experience. By acting thus, the consumer is refusing to be restricted to a mere walk-on role in a play put on by the consumption system. S/he is engaging in an overt and conscious act of protest, whose underlying intention is non-commercial in nature. As shown by Jocelyne's story, the only thing that matters is the consumer's own intention. After all, in this one instance, the hypermarket, the website, and the local grocery store all belonged to the same group (Carrefour). Of course, Jocelyne did not know this.

CDES AS NEW SPACES OF INTERACTION WITH THE MARKET: INTERCOMMERCIALIZATION

Far from allowing themselves to be benignly manipulated (as the popular image of trickery underlying the company-driven experience would have it), but also far from manipulating the company (as anticommercialization CDEs would have it), consumers can simply juggle with commercialization without falling prey to it. They can use complicity and malice to play around with the supplier's product offer. In this view, consumers are not at all naive about experiential strategies of this ilk. As they know they are being partially manipulated, they can choose to what extent this is being done to them and work around the manipulation so that it ends up complementing their daily existence (Cova and Cova, 2000). Instead of a direct confrontation with the commercial system, they can show some sleight of hand.

Intercommercialization manifests the estheticization of the experience being lived through by consumers who can devise for themselves, alone or as part of a group (and often acting from the wings), a zone of ephemeral and limited autonomy within the commercial system, without consciously associating any oppositional attitudes with their actions. They identify and decode what the commercial system has organized so as to be able not only to get around it but also to tame it so they can love it. After all, passion is a major driver behind these experiences. These playful intercommercialization CDEs can arise in more or less formalized contexts ranging from associative to imaginary modes.

CDEs in an associative context

Many collective experiences tend to have their own way with the commercial system. Examples include fan associations committed to (and involved in) traditionally non-commercial activities (spelling, weather, genealogy, heritage, or open air pursuits) that dig up and preserve products from the past (i.e., French vintage car fans such as the *Génération 2 CV*, http://www.generation2cv.org/; or *Confrérie des 650* groups, www.confreriedes650.org/). Associative experiences of this sort, whose aim is the consumption of passion, generate an intercommercialization experience yet continue to operate within the framework of a commercial interaction, meaning the game that the brands, companies, and institutions have devised.

CASE VIGNETTE 4.3: EXPERIENCING PASSION FOR THE THEATER

Compagnie de la Cité is a Marseille theater group that likes to bring professional artists together with people from the city, thereby setting their plays in the context of daily urban life. The troupe wants to be a hodgepodge of meetings and exchanges, promoting a cross-fertilization of everyone's past histories, dreams, doubts, and hopes. It tries to mediate between the written and oral arenas, and between those who talk and those who listen. Everyone is free to construct his/her own artistic experience in a space that people visit not so that they can consume an activity but, rather, so that they can get involved in an act of creation. This space is characterized by a perpetual back and forth of movement; by the giving of gifts (and receiving of others in return); and by sharing. It is a veritable melting pot. The theater blurs the borders between spectators and players, and between actors and their roles. For example, every participant in its amateur workshop crafts a singular account conveying his/her own experiences, and writing and playing their own stories. As such, each participant becomes the author–actor of his/her own past. In this sense, actor and director Michel André's work is not isolated from daily life, but instead very much a part of it. This is not an innocent approach. Its subtext hides people's refusal to allow themselves to be dominated and contaminated by the commercial system. Compagnie de la Cité is a place where pretences explode. For Michel André, this helps people to "have a better understanding of the contrast between our inner nature and what we show the outside world whenever we find ourselves being influenced by a society that is constantly and increasingly forcing us to try and look like it." In other words, this is an ongoing search based on the sincere and shared emotion that each individual should be able to live and weave his/her own experience.

Compagnie de la Cité's dependency on subsidies, precarious resources, and vulnerability to the strictures of its associative structure are all factors of fragility. To cope, survive, and thrive, it counts on its ability to get around commercial constraints; avoid relationships based on self-interest; and not give into commercial temptations. Experiences of this sort, which participants can have when they find themselves functioning in an associative mode, flirt with the commercial world even as they try to emancipate themselves from it entirely. People's intentions are full of passion – there is nothing commercial about passion, be it from an individual standpoint (I put on plays because it's useful to me) or from a collective one (I put on plays to defend some social cause or the other). Self-interest does not enter the equation. The experience is first and foremost a shared instance, one that places itself on the edges of the commercial sphere without casting a shadow over it. Examples of this include everybody's frantic race to receive subsidies or free media publicity.

Intercommercialization CDEs are also present in the rise of new market forms, one example being the growth and positioning of the organic sector. From its very outset, this movement has worked to redefine commercial/non-commercial relationships. In its varying avatars, the sector has often tried to define a different type of commercial functioning, one that reintegrates strong social relations by putting people through experiences that are more authentic and natural in tone. This is not some attempt to flee the market or to struggle against it. Instead, it is a desire to interact with the market, using its rules to create spaces that are less commercial (and even non-commercial).

CDEs in an imaginary form

In intercommercialization CDEs, consumers are free to decide to what extent they will be tricked in their consumption experience, narrating their own (mostly non-commercial) stories about the product, brand, or company. Unlike the established creed in marketing, it is essential neither that all of the messages that a company sends to the market be coherent nor that all such messages mesh with reality. It is possible for a gap to exist between a company's identity and the image it projects in the market. This gap can create a positive role by generating a greater space of freedom for the consumer (Voss and Giraud-Voss, 2000). Consumers often prefer ambiguity to clarity in a company's image. As such, intercommercialization CDEs can accommodate both a whole host of consumption re-enchantment initiatives as well as hyper-reality. The consumer does not need everything to be true and coherent.

The Provence markets example (de la Pradelle, 2006) illustrates the extent to which intercommercialization CDEs are rooted in the imaginary. The atmosphere surrounding these playful interactions is omnipresent and offers a communitarian ambience. The market offers a stage for the pleasure of meeting up with friends, a feeling that is supposedly characteristic of traditional societies. Here, people benefit from anonymity, the fact that they know one another and the ease with which relationships can be created or unwound. Estheticism and authenticity create what the author calls "the commerce of the imaginary," composed of "rounder pumpkins" or "a typical pâté for you." This engenders a seduction-based economy in which people cultivate "the art of taking your time" and wandering about. As they run into each other, they start to watch this "festival time" spectacle, which constitutes a break from their daily lives. The market invites people to follow a certain course, one in which hesitation (and even versatility) become useful commodities. More than price, choice, or quality, what is important here is the market's ambience and friendly atmosphere, and the fact that its authenticity-based exchanges are run according to a non-commercial mode. Liking markets means accepting from the very beginning that people will be able to lure you into their traps, even if you don't believe them. It also means agreeing to be dragged into their imaginary commercial world by means of paralipsis, a mode wherein people pretend not to want, think, say, or do something they clearly want to think, say, or do.

In a sense, an intercommercialization CDE asks consumers to mobilize specific competencies and is anchored in their freedom of choice and ability to create an experience autonomously within a given experiential context. It is at this level that this type of CDE contributes to the design and realization of consumers' own experience. The meaning and usage that consumers create are more akin to poaching and cherry-picking than they are to any programming.

CONCLUSION

CDEs are geared toward situations in which consumers act as autonomous protagonists living their consumption experiences when, where, and how they desire. Whether this involves anticommercialization CDEs, more or less extraordinary protest experiences, intercommercialization CDEs, or more or less imaginary playful experiences, CDEs have the particularity of being engendered by one and only one intention, that of the consumer him/herself. Yet this intention is not utopian in nature, given that it draws from the consumer's ability to project himself/herself as the actor. The CDE may be a question of getting the customer to live through an experience that has been designed, staged, and piloted by the company – but in a CDE, customers design their own experience, above and beyond the traditional notion of customer participation as encapsulated in the company-driven experience. Here, the consumption experience does not stem from the offer of an experience that the firm is marketing, but is generated instead by the consumer him/herself, in accordance with his/her intentions, on the occasion of those interactions that s/he will be living through with the thing (product or service) on offer, or with any staff members or other persons who may be present.

DISCUSSION QUESTIONS

- What driven experiences do you find when you analyze your daily consumption?
- How do these driven experiences relate to the market?
- Why is the consumer intention level the most relevant one for apprehending customer-driven experiences?
- Based on which elements can companies try to respond to customer-driven experiences?
- In light of these customer-driven experiences, do you consider it more relevant to talk about society's commercialization or the market's socialization?

REFERENCES

Anscombe, G.E.M. (2000) *Intention*, 2nd edn. Boston: Harvard University Press.
Belk, R.W. and Coon, G.S. (1993) "Gift Giving as Agapic Love: An Alternative to the Exchange Paradigm Based on Dating Experience." *Journal of Consumer Research* 20(December): 393–417.

de Certeau, M. (1984) *The Practice of Everyday Life.* Berkeley, CA: University of California Press.

Cova, V. and Cova, B. (2000) "Exit, Voice, Loyalty and . . . Twist: Consumer Research in Search of the Subject." In: Beckman, S.C. and Elliott, R.H. (eds) *Interpretive Consumer Research: Paradigms, Methodologies and Applications.* Copenhagen: Copenhagen Business School Press, 25–45.

Desmond J., McDonagh, P. and O'Donohue, S. (2000) "Counter-Culture and Consumer Society." *Consumption, Markets and Culture* 4(3): 207–343.

Fournier S. (1998) "Consumer Resistance: Societal Motivations, Consumer Manifestations, and Implications in the Marketing Domain." *Advances in Consumer Research* 25: 88–90.

Gabriel, Y. and Lang, T. (1995) *The Unmanageable Consumer: Contemporary Consumption and its Fragmentations.* London: Sage.

Klein, N. (2000) *No Logo.* Toronto: Alfred A. Knopf.

Kozinets, R. and Handelman, J. (2004) "Adversaries of Consumption: Consumer Movements, Activism, and Ideology." *Journal of Consumer Research* 31(3): 691–704.

Marcuse, H. (1964) *One-Dimensional Man. Studies in the Ideology of Advanced Industrial Society.* Boston: Beacon Press.

Penaloza L. and Price L.L. (1993) "Consumer Resistance: A Conceptual Overview." *Advances in Consumer Research* 20: 123–128.

de la Pradelle, M. (2006) *Market Day in Provence.* Chicago: University of Chicago Press.

Shankar A., Elliott R. and Goulding C. (2001) "Understanding Consumption: Contributions from a Narrative Perspective." *Journal of Marketing Management* 17: 429–453.

Voss, G. and Giraud-Voss, Z. (2000) "Strategic Orientation and Firm Performance in an Artistic Environment." *Journal of Marketing* 64(1): 67–84.

Zavestoski, S. (2002) "Anticonsumption Attitudes." *Psychology and Marketing* 19(2): 121–126.

Chapter 5

Consumption experiences and product meanings

Pasta for young Italian consumers

Daniele Dalli and Simona Romani

KEY POINTS

■ The consumption experience cannot be fully understood without considering the individual's social and cultural context.

■ The consumer reappropriates, renews, and transforms the values and meanings of the product, removing it from the ideology of the market system.

■ The richness and depth of the consumption experience depends on the individual's capacity to prepare the product.

■ The preparation of most of the products consumers use on a daily basis provides them with intense and intimate experiences.

■ Daily preparation and consumption integrate common products into consumers' knowledge structures.

In the postmodern context, consumption is no longer considered simply a practical act of using products, but a productive moment of individual and collective meanings and experiences (Firat and Dholakia, 1998). Individuals are continuously engaged in the symbolic appropriation of goods and services, and use them to construct their own individual identity (Miller, 1995). Through these symbolic transformation and recontextualization processes, goods can become the means of reappropriating the identities of both individuals and social groups.

Obviously, the capacity for recontextualization is not synonymous with the complete autonomy of the consumers who, with their own work on the purchased object, must deal with the object's history, with the remnants of meaning sedimented in the layers of meaning through which it has passed, and with the persons involved in the process of validation and sharing of their appropriation rituals and, therefore, in their collective consumption experiences.

Social relations define consumption experiences. More and more, we discern the important roles of the subjects and of their social and family groups in the meaning-making process.

In this chapter, we analyze the experience of the consumption of pasta by young Italians. This context is interesting because of the characteristics of pasta, characteristics that engender the possibility of appropriation and use in the creation of the subject's self-image, as well as the construction of important collective consumption experiences.

We illustrate how a common, everyday Italian food represents a particularly complex and varied cultural reference for young consumers. Young Italians have developed a close relationship with pasta because of its intrinsic characteristics (it is versatile, natural, healthy, and inexpensive) and its symbolic values (traditional food, temptation, social glue). To a significant degree, these meanings depend on the consumption experiences in which individuals have interacted with their culture, linking their knowledge to episodes, people, and places which together constitute the narrative framework for describing the relationship between young Italians and pasta.

The results of the processes of decommodification and the retranslation of the meanings of the product are clear. Individuals have decisively distanced themselves from the communication protocols typical of production and mass communication in favor of social and cultural relationships and the recollection of the emotional components of a consumption experience.

Although advertising is one of the main means through which meanings are transferred from the culturally constructed world to consumption objects (McCracken, 1986), in this case, its role is marginal because of the subjects' appropriation work in meaning-making.

PASTA IN THE CONSUMPTION CULTURE OF THE ITALIANS

It is difficult to think of pasta simply as one of the typical foodstuffs of Italian cooking, created from flour and water, molded into various shapes, dried, cooked in boiling salted water, and seasoned in a variety of ways. In Italy, pasta is a social phenomenon; it is part of the culture of a people and has profound links to their history, their geography, and, above all, their lifestyle.

Toward the end of the 1950s, Italians became more prosperous after the poverty and hardship of the prewar and wartime years. The country was gradually being rebuilt and reformed into a modern and prosperous nation. Italians – spectators, architects, and builders of the economic miracle – were transformed from a life of rural poverty into a relatively affluent society of mass consumption. Widespread prosperity altered the collective mentality: material aspirations grew, the economic and cultural implications of consumption changed, and the function of goods as aids in building the identity of individuals and defining their role in society became widespread.

This process necessarily involved food. Now that the specter of famine had receded, the increase in family incomes led to the widespread conversion from traditional and frugal foodstuffs to the edible symbols of opulence (Vercelloni, 1998).

In the collective imagination during the boom, pasta was seen as a food for the poor, denigrated and believed to be of little nutritional value. It became a symbol of the past that people wanted to leave behind, a past in which hunger was widespread and pasta was cheap and filling (La Cecla, 1998). Furthermore, it should not be forgotten that, during this period, infatuation with all things foreign led the Italians to copy American consumption models and to prefer foods that were status symbols of acquired wealth.

CASE VIGNETTE 5.1: *UN AMERICANO A ROMA*

Un Americano a Roma (a movie directed by Stefano Vanzina, alias Steno, in 1954) is a comedy which ridicules the grotesque character Nando Moriconi (Alberto Sordi), a lazy young man dazzled by the American dream, of which he has superficial and stereotypical images obtained from the cinema. Actually, he has never been to America, he doesn't speak English, and he doesn't know any Americans, but he pretends to a familiarity with American culture which is the source of hilarious jokes.

The most famous is a conversation with a plate of macaroni which is sneeringly refused and pushed aside in favor of an ''American dish'' (toast, milk, mustard, and marmalade). The concoction is inedible (''How disgusting!''), and Nando returns to his pasta and a bottle of red wine: ''Macaroni, you have provoked me and I will destroy you'' (Figure 5.1).

The film ridicules the excesses of Americanism among certain young people in the 1950s, using, as in the scene described above, cultural elements, such as a plate of macaroni, indispensable for the average Italian.

Figure 5.1 *Conversation with pasta.*

The social groups that emerged during the early years of the economic boom declared the end of pasta.

> Pasta was an object of social shame. As it was no longer eaten in the most developed countries, it was accused of provincialism, as well as of having no gastronomic quality. Guides to etiquette even forbade its use at elegant dinners. Pasta was further tainted by the fact that it was a food of the common people, an embarrassing hangover from poor rural Italy, in contrast to meat, a true object of social aspiration. Worse still, pasta was condemned as an example of bad nutrition, a presumed source of weight gain.
>
> Vercelloni (1998, p. 979)

These negative stereotypes began to fade in the 1970s, and a central role in this change must be attributed to the "invention" of the Mediterranean diet (Keys and Keys, 1975). This was to have the benefit of promoting pasta in the rest of Europe and America, making its main nutritional benefits known, while destroying other prejudices.

Pasta then began to gather ever greater social support in Italy, significantly from the most cultured and innovative segments of the population. From the beginning of the 1980s, the image of pasta changed. Its nutritional value was redefined, its cultural meaning was reinforced, and its role as a building block of national identity was legitimized. This came about partly as a result of the glorification of pasta in the Mediterranean diet and partly with a rediscovered sense of national pride, of which a return to pasta was a part.

The most recent Italian market data (source: *Cirm*, 2003, 2004) show that, on average, Italians consume about 28 kg of pasta a year, in 85-g portions, at least five times a week. The most common recipes are the traditional ones (spaghetti with tomato sauce, macaroni with meat sauce), even if every Italian knows twelve pasta recipes well and tries six new ones every year. Consumers keep an average of 5 kg of pasta in stock, in at least five different shapes, of which two are brand names. Short pasta is preferred to long pasta but, for 36.7 percent of Italians, the shape does not matter. Instead, they choose between smooth or ribbed pasta, with a clear preference for the ribbed. Nevertheless, Italians are traditionalists, and the most popular pasta shapes are spaghetti followed by penne, with rigatoni, macaroni, and fusilli some way behind. These five shapes account for 77.5 percent of the pasta consumed.

PASTA AND ITS MAIN MEANINGS

The primary purpose of this study is to describe the meanings that young consumers associate with pasta. Our research methodology – collages and introspective reports – belongs to a group of projective research techniques that have proven valuable in other consumer knowledge research studies seeking to describe symbolic and abstract components (Zaltman, 1995; Boddy, 2005). Collages and other projective techniques have been part of consumer culture research, but their use has been relatively limited (Belk *et al.*, 2003).

In our study, the collages focused on intrinsic and symbolic components, while the written documents (relating to personal experiences and events) described situations in which the subject interacted with the product and other people. These episodes revealed the product's role in the creation of meanings, symbols, and metaphors that are instrumental in interpersonal communication and the construction of individual identity.

The informants were 280 students at the Business School in Pisa. For the collage, they were divided into groups of ten to fifteen and given 70 × 50 cm pieces of cardboard on which they had to glue images cut from various magazines (weekly and monthly publications with large circulations). They were asked to select the images that best described the ideas or concepts of pasta shared by the members of the group. The collages were completed in about two hours. Then, a representative from each group explained the group's collage to the whole class so that a common interpretation could be agreed. The individual presentations were tape recorded so that they could become part of the data set.

In the introspective report, each informant described what came to mind when thinking of pasta. There were no rules about form; options included a short account of a personal experience, a poem, an outline of a scene for a play, a short story.

Each of us analyzed the data independently to identify the key themes. We then compared and combined our individual results into a single assessment scheme; this was presented to the students for critical analysis and subsequent validation. The most important elements of the meanings associated with pasta by the students in the study are presented in the next section.

Pasta's intrinsic characteristics: versatile and adaptable, natural, healthy, inexpensive, quick

Our list of the intrinsic characteristics of pasta, those which constitute its essence, were found in a significant number of the collages and the written documents.

Versatile and adaptable

Pasta can be transformed into both simple and complicated dishes. It adapts itself to everyone's palate and to the most varied requirements and situations. "There are no other foods, either natural or industrially manufactured, which show the same qualities as pasta in adapting to combinations and associations of tastes and consistencies" (Serventi and Sabban, 2004, p. 327). This is clearly illustrated by the following extract:

> For me, pasta is a constant feature of my daily life. It is a dish which, with a more or a less complicated sauce, can be presented on any occasion and on any menu. For example, fettuccine with prawns and courgettes is a dish which I eat on special occasions, but the classic spaghetti with garlic, olive oil, and peppers, prepared with friends on a late summer night, is another example of how the same product can be right for completely different occasions.
>
> Andrea (m)

Note that pasta takes on the characteristics of versatility and adaptability thanks to the sauces and the recipes. Indeed, although the shape varies, pasta is a basic, standardized product.

> Pasta without sauce: the thousands of occasions on which I have tried more or less in vain to follow a diet in order to look like one of the many fashion models I see every day in the media [. . .] Pasta with garlic, olive oil, and peppers: The smell of summer, crazy nights, where everything seems more like a dream than reality [. . .] Pasta with pesto: exam time, when we shut ourselves up in an apartment and lose all sense of time and the only meal which we cook is pasta with ready-made pesto [. . .] Pasta with meat sauce: strength, tradition, the joy of having known the woman (or rather my grand-mother) who prepared the best meat sauce in the world [. . .] Seafood pasta: Shudders. The most intriguing evening of my life. Hidden glances, laughter. The only bitterness in not being able to eat, but no regrets! [. . .] Pasta bakes: the years pass, but everything remains the same – wherever I find myself, my mother always succeeds in sending me a portion of pasta bake on January 12th, which is now a symbol, an unwritten pact between us both. The smell of pasta made with true love.
>
> Teresa (f)

Natural

The ingredients (flour and water) are basic and simple. Sometimes, the pasta is mixed with other simple and natural ingredients such as olive oil, tomatoes, garlic. The secret of pasta's huge success is also linked to its natural, simple, and neutral characteristics, which do not limit the search for new taste combinations.

Healthy, if in moderation

Young people now seem convinced that pasta is good for you. Pasta helps them to satisfy their energy needs in a light, healthy way. Some also attribute miraculous effects on their mood to pasta. Even those obsessed with their weight seem to have been converted to the Mediterranean diet, as long as the pasta is eaten in moderate portions with low-fat sauces. In the collages, kitchen scales were often used to express this characteristic.

Inexpensive

Pasta costs little, but provides high value. This has been central to its diffusion over the centuries. Young people dedicated a lot of space to this aspect in their written documents.

> A student away from home doesn't have his mother, doesn't have money, patience or time to cook. But the same student is hungry, wants tasty food, has many friends who find any excuse to eat at his place and – hopefully – to enjoy his company as well. Just as well there's pasta! You can cook it quickly on your own, without serving elaborate sauces, it doesn't cost much, and it can be shared among a lot of people.
>
> Pierluigi (m)

Quick

Pasta has a lot to do with time. Although preparing a dish of pasta does not require much time, time is a determining factor for a successful outcome: the pasta must be cooked al dente, and no mistakes are tolerated. Cooking pasta is a simple and quick, but at the same time delicate, operation that reveals the cook's ability. The culture of a short cooking time, leaving the pasta fresh and with an elastic, solid "backbone," began in Naples. After the political unification of Italy and with the increase in manufactured pasta, the Neapolitan method gradually won over the whole country. Pasta "cooked for a short time in a lot of water" was the norm (consecrated by the expression al dente) and became common after World War I (Serventi and Sabban, 2004). Having gained worldwide popularity, cooking al dente is now a symbol of the Italian gastronomic model.

> Pasta comes to our aid in many situations, thanks to the speed of preparation. When we are in a hurry and there is no time to cook, when we have unexpected visits from friends, a good plate of pasta is always very welcome.
>
> Romeo (m)

> You cannot eat overcooked spaghetti: You need to pay attention, sometimes 30 seconds make a difference. The trouble is those 30 seconds are not a problem when the pasta is very good. However, I am learning to cook it al dente, which makes it more difficult to wrap around the fork, but is much, much better!
>
> Silvia (f)

In sum, pasta has positive qualities and benefits. There are only two caveats: to enjoy all its healthy characteristics, it has to be eaten in limited portions with light sauces, and it must be cooked in a short period of time and drained slowly.

Pasta's symbolic values: pleasure, well-being, temptation, fun and sociability, domesticity, Italianness

Beyond the practical aspects discussed in the previous section, pasta is associated with more abstract concepts and values that show how it has been integrated into an intricate cultural and symbolic system.

Pleasure, well-being, temptation

Pasta is first and foremost a pleasure because it tastes good. As with other pleasures, it has two sides: a positive one linked to the well-being brought about by its consumption and another, more ambivalent, aspect. The majority of representations and descriptions of pasta were focused on one side or the other. First, pleasure is interpreted as physical and psychological well-being when linked to eating healthy, tasty foods that are part of the Mediterranean style. Second, pasta is interpreted as a pleasure on the grounds that it is a temptation. Indeed, it is often admitted that winning over one's partner by cooking a delicious meal is a possible move in a seduction strategy, and pasta lends itself to this role.

71

CASE VIGNETTE 5.2: PASTA AGNESI, FROM SILENCE, TO SENSING, . . . TO SENSES

Agnesi has produced interesting innovations in the field of television advertising. The first and perhaps most famous is "Silence, Agnesi is talking" (1980s). Images of people sitting at the table eating pasta without background voices. There is no space for anything other than the full enjoyment of the good flavor of the pasta (Figure 5.2).

In the 1990s, the company turned to more explicit and high-impact emotional levers: "Where there's Agnesi, . . . there's Agnesi". A young, good-looking, sexy couple returns home and begins to prepare dinner. While preparing the pasta, they begin to remove their clothes and throw dishes and cutlery on the floor with their clothes. At the end of the commercial, the pasta is placed on the by now semi-nude girl's back, together with the sauce.

In 2002, the consumption experience was further enriched with "Agnesi. The pasta with more taste." Added to the close and affectionate relationships that exist between the protagonists (three young couples dining together) are the sensations deriving from the stimulation of all five senses: hearing, touch, smell, sight, and taste.

Figure 5.2 *The flavor of a pasta dish.*

Fun and sociability

Pasta reminds young Italians of fun, the pleasure of sitting together at the dinner table to socialize and eat. The collages often showed couples, families, and happy and radiant groups having fun cooking and eating together. Other collages included people of different ethnic origins to show the versatility and global nature of pasta.

Domesticity

Although pasta originated as a street food (the figure of the *maccaronaro*, who for a modest sum served the passer-by a dish of steaming macaroni at any time of the day, was a symbol of Naples in the late 1800s), it developed in the home; pasta became the first in the series of courses that made up the meal. Both the collages and the written documents make reference to all the elements and accessories related to cooking. Pots, colanders, ladles, forks, and spoons take on a symbolic dimension because of their link with the product. They represent a culture in which preparing and consuming food at home has great importance.

The difference between pizza and pasta, the two foodstuffs typical of Italy, is that pizza is a dry food with a topping, while pasta is a food with liquid (La Cecla, 1998). Pizza has a public role; it can be eaten on the street, even without a plate, while pasta needs to be eaten mainly in the home, with family and friends. It is the most typical home-cooked product, made by the mother for the family, requiring knowledge of cooking and sauce preparation, as well as a private atmosphere.

Italianness

Italy is usually identified abroad by its artistic and cultural heritage. Although they know about and are proud of these national treasures, many young people also identify pasta as an important symbol of their national identity. Pasta is an expression of their material culture; the collages included maps of Italy, the Italian flag, and the word "Italia", and even natural environments and artistic treasures.

The associations described above impose a symbolism on pasta which seems to be tied to the essential elements of the individual and collective identity of the Italian consumer. It satisfies taste and gives pleasure; it is a common denominator of Italian culture; and it plays many different, positive and gratifying, roles.

Pasta and personal experience: the family and pasta, friends and pasta

Pasta brings to the mind of young consumers their firsthand experiences. In general, they recounted episodes in which social relations were particularly important. They emphasized people's ability to interact in a personal and creative way with the product and with others, expressing themselves and contributing to the definition of the social and cultural environment.

In every account of a personal experience, pasta plays a supporting role, together with the people involved. There are no direct or indirect references to the role of manufacturing or of advertising (the market system) in the creation of the experience itself. This results in the decommercialization of the product and the redefinition of some of its meanings; individuals reappropriate the consumption process, partly removing it from the ideology of the market (see Chapter 3 in this volume).

From this point of view, the experiences described by the students can be classified on the basis of the social contexts in which they take place – with the family and with friends.

The family and pasta

As confirmation of its versatility, pasta is involved in various family rituals, from the most simple and everyday to those of great importance and depth (Rook, 1985). It is a common denominator of get-togethers and celebrations.

> I'm in the car, I'm returning home. I've covered a number of kilometers, I'm close. The road is clear, perhaps because it's one o'clock! There's no one around, but perhaps because it's Sunday! Keys in the door, affectionate embraces from all. Then the usual voice "Sit down, it's ready!" The smell of meat sauce! It's Sunday, pasta with meat sauce . . . my favorite! Wonderful smells and the beginning of another lovely day with everyone finally together.
>
> Esterino (m)

From this brief extract, it is clear how the pleasure of pasta is tied not only to the quality and quantity of the food, and therefore to the product itself, but also, and perhaps above all, to the social dimension of eating together with family and friends. The consumption experience takes on a particular significance in the light of the social bonds that it helps to strengthen. Eating together allows people, within certain limits, to articulate their identity and to define their role with regard to others. This is why eating pasta alone is not seen by young people as positive.

Pasta often plays a role in lifestyle changes, for example leaving home to study in another city. In this case, the classic problem of new responsibilities and tasks presents itself, including shopping and cooking, previously undertaken by other members of the family. Here pasta, linked to family experiences and the techniques learnt from mother or grandmother, takes on a fundamental role in the definition of a new identity:

> It was all perfect apart from a perhaps not completely irrelevant detail. What would I eat? I had never cooked anything in my entire life, perhaps once or twice I had made some toast, a boiled egg, but nothing more. How would I resolve the problem? Would I have to eat rolls, pizza and sandwiches for years to come? Perhaps it was better to learn to cook something. I then went to my mother to ask her advice and she told me to begin with pasta: "Fill a pan with water, when it boils put in a little salt and then put the pasta in and it will be ready more or less in about the time indicated on the

package. After that you can add to it what you want." It was easier than I had thought. Just to be sure, I learnt how to make the sauce as well. That is how my relationship with pasta began.

Stefania (f)

The progressive socialization of preparing pasta happens not through the intervention of the market (for example, through cookbooks or television programs), but through the key role of the mother. This confirms the central role played by family, social, and cultural relationships in the creation of the consumption experience.

Friends and pasta

Young consumers also describe the central role of pasta in creating and consolidating friendships and relationships with their contemporaries. Relationships are formed and cemented around the table; even emotional relationships can begin to take on meaning with pasta.

At the end of the evening, my suggestion to my friends was not "I'll make you some spaghetti" but "Let's make some spaghetti." However, at that time of night and after a few drinks, the collaborative spirit was very low and I found myself in the kitchen preparing the sauce on my own, when I heard "her" voice behind me offering to help. It was the best part of the evening, and when I realized that I was not the only embarrassed one in the kitchen, any excuse was good for making us laugh. I hoped that the pasta would never finish cooking, because I really liked the subtle complicity that had been created between us in every glance and every small gesture. The spaghetti with tomato sauce and tuna was a success and everyone asked for seconds. The evening finished shortly afterwards, but the icing on the cake had yet to arrive: I was saying goodbye to everyone when "she" came to me and whispered in my ear, "Why don't we make spaghetti together tomorrow evening?"

Francesco (m)

In this episode, the role of "consumption" is clearly secondary to that of preparation, which creates the conditions for the development of an emotional relationship, the importance of which goes well beyond any material or commercial consideration. That the "product" then appears to be appreciated by the other players is completely secondary. Many of our informants reported similar experiences, showing how the complex "preparation–consumption" ritual is intimately linked to social relationships; the economic and ideological aspects of the market are lost.

In sum, consuming pasta is almost always a collective experience in which family, friends, and acquaintances assume important roles in defining the boundaries of the experience itself and determining the satisfaction that the consumer feels. Economic organizations (companies, the market) and the mass media do not play an important part in these episodes; the contribution of market ideology is also limited.

CONCLUSION

In this chapter, we have described the depth and complexity of the bond that links a basic product, pasta, to the consumer. Despite the fact that the individual episodes of consumption belong to the most simple and repetitive part of daily life, over time they overlap and determine a highly subjective structure of meanings strongly linked to the culture of belonging, to people's history, and to their social network. It is in this context that the experiential dimension (Addis and Holbrook, 2001) of the pasta consumption experiences of young Italians should be understood.

Very generally, the sensorial experience is tied to the product's attributes and its immediate effects. Flavors, recipes, and sauces, combined with the variety of possible occasions for preparation and consumption, make eating pasta a unique and always new experience, but one that is at the same time integrated in previous experiences and culture.

Young consumers clearly display a knowledgeable and explicit ability to link pasta and its attributes to elements of their culture. Pasta is a symbol of Italy in the world and, along with other values, it is one of the elements that constitute national identity, both in Italy, where it unifies, as well as abroad, where it symbolizes Italy and Italians. It respects the values assigned to food and can be seen in different ways in the debate on the healthiness of the Mediterranean diet (Keys and Keys, 1975).

Furthermore, the experience of consuming pasta has important social implications. Our informants were well aware of the rules and principles that underlie the preparation and consumption of pasta in different contexts. Whether alone, in the midst of the family, with friends, or with one's partner, preparation and consumption take on different content and values.

In this sense, the experience of consuming pasta is always sustained by the cultural and social fabric. It cannot be reduced to a simple relationship between consumer and product, as demonstrated by the fact that occasions when subjects talk of eating pasta alone are considered in a negative light. Rather, in the vast majority of cases, eating pasta is an important meeting point of individual, social, and cultural values where individual identity can be affirmed and one's social position established.

This is also confirmed by the fact that the events related in the introspective documents generally refer not to the particularity of pasta as such, but to the social relations within which pasta is consumed. This implies that the respondents see pasta mainly as a sort of social glue, a unifying element in interpersonal experiences. All of this brings to mind the concept, so dear to the sociologists of food, of a "proper meal," defined as cooked, hot food served as the main meal of the day and eaten with the entire family gathered around the dinner table (Charles and Kerr, 1988). Independently of the composition and nutritional characteristics of this dish, what is significant is its contribution to the construction of the family, to the definition of the relationships between the various components of the family nucleus, and to the construction and expression of their individual identities. Something that persists even after the young members have left the family nucleus: using pasta to develop and maintain one's ties of friendship, love, and hospitality.

The daily reconstruction of these meanings helps to link individuals closely to their culture and to satisfy their need for authenticity and self-awareness. These experiences are not intense or revolutionary; they do not lead to fully fledged transformations. For all Italians, pasta is a material and cultural object about which they know almost everything. It is consumed almost daily and does not cause deep or radical change. Nevertheless, every single consumption episode is accompanied by symbolic and emotional values and past experiences; this emerges clearly from the research data.

We also highlight the importance attributed by the participants to cooking the pasta. Young consumers are knowledgeable and competent pasta cooks and, in this way, show the peculiar postmodern trend in consumption, as predicted by de Certeau (1984).

Despite the fact that pasta is "threatened" by precooked products, the consumption culture seems to be strongly anchored in a model in which the goodness of the product and, therefore, the fullness of the consumption experience derive from the correct organization of the cooking. These are not exclusively instrumental (cooking a good dish of pasta), but rather social – they allow individuals to compare and exchange ideas, meanings, and memories. As in other sectors (Ladwein, 2003), the preparation and consumption of the product/ service are often part of the same ritual, and both contribute to the final satisfaction.

Because the cooking is so important, consumers assign themselves ownership of the finished product. Pasta is made of flour and water, and it is thanks only to the creative touch and skill of the cook that it is transformed into a memorable consumption experience. In this sense, cooks take on the values and meanings of the product, often modifying, renewing, and transforming their significance. Recipes combine special ingredients to transform and decommodify purchased products.

By co-opting mass-produced brand-name products in creating a meal, the cook demonstrates that familial values can triumph over the powerful homogenizing influences of consumer culture (Wallendorf and Arnould, 1991, p. 28). Brand-name products are reclaimed from the world of commodities and reassembled into traditions and daily practices. Through such transformation processes, individuals define their immanent productive power, their ability to produce for others.

DISCUSSION QUESTIONS

- Do you think it's possible to create a memorable experience with a convenience product?
- What are the most experience-favorable characteristics of a convenience product?
- How do consumers manage to daily reconstruct the meanings of convenience products?
- In what sense do consumers perceive some convenience products as a means of interpersonal interaction?
- What is the role of preparation in the experience of consuming pasta?

REFERENCES

Addis, M. and Holbrook, M.B. (2001) "On the Conceptual Link between Mass Customisation and Experiential Consumption: An Explosion of Subjectivity." *Journal of Consumer Behaviour* 1(1): 50–66.

Belk, R.W., Ger, G. and Askegaard, S. (2003) "The Fire of Desire: A Multi-Sited Inquiry into Consumer Passion." *Journal of Consumer Research* 30(3): 326–354.

Boddy, C. (2005) "A Look at the Evidence for the Usefulness, Reliability and Validity of Projective Techniques in Research." *International Journal of Market Research* 47(3): 239–255.

de Certeau, M. (1984) *The Practice of Everyday Life*. Berkeley: University of California Press.

Charles, N. and Kerr, M. (1988) *Women, Food and Families*. Manchester: Manchester University Press.

Firat, A.F. and Dholakia, N. (1998) *Consuming People: from Political Economy to Theatres of Consumption*. London: Routledge.

Keys, A. and Keys, M. (1975) *How to Eat Well and Stay Well: the Mediterranean Way*. New York: Doubleday.

La Cecla, F. (1998) *La Pasta e la Pizza*. Bologna: Il Mulino.

Ladwein, R. (2003) "Les méthodes de l'appropriation de l'expérience de consommation: le cas du tourisme urbain." In: Rémy, E., Garubuau-Moussaoui, I., Desjeux, D. and Filser, M. (eds) *Société, Consommation et Consommateurs*. Paris: L'Harmattan, 85–98.

McCracken, G. (1986) "Culture and Consumption: a Theoretical Account of the Structure and Movement of the Cultural Meaning of Consumer Goods." *Journal of Consumer Research* 13(1): 71–84.

Miller, D. (1995) *Acknowledging Consumption*. London: Routledge.

Rook, D.W. (1985) "The Ritual Dimension of Consumer Behavior." *Journal of Consumer Research* 12(3): 251–265.

Serventi, S. and Sabban, F. (2004) *La Pasta. Storia e Cultura di un Cibo Universale*. Bari: Laterza.

Vercelloni, L. (1998) "La modernità alimentare." *Annali della Storia d'Italia* 13: 951–1005.

Wallendorf, M. and Arnould, E.J. (1991) "We Gather Together: Consumption Rituals of Thanksgiving Day." *Journal of Consumer Research* 18(1): 13–31.

Zaltman, G. (1995) "Amidword: Anthropology, Metaphors, and Cognitive Peripheral Vision." In: Sherry, J.F., Jr (ed.) *Contemporary Marketing and Consumer Behavior: An Anthropological Sourcebook*. Thousand Oaks, CA: Sage, 282–304.

Chapter 6

The blandness and delights of a daily object

Benoît Heilbrunn

KEY POINTS

- An object is more than a mere system of signs.
- A consumption experience can be broken down into four essential modes.
- The experiences we engage in with objects can be analyzed at different levels, ranging from the substantial to the interactional.
- An object can be seen as a real partner in a consumer's life.
- An object's banality and blandness constitute experiential principles in and of themselves.

Marketing talks often about products, but seldom about objects. Moreover, when people evoke products, they are often referring to sign systems. The semantic approach makes a clear distinction between the material dimensions of objects (the signifier or the expressive level) and their idea-related dimension (the signified or the contents level). This perspective analyzes objects in terms of their specifically ideological dimension, to the detriment of their corporal and sensorial dimensions. Have the instrumental and symbolic dimensions that are traditionally associated with objects in our western culture put paid to all other possibilities for ascribing coherence and meaning to objects – despite the fact that these other possibilities continue to crop up, as if by stealth, in people's daily lives? But how is it then that objects are still able to surprise us time and again, enchanting us despite the familiar place they have in our daily lives? By no longer focusing only on the symbolic dimensions of products and brands, the experientialization of consumption may pave the way for an approach that will do a better job of incorporating the specifically material embeddedness of our relationships with objects. Now is probably the time both to try and understand the infraordinary mode that surrounds us, and also to transcend the saturation of the effects on our senses as well as the tyranny of symbolism. Both these factors have imprisoned objects in a register that tends to empty them of their meaning and emotionality, and very probably of their effectiveness. The present chapter aims to reveal insights into the objects that surround us on a daily basis, insights that will marginalize the commonplace and the spectacular, and help show how our daily experiences with such objects epitomize a sort of constant iteration with the moral and physical constraints of daily living (Kaufmann, 1997). The idea argued here is that, to understand key issues in marketing, and to truly reacquaint ourselves with consumers' actual experiences, we will have to go beyond the rhetorical and the spectacular fields that have become so intrinsic to commercialization.

THE DISENCHANTMENT OF AN OBJECT

The excessive semanticization of consumer goods has caused an irreversible shift in the analysis of objects. Whereas objects were viewed as material entities, now they are seen as systems of signification. We could even say that, ever since Baudrillard's seminal work in this field, studies here have continually analyzed the signifier in terms of the signified, thus destroying the material and sensorial dimensions of objects. It is clear that an object will at the very least speak to us and tell us about the various ways in which it can be used:

> A pocket knife always says more about the person who owns it . . . In our opinion, it is legitimate to imagine that a knife's handle can be extended by the various ways people use it, and that this ultimately attests to a certain way of living and being. By broaching the question in this manner . . . we are trying to identify if not a culture . . . then at least a form of thinking and a particular mode of interaction between oneself and the world.
>
> (Floch, 1995, p. 181)

In other words, pocket knives are mountain knives that suggest one and only one response for each function, a generalist that seems to be telling users, "Sort yourselves out." Inversely, a Swiss army knife that acts like a specialist by offering a specific answer for each type of utilization seems to be telling its users to "Go ahead" (Floch, 1995).

This raises questions as to the role played by a specifically sensorial and corporal experience in the choice and utilization of an object. After all, experiential marketing orchestrates a constant scenarization, which can readily intimate that signs have become the principal suppliers of meaning and therefore of enjoyment, reducing consumption or interaction to a semiotic experience. Is it possible that marketing's undeniable capacity for theatricalization has been replacing senses with signs by obliterating the sensoriality and gesturality with which all experience is necessarily imprinted? We can turn this question around by wondering aloud whether an object is capable of provoking affection, feelings, and emotions.

In actual fact, this constitutes one of anthropology's main criticisms of the semiotics of objects. An object cannot be reduced to a system of signs, because social significations are not the only things that it conveys. In other words, an object will not always be bogged down in cultural and social significations that inexorably cause an a priori determination of its senses and functions. It can also be appropriated by individuals and strengthened using signification and personal values even as it refers to something other than its utilization value or its value as a social sign. The big risk of equating an object with a quasi-language is that, once the signified has been identified, the signifier becomes surplus to requirements. After that, an object will no longer be seen as anything more than a simple system of connotative signs that run at high emotional temperatures (Eco, 1985). This kind of practice, from which a certain number of semioticians are not exempt, can nullify the very idea of objects being incorporated by individuals. In other words, structural and semantic approaches to objects can be criticized as being reductionist. This is because they ignore materiality per se, in terms of its relationship both to the construction of the subject and to its objectification within action.

Reducing a material object to a sign or "quasi-word" means that material culture tends to be viewed as a "simple twinning of discourses" (Warnier, 1999, p. 124). In other words, by replacing objects with words, semiotics seems to be depriving itself of everything that is original about a substance, in particular its ability to structure and diversify instruments of action or its environment, thus shaping the subject in a way that cannot be reduced to mere discourse. At the same time, by manipulating objects, a subject becomes embodied, expressing itself through gestures and substance, hence the irreducibility of the material expression, something that becomes particularly necessary whenever discourse no longer has the words to describe this. Even if some objects could be translated into words (as a result of their structural and communicational dimensions), their most opaque substrata rebel against notional and verbal expression, even though they represent a powerful factor for building subject and meaning.

And yet, modern humankind seems to suffer when faced with an object. At a time when technological progress has enabled almost all conceivable combinations of the forms, materials, and colors that are now possible, objects scarcely provide any more the kind of initial resistance that once explained their charm. The infinite malleability that design offers has detracted from the objects themselves, insofar as the profusion of objects has tended to empty them of their signifying substance.

Objects become sorts of slaves, having lost their nobility, as we are told, in the service of humankind. They have become too obvious, too familiar, and too docile. To what extent can they continue to surprise and amuse us? What awaits and threatens an object is a real neglect stemming from the continuous rationalization of the production and consumption processes. This sort of disenchantment with the world of objects basically harks back to the mass production of objects and to the ensuing depersonalization of contacts (how can we have a personal contact with an object that is replicated ad infinitum?). As Max Weber pointed out, this process of disenchantment with the world is one in which spontaneity, idiosyncrasy, and superstition have been erased and replaced by values such as effectiveness, predictability, and replicability. Here, the consumption object appears to be abundant and at the same time in shortage. It is abundant because of the profusion of objects in individuals' daily lives (people supposedly encounter 20,000–30,000 objects in just one day). It is in shortage because the profusion of objects, resulting from their repeated production, tends to empty them of their signifying substance. Now, an object can exist only if it entertains a relationship of signification with its user. It must necessarily be imbued with values superseding its function alone. When redefined thus, an object (with its substance and meaning) carries with it a past and a future. More specifically, it is able to scenarize consumption by projecting it into a universe that is rich with meaning and emotion. We feel that this is what imbues an experience with its full meaning, signifying here a transformation process, as well as people's ability to use the power of objects to become something different.

81

OBJECTS, BETWEEN ROUTINE AND SURPRISE

People have relatively paradoxical expectations of the objects that make up their daily lives. In turn, these expectations evoke a repetitive flow of actions taking a simple psychological approach that views an object in terms of its utilitarian purposes, and also expresses people's desire to be surprised and enchanted when objects become endowed with a certain mystery, magic, and even aura. An object takes part in a sort of reassuring routinization of gestures, incarnating a form that incorporates the object into daily gestures and ensures an embodiment in one's daily actions. Individuals wield undeniable control over the objects they use. This allows them to control their environment, notably their interpersonal environment. Thus, in terms of an object's instrumental functions, we should not forget the crucial value of freedom that is associated with material ownership, and specifically makes it possible to predict a result and to experiment with causal efficiency and control (Furby, 1978). In short, the most salient benefit that an object offers is very probably the fact that it can be controlled, as this makes it possible to characterize ownership, regardless of the age of the person involved (Furby, 1978). Objects constitute benchmarks for an individual's identity and truth. Thus, routine is the vehicle that will enable the individual to live in an illusion of stability such as seen in the devotion to household chores (Kaufmann, 1997).

Above and beyond the control function, an object contributes to emotional stability, as the environment it creates is a familiar one. Some children, for example, can eat only from a plate that is familiar to them. Similarly, some adults feel at home anywhere as long as they can listen to their usual music on their iPod: objects help to garnish an emotional screen that makes people feel secure. A child never feels alone when his/her teddy bear is around, and the same can be said of many adults with some of their favorite objects. Objects accompany us in many different ways (Tisseron, 1999), for example by offering children a training pitch where they can practice potentialities that will be of use to them for later interpersonal relationships, such as patience or the ability to test one's own limits when encountering an obstacle. An object can specifically mollify the tensions that are created by life in society, one example being when pupils use pocket knives to carve complaints about school life in their wooden desks. Objects also surprise us when they break down or when incidents occur that transform the continuous and monotonous thread of our daily lives into a major event. At the same time, even the most familiar objects can be imbued with different values enabling an emotional release. Such values can be based on varying emotional registers such as contemplation, nostalgia, connection, self-projection, etc. To understand this intrinsic ambivalence in our relationship to an object, maybe we should shift the starting blocks that determine our representation of an object or an experience (often by subjecting this representation to the sort of logic that applies to major events) and envision other modes for relating to an object.

CASE VIGNETTE 6.1: ALESSI'S "OBJECT-GAMES"

The Italian firm Alessi, which has been making kitchen utensils for three generations now, is a prime illustration of what the poet Francis Ponge calls "object-games." What is a game if not a discontinuity inserted into the framework of our shared representations, a displacement of the way we see an object, a way to reconsider an object as if we were seeing it for the first time, in terms of both its form and its function(s)? We could say that a game is akin to having some slack in a rope. An object that used to depict itself as something self-evident, characterized by a sort of routine and monotonous limpidity and banality, is now resisting the way people look at (and handle) it and no longer acting as it once did, so that playing with an object signifies being played by it and letting oneself be surprised by it. Whereas it used to be something that could be handled without any special attention or emotion, it once again becomes an "ob-ject", i.e., an object reimbued with meaning. As Alessandro Mendini, designer of the Fastaf pot, has said:

> With their simple elegance, Fastaf pots try to present a group of utensils that are in harmony with their kitchen surroundings and enhance the practice of the supreme domestic culinary art of gastronomy [. . .]. At work and at rest, they form a bouquet of reflectively polished, convex objects. Sometimes theirs is a discrete and slightly invisible presence; on other occasions, they constitute brilliantly visible and even poetic kitchen sculptures. Perhaps they are actors with mysterious tales to tell us while we cook . . . The ideas they highlight include playfulness, magic, invention and ritual . . . They enhance the pleasure of performing many age-old actions that used to be a chore but are now fun – like the art of cooking itself.
>
> (based on information included in the Fastaf collection presentation catalogue, Alessi, Milan)

FROM SUBSTANCE TO INTERACTION

If objects play such an important role in our lives, it is because they occupy a physical space, a symbolic space, a mental space (by filling our minds with dilemmas about choice, utilization, storage, and rejection), and a temporal space – as well as a mixture of sensations and emotions. In other words, an object becomes an essential mediator between individuals and their daily environments, helping them to reconsider their surrounding spaces. Objects all summon up practices, rituals and, therefore, a specific type of corporal experience. Objects present "ways of doing things," illustrated, for example, by the ritualized act of perfuming oneself – people do not perfume themselves at any time, in any place, and especially not in any way. The perfuming act can be broken down into a precise syntax of gestures that enable an appropriation and even an incorporation of the product and the brand. This frequent ritualization of perfuming gestures reminds us that perfume brands are often "factitive" insofar as they induce specific gestural sequences.

We may also deduce that all sensorial experiences are inseparable from a specific corporal experience. In this way, one can notice that linen constitutes the backdrop for a sort of eternal new beginnings that can be attributed to the reproduction of gestures facilitating the transmission of ways of seeing things, as well as ways of doing things. From mother to daughter, household knowhow is perpetuated by imitation and technical learning, until women begin to identify deeply with linen, an attachment materialized through simple gestures whose nature seems self-evident and natural. It remains that the experience of an object evokes, above and beyond any sensorial imprint, a universe of consumption that is emotionalized and socialized (Boutaud, 2004). In short, our relationship to objects always more or less mediates a relationship to someone else. We distinguish between two main ways of relating to an object, relationships that are in fact never entirely independent of one another:

- An autospheric type of relationship that refers to the exploration of one's own corporal sensations and corresponds to the fact that "individuals are not satisfied with considering, contemplating, examining, desiring, and admiring objects, but must touch, taste, and feel them in a constant collaboration of the five senses" (Löfgren, 1996, p. 143). This type of experience mainly emphasizes an object's hedonic dimensions.
- A microspheric type of relationship accounting for an individual's relationship to his/her close environment. The main issue here is microsocial interaction. An object is important because it makes it possible to situate the individual within a relational fabric of proximity.

CASE VIGNETTE 6.2: THE POWERS OF A CLOTHES IRON

In his analysis of household actions, the sociologist Jean Claude Kaufmann (1996) clearly showed the connections that are likely to run between the autospheric and the microspheric domains. For example, a few extracts from his *Lettres d'amour du repassage* show how a clothes iron can become a clear mediator between relations of love and tenderness:

There is also this very special moment when you can touch and stroke clothes worn by a loved one as if it really is this other person you are touching. Straightening out a shirt, for example, is like a sensual caress. You start with the collar which fits so perfectly around the neck and go on to the wrists, the sleeves and then the body which, when laid out flat, is reminiscent of a very large and comforting bust . . . Buttoning up this same shirt is reminiscent of the protective maternal gesture that is so easily forgotten once children no longer let you dress them. Ironing a soon-to-be-born baby's bib means visualising the small person who is coming. And when the child is finally there, ironing baby clothes is like an extension of hugging.

(Letter 15, p. 40)

I can tell you why people like it (ironing). It is because out of a crumpled cloth you can make something that is really neat, adding value to the item's fabric, form or embroidery. You get a feeling of order, beauty and also the pleasure of preparing, on behalf of the people you love, something you have done out of love for them.

(Letter 14, p. 40)

Between these two levels stretch several gradients represented in Figure 6.1, depending on whether one focuses on the:

- specifically substantial level, involving a holistic and synesthetic approach to objects, construed here as an interplay of sensorial correspondences;
- analytical level, involving a polysensorial valuation of objects;
- referential level, referring to all of the evaluations that are projected onto an object and are tied either to the person's personal history (with the object reminding him/her of someone or of some past experience) or to the object's sociocultural history (with the material culture analyzing all signifiers in terms of the object);
- situational level, which refers to the framework of an object's consumption;

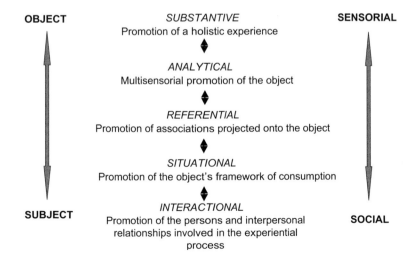

Figure 6.1 *The scales of experience of an object.*

■ interactional level, which refers to ways of doing things and to the interpersonal relationships involved in using an object (sharing, offering, etc.).

An object enables a reconfiguration of relationships between people. It turns something unpleasant into something pleasant, relieves tension, and offers harmony. In short, in this approach, there is nothing neutral about an object. Instead, it becomes an essential mediator for human relationships, notably within the space of the family home. An object is a relational entity that can allow individuals to create more pleasant and harmonious relationships with their loved ones – but also with themselves.

CASE VIGNETTE 6.3: THE HEALING SOFA

Psychotherapists have long recognized that our love for objects constitutes a replacement for difficult emotional relationships. One interesting example was found by Serge Tisseron (1999), who tells the story of a young man who used to greatly enjoy repairing old sofas. This activity was an extension of what he did as a child to "repair" his parents, whom he always saw as being broken down and used up. Having failed in this task, he tried to do better with sofas. The choice of this particular piece of furniture was symptomatic of his desires, as a sofa is a lap that people can sit on. Moreover, sofas have arms that can hold you, which is more or less the expectation that any child has of parents. As the young man's therapy sessions progressed, he began to concentrate on renovating the kind of veneer wood that is used to decorate early twentieth-century sofas, discovering how gestures such as sanding, polishing, varnishing, and cleaning the wood's "skin" could help him to unconsciously work through early experiences in which he had been the object of too much hugging from his parents. This had happened because the young man's parents used him to give free rein to their own frustrated needs for closeness and contact. Once their son had grown up, they reacted to their own incestuous desires by adopting attitudes of coldness and distance that the child found all the more difficult to explain because they would occur after periods of excessive intimacy. What the young man was trying to heal through the various facets of his DIY activity were these two traumas, the invasive contact followed by the sudden distancing.

OBJECTS AS SOMETHING IN-BETWEEN

The psychoanalyst Donald Winnicott introduced the notion of a transitional object to designate a material object that is imbued with an elective value for an infant and a young child, notably at bedtime (a corner of a blanket or a towel that the child sucks on). The transitional object is halfway between the internal and the external world and specifically presupposes the existence of a transitional space. This idea of a kind of initial indistinction is reminiscent of certain studies of emotions and passion. For example, at the origin of an emotion, there is always a meeting. According to Sartre, "the emotion is a certain way of apprehending the world," one where "the subject feeling the emotion and the object of the emotion are united in a synthesis that cannot be dissolved" (Sartre, 1965, p. 37). As indicated by its name, e-motion is not a purely internal state, but more of a movement that brings the subject feeling the emotion out of him/herself, with the subject then being able to express him/herself by modifying his/her relationship to the world. Consciousness projects emotional significations upon the surrounding world and, in return, "vibrates at its most intimate level, 'living' this modification of the world and providing it with consistency through physical reactions that serve as its 'substance'"(Sartre, 1965, pp. 50–51). The being that feels the emotion is overwhelmed both internally and externally. Through its emotional power, an object plays an essential mediator's role that makes it possible to express some of its user's character or personality traits via a sort of mechanism based on an incorporation and marginalization of the individual's psychic life.

The emotional power of objects raises question as to where they begin or end. Are objects defined in opposition to "living substances" or rather by their own functions? Should they be contrasted with humans? Can they occasionally supplement humans or become part of them? Furthermore, the distinction between subject and object is a relatively recent one. Its premises go back to Roman times (notably the distinction between *persona/res*), even though it has only really developed in what we call modern times. So what is the definitive definition of an object? Etymologically, object (*objectum*) means "thrown against," a thing that exists outside of ourselves, that is placed in front of us, and has a material nature. An object, insofar as it can become non-transformable, impenetrable, offering us smoothness and an indifferent nudity, is first and foremost something that resists.

Yet to understand the emotional power of an object over a subject, we need to hypothesize the existence of an exchange between subject and object, an idea that the western mindset particularly dislikes. The same does not hold in other traditions that recognize no such chasm. For example, Chinese thinking is based on a participation of both the body and the human mind in the winds that blow through the cosmos. Poetry specifically (Liu, 1975) affirms the solidarity of the I (*wo*) with things (*wu*), as well as the inseparability between emotions or internal experiences (*ch'ing*) and the "setting" or the outside world (*ching*). Similarly, in the African tradition, emotion occupies an eminent position not as the expression of personal feelings, but as an openness to the world. For a black African, a work of art expresses confrontation, an embrace of a subject and an object (Senghor, 1977). Esthetic emotion supposedly has traces of this kind of indistinction, or feels nostalgia for it. The differentiation of this state entails an investment in the object that specifically implies an exchange between the inside and the outside worlds, one based on a mediation of the body that feels something. What we mainly remember here is the continuity of the psychic processes that invest, in one and the same movement, the body as well as the objects that surround it. But doesn't this psychological continuity mean that we should in fact view objects as if they were our partners?

OBJECTS AS PARTNERS

The positions that our western cultures attribute de facto to objects exist in relation to a subject. But if we accept that an object entails an experience, would this not be tantamount to hypothesizing the reciprocity, or more precisely, the reversibility of objects? This would intimate that the consumption experientialization paradigm means that objects and brands constitute fully fledged actors in consumers' emotional and daily environments, much as relatives or friends. One significant analysis here is on the relationship that individuals can have with mobile phones: "we sometimes touch them delicately as we would a dearly beloved friend" (Tisseron, 2000, p. 20).

Indeed, if the relational paradigm is to be something other than purely metaphorical, we must accept some symmetry in the exchange between an individual and an object. The wealth of the relationships we entertain with objects stems from their reversible nature, for example from the fact that an object may only be an object yet, at the same time, it is capable of mutating into a true subject partner. Take, for example, something that is "treated like a face, hence 'envisaged' or 'given a face,' and which in turn faces us and looks at us . . ." (Deleuze, 1983, p. 126). What this means is that a "face-giving" process exists for objects, and that "even an object we use (a house, a utensil . . . a piece of clothing, etc.) will be given a face. We will say that they are watching me, not because such objects resemble a face, but because they are connected to the abstract machine of face-giving" (Deleuze and Guattari, 1988, pp. 214–215). Imbued with curative powers, an object becomes much more than an object. It is this person who remains alive, as long as the being who desired it continues to exist.

CASE VIGNETTE 6.4: THE ANTHROPOMORPHIC OBJECT AS A PARTNER

The rise of anthropomorphic products clearly illustrates objects' ability to become partners in our daily lives. One example is Ketchupy, the first anthropomorphic flask, which Amora launched in 1994. This anthropomorphic object helps children to restore meaning to the act of eating by transforming a formerly impersonal and glum bottle of tomato sauce into a little person, a companion with whom a child can create a relationship of complicity. This turns meals into small parties, moments when the child can tell things to an object and talk about him/herself. This practice of anthropomorphizing objects has been extended to include many products such as toothbrushes (Signal's "JoJo" toothbrush) or culinary utensils designed by Guido Venturini, Mattia Di Rosa, or Biaggio Cisotti for Alessi, items that reproduce an object's creation and operationalization process, shared by the world of children and by primitive cultures, and based on a transcending of any esthetic, stylistic, and cultural discourses.

(based on information included in Alessi, *L'usine à rêves*)

In short, marketing, even in its experiential avatar, continues to depend on a rhetoric of effects that is specific to western culture. The aim is both to make an impact that is overt and voluntarily spectacular, and also to highlight the brand's distinctive signs, as either a product or a trademark. In other words, experiential marketing still falls very much in line with the esthetic view, such as was defined in the eighteenth century by Baumgartner in *Aesthetica*:

> The more a perception includes distinctive signs, the stronger it is. Some obscure perceptions contain a greater number of distinctive signs than some clear perceptions and are stronger than the latter. Those perceptions that contain the greatest number of distinctive signs can be described as poignant. Poignant perceptions are the strongest ones . . . . Terms whose signification is poignant are emphatic.

And here we come to the terms empathy and emphasis. When we scrutinize marketing, we realize that it can basically rely on two modes for accessing a subject: the *emphatic* and the *empathetic*. The former involves a spectacular and grandiose saturation of the effect by relying on that which is bombastic, extraordinary, etc. The latter involves creating complicity with the consumer by playing on the referential and interactional levels of an object's experience.

What we are suggesting here is that consideration be given to two other registers of experience: *pathos*, which relates to the emotional register and an object's ability to play its in-between role; and the *phatic*, corresponding to a contact and reassurance register that is tied to a sort of banalization of the object (Domecq, 2004). We need to consider the power that can be carried within the banality and the blandness of a daily object (Figure 6.2).

BLANDNESS OR AN OBJECT'S CHINESE DESTINY

Without a doubt, marketing has chosen spiciness over blandness. But how should we deal with the vital energy that an object may be carrying? After all, this is a principle that covers a number of sensorial modalities: the power of a form, substance, color, space, and movement. How can we ensure that this emotional condensation is ascribed at least some

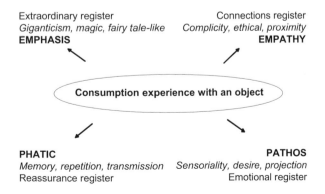

Figure 6.2 *The different registers of a consumption experience with an object.*

meaning in our western universe, and that it can really reach us, without making too many waves or setting off any fireworks, i.e., without causing any major deviations from our usual modus operandi, which involves provoking, upsetting, and disturbing the world that surrounds us? Isn't the best deviance from the norm for us to remain quiet when everyone around is all up in arms, and to let our silence be heard in the generalized uproar?

> But even if we could isolate this silence in the general noise, something that would already be quite a challenge and a feat, this does not mean that it would be ascribed any meaning outside of its phatic power.
>
> (Boutaud, 2004, p. 88)

To achieve this, we mobilize an esthetic of blandness (Jullien, 1991) that allows us to imagine other categories conducive of a new vision of objects: the vague, the indistinct, the quiet, the transformative, etc. This prism helps us to realize the extent to which brilliance fades because its underpinnings are at best topical and ephemeral, whereas blandness expresses openness to all potentialities as well as the propensity of things just to exist, even those things that are not yet visible or cannot be distinguished. Blandness engages a logic that tries to "infuse" meaning instead of exposing it and hanging it out for all to see. This is also a logic that revolves around an object's underlying ability to express itself through ellipsis and enigma, drawing on the efficiency that an object finds in a discrete existence, one in which it does not try to create any major effects – as if an object is all the more effective when people do not notice it or see it at work, only remarking its effects. Instead of valuing that which is spectacular and lauding effort and risk, Chinese thought is attentive to the realm of the discrete, recommending a sort of efficiency that is non-confrontational and does not force things, a drive that advances seamlessly and without spending itself. Hence, its gray effectiveness, flowing through the course of daily objects that refuse to stand out. The better these objects perform, the less people notice them.

Meaning should be "infused" rather than exposed and hung out for all to see. Blandness corresponds to a particular experience of the world, one based on an internal detachment. In the same way that spiciness binds us, blandness frees us. The former captures us and we are obsessed by it. The latter liberates us from outside pressures, sensations, and artificial intensity. This elegy of blandness, which is a basic characteristic of Chinese thinking, could be understood as an antidote to western culture's inherent ideology, which is based on an oversemanticization of objects. Considering an object's blandness also means trying to transcend the saturation of our senses' effects while overcoming the tyranny of the symbolic – both of which imprison objects in a register that tends to empty them of their meaning, emotionality, and very probably their effectiveness.

DISCUSSION QUESTIONS

- What are the limits of the approach that views objects as sign systems?
- To what extent does experience tie us to objects?

- Can a routine be contrasted with an object's emotional power?
- To what extent can blandness become the basis of a veritable experience for an object?
- What are the four main registers for a consumption experience with an object?

REFERENCES

Boutaud, J.J. (2004) "De la difficulté de communiquer un concept polysensoriel, Kenzoki de Kenzo." In: Boillot, F. and Grasse, M.C. (eds) *Olfaction et patrimoine: quelle transmission?* Aix-en-Provence: Edisud, 79–89.

Deleuze, G. (1983) *Cinéma 1. L'image-mouvement.* Paris: Editions de Minuit.

Deleuze, G. and Guattari, F. (1980) *Mille plateaux.* Paris: Editions de Minuit.

Domecq, J.P. (2004) *Traité de banalistique.* Paris: Mille et une Nuits.

Eco, U. (1985) *La guerre du faux.* Paris: Grasset.

Floch, J.M. (1995) *Identités visuelles.* Paris: PUF.

Furby, L. (1978) "Possession in Humans: An Exploratory Study of Its Meaning and Motivation." *Social Behavior and Personality* 6: 49–65.

Jullien, F. (1991) *Eloge de la fadeur. A partir de la pensée et de l'esthétique chinoises.* Paris: Philippe Picquier.

Kaufmann, J.C. (1996) "Lettres d'amour du repassage." *Ethnologie française – Culture matérielle et modernité* 1(Mar): 38–49.

Kaufmann, J.C. (1997) *Le cœur à l'ouvrage; théorie de l'action ménagère.* Paris: Nathan.

Liu, J. (1975) *Chinese Theories of Literature.* Chicago: University of Chicago Press.

Löfgren, O. (1996) "Le retour des objets? L'étude de la culture matérielle dans la culture suédoise." *Ethnologie française – Culture matérielle et modernité* 1(Mar): 38–49.

Sartre, J.-P. (1965) *Esquisse d'une théorie des émotions.* Paris: Hermann.

Senghor, L. (1977) *Liberté 3: Négritude et civilisation de l'universel.* Paris: Seuil.

Tisseron, S. (1999) *Comment l'esprit vient aux objets.* Paris: Aubier.

Tisseron, S. (2000) *Petites mythologies d'aujourd'hui.* Paris: Aubier.

Warnier, J.P. (1999) *Construire la culture matérielle. L'homme qui pensait avec ses doigts.* Paris: PUF.

Part III
Co-driven experiences

Chapter 7

Consumption experience, self-narrative, and self-identity
The example of trekking

Richard Ladwein

KEY POINTS

- Risk-taking contains the promise of an extraordinary consumption experience.
- An extraordinary consumption experience is motivated by self-renewal.
- Self-narrative about a consumption experience implies a dramatic situation that the consumer-hero will ultimately overcome.
- Self-narrative about a consumption experience enables the structuring and memorization thereof.
- Telling other people about one's own experience structures a consumer's future identity by insuring that his/her past has been memorable.

We can't understand everything. A narrative is an endless journey.

H. Mankell, *The White Lion*

The experiential approach to consumption is present in many compartments of life. Although it is likely to apply to relatively ordinary consumption phenomena, it quite naturally finds a vast field of investigation in the arena of leisure as well. This can involve cultural practices or tourism (Holbrook and Hirschman, 1982). When seen in this light, risky practices are particularly attractive to many consumers (particularly young adults), as they are likely to generate a whole range of emotions. Indeed, we believed in the existence of a mythology of modern adventure (Le Breton, 2000), one that, based on an intense commitment, would induce individuals to associate (at least symbolically) with death. We view risky practices as modern ordeals whose vocation is to provide answers to questions about the meaning of life. By turning to external forces and thereby imitating the classical ordeal with its reliance on divine sanction, individuals seek a definitive sanction that will supposedly resolve the tensions they feel with their social or cultural environments. From this view, the experiential approach is not the only driver behind the practice of risky activities. The symbolic aspects and finalities that the protagonists are pursuing can also help to inject value into the consumption experience.

By deciding to focus on trekking (in the sense of hiking), the present chapter tries to qualify the nature of such a consumption experience and ascertain its meaning for young adults. This will notably involve investigating the role that risk plays when such activities are being practiced. The goal here is to apprehend all facets of the risky consumption experience, from the project's genesis through participants' final report of their experience. This analysis will allow us to question consumption experiences' control rationalities from a managerial point of view.

TREKKING AND EXPERIENTIAL CONSUMPTION

The experiential approach to consumption was for all intents and purposes initiated by Holbrook and Hirschman (1982), who tried to show how consumption could not be reduced to the utilization value of a product's supply or function. By championing this approach, they were mostly trying to free consumer behavior studies from analyses that focused solely on decision-making, by creating a space in which consumption could be treated as the fully fledged activity that it is. Applying this same logic, many other authors then analyzed the nature of a slew of consumption experiences, with practices such as rafting and skydiving turning out to be the most fruitful (Arnould and Price, 1993; Celsi et al., 1993). What these analyses had in common is the importance of the emotions felt during the course of such consumption experiences. Emotions were having a major impact on people's evaluation of their experiences. Analysis of such consumption situations also revealed the role played by people's involvement in the consumption experience and, in particular, by their active participation in producing the experience, often within a social or even tribal framework. Furthermore, in these kinds of situations, individuals did not simply find themselves in a state of immersion, something that would have implied passive enjoyment. They also had to develop methods and appropriation logics that could pave the way to a satisfactory consumption experience.

As a tourist activity, trekking offers a new field of investigation for experiential consumption. It presents the attribute of being considered a risky practice, much like rafting (Arnould and Price, 1993) or skydiving (Celsi et al., 1993). Trekking as an activity involving hiking in the wilderness (mountains, deserts, or near the poles) fits into consumption logic such that the experiential value is a priori extremely intense. Under these conditions, what we need to investigate is the nature of this consumption experience, to discover whether it is limited to a phenomenological experience. The point of convergence could be found in an experience's magical nature and, because of their emotions, people in these circumstances would relate very differently to one another than they do in daily life (Arnould and Price, 1993). Furthermore, this is an experience mediated by a guide, who imbues it with magical and sacred tones by initiating the relationship to nature and structuring people's relationships with one another. This enables the participant to experience an internal transformation. This also introduces the idea that the value of a consumption situation cannot be defined by the experience's phenomenological nature alone, the idea being that the subject has to be reintroduced into the perspective of his/her own history (Arnould and Price, 1993). In the same vein, in the study of skydiving, the extraordinary experience is characterized by a dramatic situation that implies different phases (namely a beginning, a middle, and an end). The analysis mobilizes (Celsi *et al.*, 1993) this dramatic model, which is considered to be seminal in western imagination. The media have given abundant airplay to this concept, particularly on TV and in films. Without a doubt, this has enhanced its relevance for structuring people's lives.

These various ideas on the nature of the risky consumption experience suggest that, despite the importance of the consumption experience's phenomenological aspect, this is probably not the only facet being mobilized. By hypothesis, the experience's dramatic and sacred aspects are likely to have had an effect on individuals' internal transformations, particularly with young adults (Le Breton, 2000). We will be limiting our investigation to this group, comparing our findings with those obtained using older people. To appreciate the nature of the trekking experience for young adults, we chose to proceed under the egis of an interpretative type of exploratory approach, specifically by applying analytical induction based on grounded theory. This methodological option is rarely used in marketing and the study of consumer behavior, although it can be especially relevant in a postmodern approach to marketing. To carry out the study, a personal interview technique was chosen, with limited recourse to guided interviews. Respondents were asked to give an in-depth description of their experiences and their reasons for taking part. They were also asked to report on what they had gone through. The interviews were retranscribed in their entirety, following which a contents analysis was carried out. An initial series of fifteen interviews was mainly conducted in respondents' homes. Individuals were recruited in various ways, through associations, online, and also via acquaintances. Interviewees were young people between the ages of 23 and 42 (the median being 26 years). Interviews were conducted in a way that complied with theoretical sampling constraints. This principle led to the conclusion that the diversity of cases used was such that semantic saturation had been achieved, so that the later interviews provided little new incremental information. In line with any inductive approach, the first stage consisted of a microanalysis focusing especially on the stated concepts, but also on the way in which they were being stated. Then came a more formal type of categorical encoding. The final stage was based on axial coding that, by interconnecting the various categories, helped to restore the overall coherence of the phenomenon under study.

FEARS, RISK, AND DANGERS

The heart of the consumption experience's organization resides in notions of perceived risks and dangers faced. The two aspects focus mainly on an experience's emotional side.

Perceived risks and dangers faced

Perceived risks in the context of an experience vary in nature. Schematically, fears can be split into three main categories: oneself, other people, and the natural environment. Natural environments are potential sources of danger because they appear as something unknown and possibly unpredictable. Even when a journey was sufficiently prepared, there remained a great deal of uncertainty that couldn't be overcome before the departure. Scorpions, desert sandstorms, bears in certain regions, rockfalls in mountainous areas and, above all, bad weather all constituted potential sources of anxieties that many mentioned. Most fears related to the group's human environment, i.e., to other expedition participants. Interviewees mentioned the risk that a group member might not be up to scratch. This category notably included fears about testing relationships with other people. Fears about the human environment also included relations with locals, albeit more infrequently. The fear of being robbed or duped by guides or the local population was also mentioned.

A final focus was the individual him/herself. Interviewees wondered whether they would be successful at the experience they had embarked upon. In particular, they hoped that they could keep up physically and not fall behind. A second aspect pertained to psychological resistance. Individuals hoped that they could cope with any difficulties and be mentally solid enough to resist adversity throughout the expedition. These uncertainties, all of which can cause a feeling of fear, were not independent of one another. Clearly, a relationship exists between "oneself" and the natural or social environment. Natural and social environments constitute little more than a framework that is likely to interact with people's fears in this area. The commonality of all these fears is that they could curtail the expedition, as so many different events might lead to failure. It is therefore unsurprising that people ascribed so much importance to them. A final comment concerns the status of these fears, portrayed both as factors that might have a negative impact on the experience's outcome yet also as a sort of promise, insofar as they related to challenges that our young adults would have to overcome.

Interviewees were happy to portray their experiences through a prism of danger – although one should question how much danger they really faced (case vignette 7.1). Even if we cannot deny that this type of activity does contain some risk, in many respects this had been measured and channeled. Individuals who chose to travel with an agency or an association found themselves in a situation where the danger seemed very limited indeed, notably because of the help they received from local guides, who were not only familiar with the terrain and the local weather, but also experienced in handling tourists, i.e., capable of keeping any overly ambitious clients under check. Note also that the trek organizers' risk control methods received scant approval whenever they became too obvious, as this undermined the representation of authenticity that is associated with trekking, with participants feeling deprived of the possibility of controlling themselves and the risks they had chosen to take. Supervision, when construed as a set of constraints or obligations, is apt to devalue the quality of an experience. It makes an extraordinary experience ordinary, thus taking away its magic.

In short, organization can either seem like a constraint that gets in the way of a completely fulfilling consumption experience, or else like a support structure that offers a semblance of risk without letting this get out of hand. Whatever the individual's preference, the consumption experience must preserve, or at least help generate, a portion of the risk that is consubstantial to the experience.

CASE VIGNETTE 7.1: FEAR AND DANGERS OF THE TREKKING EXPERIENCE

Kilimanjaro is full of checkpoints with guards carrying Kalashnikovs. Africa is like that, it's very militarized and you're forced to take a guide and one baggage carrier per trekker. Meaning all in all you have 11 people to pay. That's how they make their living but honestly we really didn't need them . . . . The next day a guide took us through the park with our permits, because you do need to have a permit. All we had to do was climb. We didn't even buy our own food. We had nothing to do, nothing at all.

(Samuel A., 32, teacher)

You know that from time to time there will be crap to deal with, it'll be a real hassle but in the end you'll be fine. Things happen to you afterwards, really spectacular moments, and you'll have a bunch of stories to tell. That's the best thing about adventure travel, you have no idea what's going to happen, just that you are heading off into the unknown.

(Eddy A., 25, teacher)

Basically all this makes for wonderful memories, what else can you say? Although I did see a bear in Quebec and the guys who were with me were scared and hid behind me wondering what to do, whereas I wasn't particularly afraid. It was like the Pointe de la Percée and I'm really proud of that (laughs) . . . especially because we also had a Canadian with us and when he saw the bear, he took off running.

(Marilyne P., 42, IT specialist)

The imaginary side of the danger and the need for an event

The ongoing ambiguity that consists of both soliciting danger yet hoping that the risks are not excessive (or are at least under control) can be grasped via the notion of an "event." An event is one of the fundamental theories (construed here as a representation) of the social individual (Augé, 2003). First and foremost, it is something remarkable that arises in the individual's environment. In the framework of a trek, this can be confused with a test however. At a basic level, this means winning, and also being able to contextualize oneself.

From a social perspective, events fulfill a function and are necessarily situated in a person's discourse (Augé, 2003). In and of itself, the vocation of an event is to create a connection and contribute to social cohesion during the trek. Events are mainly found in the dangers that participants face when compared with other individuals who have not had the same opportunities. Although perceived dangers are very subjective and depend on an individual's own experience, almost all interviewees referred to the dangers they had faced. This featured almost systematically in their narratives. Moreover, it was often vicariously that participants evoked the dangers they had faced during an experience. In practice, this invocation consists of benefiting from all of the stories told by those individuals who, in identical circumstances or in the same location, had struggled or had an accident, or else who met other people who had witnessed dramatic situations that could have been fatal. These dramatic situations were never experienced directly. They were always mediated by narratives of dramatic episodes that were transmitted orally, much like myths in traditional societies.

Without judging the real dangers that people faced as part of their experiences, there is little doubt that narratives made it possible for them to get the most mileage (and value) out of the events encapsulating the danger in the situations in which they had found themselves.

THE CONSUMPTION EXPERIENCE AND THE QUEST

Although trekking fans assume, accept, and even seek danger, an experience never involves adversity alone. The participant is on a quest for experience. This can be broken down into several facets.

The trek as a break from the ordinary

Trekking, like other sporting activities of its kind, presents the particularity of being very limited in both time and space. This attribute is not without consequences for the way people approach this phenomenon. By being limited, it features discontinuities that isolate it from daily life, meaning that it can be defined as a fully fledged episode in one's life. These discontinuities are particularly meaningful, because the journey is over so quickly, and because it causes a sudden sense of being away from home.

One position that respondents commonly adopted was the notion of a break from the ordinary. In general, the trekking experience marked a discontinuity in the flow of people's daily lives. This was something they sought. Adepts of this practice were quick to recognize that a trek was a consumption experience that would enable them to organize a clear-cut discontinuity in their daily life flows, while immersing them in another world. It could be viewed as a response to an altered or trivialized self in one's daily life.

This discontinuity materialized in reference to people's selves. The outcome of the experience lay in the approach that the person took to him/herself, to the individual that s/he had been before the experience. The particular poignancy of this discontinuity allowed people to contextualize the experience by means of the changes they were going through — modifications mediated through their relationship to the natural environment and to other participants.

Authenticity

The trekking experience very much falls into the category of a search for authenticity. This is due to the discovery of landscapes that are supposed to produce a range of emotions that are very strong yet subtly nuanced, despite their intensity. The sense of wonderment when faced with new landscapes, the colors of the dawn, etc., all of this constitutes an esthetic experience that interviewees mentioned frequently. Individuals become contemplative when exposed to the riches of nature, easily discovering a state of serenity. Elsewhere, we find the fascination of being dominated by the immensity of natural spaces. People no longer necessarily felt that they were in a position to dominate their environment. Unfamiliarity with the natural world (albeit one whose risks and dangers could be controlled) meant they felt that they had to yield to it. They were forced to accept its superiority and the impossibility of being able to exert any sort of control over it. In actual fact, it is precisely because the natural environment contained the risk that the person had agreed to face that the setting became so cherished.

A person's relationship to nature is also likely to be appreciated from a fusion perspective. Interviewees spoke of an intimate and physical relationship to their natural environment during the trek. They had to stand up for themselves in this environment, with all of its challenges. This act of resistance led to a fusional relationship reminiscent of a "flow" experience. In practice, an experience of this sort signifies an intense emotional and physical involvement in the activity the individual is practicing. This can lead to perceptions of significant distortions in time. Thus, as people rose to the challenge, they found themselves in sync with their surroundings and did not notice time passing. It was the interaction between the individual and his/her environment that imbued the experience with meaning. Authenticity lay in nature's resistance to the person's action.

In general, authenticity means naturality. From a structural perspective, this is traditionally opposed to culturality, found primarily in urban living. There is nothing natural about cities. Treks, on the other hand, almost exclusively run in natural settings. Here, the opposition between nature and culture is all-encompassing, opposing daily life to life during the trek. An authentic experience means leaving civilization and urban density behind – hence participants' frequent evocation of their antipathy toward touristy destinations, as they generally do not identify with this type of travel. In any event, this was the image that the study's interviewees wanted to remember – although it did not necessarily match the reality of certain destinations. The Himalayas or Machu Picchu, for example, are veritable concentrations of tourists (case vignette 7.2).

CASE VIGNETTE 7.2: AUTHENTICITY AND INAUTHENTICITY OF THE TREKKING EXPERIENCE

It's also fairly overwhelming. You feel really small, surrounded by all these mountains and forests as far as the eye can see, it's the immensity that does it for me. Plus we had to be careful, maybe I didn't tell you but there were bears, a lot of them in fact.

(Eric P., 25, student)

> You are all by yourself, completely focused on the landscape and walking around in your own little world, you're seeing all these fantastic things and I dunno, it's a strange feeling. Sometimes I could have kept on walking, I wasn't at all tired because I was totally into the trekking.
>
> (Ludovic A., 23, student)

> By 8 o'clock it's chock-a-block and when you get to the place where you normally get your first glimpse of Machu Picchu you can't see anything because there are all these people climbing all over the rocks.
>
> (Nicolas P., 29, manager)

Cultural encounters

One component of a trek lies in the encounters with the host culture. Respondents frequently mentioned their wish to be in touch with locals, but this often remained wishful thinking. Linguistic problems and cultural differences meant that encounters and exchanges with local populations could often seem very limited.

Owing to the rarity of these exchanges, cultural exposure was mainly an internal affair, with participants feeling no qualms about projecting their own cogitations on to the local populations. In particular, we find questions relating to locals' material living conditions, with participants wondering about the nature of his/her own daily life. The main question concerned the material wealth of the western world, and it was specifically in terms of this material culture that people would muse upon the meaning of life. The discovery of locals' relative material deprivation made them wonder whether material goods and comforts brought happiness. Appreciations of such encounters varied, ranging from simple surprise to reflectivity to complete upheaval. Cultural discovery could also lead to a certain sense of guilt. Curiously, it is noteworthy that, even though trekkers almost systematically mentioned cultural encounter, the real encounter, which in respondents' opinions would have consisted of taking the initiative of actually going out to meet locals, was much less frequent. It was enough to be able to say that this was something they could at least potentially do during their trek.

Self-renewal: a reflexive approach

Participants all characterized trekking in terms of their own selves, as per the reflexive mode. People contextualized themselves in their adventure. To varying degrees, participants mentioned self-renewal as an almost systematic outcome. Moreover, the greater the self-renewal, the more they had a feeling of having had to overcome the elements. Although they found it difficult to identify their motives for embarking on the adventure, at the end of their description, they were able to verbalize what they had gained from the experience.

As much as anything else, the idea of renewal is tantamount to transformation. This is part of what is called "concern with oneself" (Foucault, 2001). The modern subject tries to restore his/her own coherence, adopting an approach that resembles a conversion. Toward this end, a reflexivity effort must be undertaken, allowing the individual to wonder about the meaning of his/her own life. Many consumption experiences offer young adults this possibility by giving them a break from their usual circumstances, allowing them to reflect upon their lives and to dream about the future. Self-renewal can also be viewed as the restoration of an authentic self – mainly when the individual is in a situation in which s/he feels a need to rediscover lost meaning.

TREKKING AS A WAY OF CREATING SELF-NARRATIVE

The analyses above justify our amending the purely phenomenological conception of the consumption experience's extraordinary nature. We should also consider narrative's role as a practice whereby participants try to normalize their experiences while stabilizing their self-identities (Escalas and Bettman, 2000).

Experience and its narrative

A transversal examination of respondents' discourse reveals great similarities. Clearly, the destinations differed, and the experiences' ostensible characteristics varied from one person to another. But fundamentally, from a structural viewpoint, there were few basic variations. The trek was presented as an adventure in which the narrator played the hero. Having had to face up to him/herself or to the elements, there was no choice but to complete the quest and return victorious. There could be failures but, even here, the individual could learn something. The narratives produced by our respondents were also far from being linear, i.e., they did not necessarily or strictly comply with sequential (contract–action–sanction) types of narratives. Under these conditions, the use of an actantial schema is particularly appropriate (Propp, 1970; Greimas, 1986). In fact, events or characters are not as important as narratives tend to indicate. Characters embody functions, i.e., "the actions of a character, defined

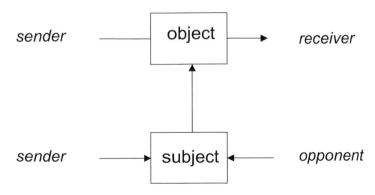

Figure 7.1 The actantial schema (adapted from Greimas, 1986).

in terms of its significance for the narrative's unfolding" (Propp, 1970, p. 36). Based on this notion of functions, we can identify (Greimas, 1986) actantial categories, i.e., structural invariants that organize respondents' productions and imbue them with a narrative quality.

To start out, the actantial schema (Figure 7.1) isolates the subject and the object. Here, the subject is the actor, the person engaged in the experience. The consumer is the hero but also the narrator. The object characterizes the experience itself, construed as a quest. This consists of living through an extraordinary experience, i.e., a destination that must enable an encounter both with a natural setting that is authentic and rough, and also with another culture, something that requires adaptation and even domination. A successful experience, or at least one containing lessons for the participant, entails the possibility of creating positive emotions and becoming memorable.

The actantial schema then separates the sender from the receiver. The former, being the person on whose behalf the subject is acting, must be considered here as one's altered self. The alteration is generally a consequence of daily life, which will drag an individual into an acceleration that prevents him/her from pursuing the sort of reflexivity s/he needs in order to develop an identity. This notion of an altered self also implies the possibility of a self that can become increasingly difficult to define or delineate. By choosing a distant destination that is very different from home, the person is seeking a break from his/her ordinary existence. Thus, the receiver is one's renewed self, a figure who, as we have seen, can be broken down into two modalities: transformation and restoration.

The final actantial categories revolve around helper and opponent. Here, we note the existence of a perfect symmetry, as an event can just as easily be a helper as an opponent. Individuals, through their minds and bodies, fit into these categories. For example, a good preparation allows the body to cope, whereas physical shortcomings are an obstacle to overcome. Moreover, the protagonist has to contend not only with him/herself but also with the other participants. Group cohesion can be a helper, as can the quality of the organization that the service provider has set up. An organization that is omnipresent can also be viewed as an opponent. Lastly, nature can in turn be viewed as either a catalyst or a hindrance. Good weather will be perceived as a helper, wild and potentially dangerous animals as opponents.

The legitimacy of the self-narrative: self-identity

At a more fundamental level, questions can be raised about the need for young adults to live through extraordinary experiences that are meant to be structured as narratives. The key issue is concern with oneself (Foucault, 2001), which is basically "a technique of existence." This particularly strong affirmation brings us to the true nature of the consumption experience. Ostensibly, a postmodern approach makes us think that it is precisely because the consumption experience is based on a spatio-temporal break with the ordinary that it can become a form of decentering allowing people to live multiple identities (Firat and Venkatesh, 1995). In practice, with trekking, it is actually the concern with oneself that legitimizes the experience. This is a type of self-identity, i.e., a specific story encapsulated in the subject's biographic past.

As a narrative, this cognitive organization of an experience allows young adults to entertain a dynamic relationship with themselves. They can think and conceive of themselves in action, and as people who are efficient when faced with adversity (Escalas and Bettman, 2000). Primitively, they can offer themselves a self-image that is idealized in its aptitude for self-renewal. Yet this primitive function appears insufficient. It is likely that the individuals involved all feel the need to be able to tell their own story to peers with whom the passion is shared, but also to an exogenous group (composed of those who do not or cannot practice this type of activity) so as to signify what it is that makes them so singular – and ultimately so they can set their story in the context defined by their own personal pasts. Here, we find the desire or need to have a story to tell in the future, to one's children for example. As such, experience is fundamentally anchored in discourse. This imbues experience with a durability that the simple remembrance of the emotions that one felt cannot reproduce. Memories of emotions are far too personal to be readily communicated. As such, self-narrative derived from an extraordinary experience of this type is the means by which young adults can structure their identities (Shankar *et al.*, 2001; Bruner, 2002) and turn their existences into something coherent. Such narratives do not have to be a true reflection of reality (remember the possible exaggeration of danger).

Self-narrative is the culmination of the definitive incorporation of the experience into the individual's identity – something called the "narrative identity" (Ricoeur, 1990). At the same time, it offers the possibility of a social diffusion of the experience, in a normalized and recurrent framework, irrespective of the surrounding cultures – namely the narrative (Shankar *et al.*, 2001).

IDENTITY CONSUMPTION AND CONTROL OF A CONSUMPTION EXPERIENCE

Narrative discusses reality "in the subjunctive tense . . . finding room for what actually exists, but also to what could happen or could have happened. This subjunctivized universe is particularly exciting, even if it has every chance of not being very comfortable" (Bruner, 2002, p.47). To a certain extent, this conception of the narrative summarizes the legitimacy thereof as a way of organizing a memorable experience and structuring an individual's identity. It is probably for this reason that this self-narrative process specifically affects young adults, who feel the need both to project themselves into the future and also to conjugate their life in the future perfect tense, something that is no longer necessary for full-blown adults, who have already moved well along their life trajectory. For the latter, the trekking experience is purely phenomenological. The narratives that our respondents gave us may not have started out with "once upon a time" – but, from a structural perspective, most productions by the young adults we questioned were based on the same actantial schema model. Our findings suggest that a narrative is a way of injecting coherency into the consumption experience by placing the actor at the center of the system. This coherency drive is a true legitimization mechanism for individuals, insofar as it helps them to singularize themselves (Bruner, 2002). Here, self-narrative becomes a powerful means for people to structure their identity. Indeed, an experience is never truly complete as long as it has not been expressed or communicated to someone else (Turner, 1982).

The findings of our study enrich certain aspects of experiential marketing. From a managerial perspective, it appears that, for young adults, the implementation of a normative framework is not an entirely satisfactory way of producing an experience, as this makes it hard to control the consumption experience. We agree that experiential marketing owes it to itself to integrate sensorial, emotional, and relational considerations with cognitive experiences and actions. What remains open, however, is how this should be done. To enhance operationalization, three major means (Filser, 2002) have been proposed to provide valuable experiences, namely decor, intrigue, and action. Decor means the stage that has been set for the consumption situation. In the case of extreme tourism, management means identifying exotic destinations and natural decors, and offering varying levels of difficulty as well as adapted logistics. Intrigue (a.k.a. the narrative) refers here to the brand, and to the epic events that have marked the brand's history and, in general, its communications. Brands such as Terre d'Aventure and Makalu Adventure (case vignette 7.3) are perfect illustrations of this type of strong discourse in a trekking framework. Lastly, action consists of getting the consumer to entertain a relationship with the product or service offer, for example within the framework of a brand community.

CASE VIGNETTE 7.3: MAKALU ADVENTURE

Makalu Adventure is an endeavor to promote Nepal to the outside world while striving to protect an age-old tradition as well as preserve the environment for generations to come. We have committed ourselves to take every step necessary to cater you an experience you will fondly look back upon not caring what it cost you, as you will be returning back a richer person full of memories. Our tour involves experiencing all aspects of a country, the great historical sites, natural beauty and wildlife, most importantly, they give you the chance to meet the local people and to see their custom first hand. Besides you need not have to be an athlete, as trekking in the Himalayas and among the people is itself an athletic experience as trekking or hiking is not mountaineering. Anyone with a pair of strong legs and a spirit of adventure to explore the exotic will enjoy the thrills of trekking and fascinating discoveries. It is important to remember, however, it requires an adequate level of physical preparation and should remember that there is also a psychological commitment in walking on the mountains. Taking care of you is a sacred duty. It's a part of our cultural heritage that is as old as the Himalayas.

Source: www.nepalmakalu.com

Although such a consumption experience production system remains perfectly valid in the case of extreme tourism, it does require definition down to the smallest detail. Our findings suggest that excessive controls, or controls that severely restrict consumers' degree of freedom, constitute negative factors in people's valuations of their consumption experience. Operators in the market that can still be called *extreme tourism* are the parties implementing these controls, which remain necessary for obvious safety reasons. What remains for them is the possibility of staging the dangers faced, although this does run the risk of offending trekking fans' desire for authenticity. What operators can do to give consumers sufficient freedom is set up experience co-production systems instead of production situations per se. This would allow for an *in situ* adaptation of an experience to its participants' specificities, facilitating their self-narrative or else offering narratives that will then help each of them to situate the experience within their own biographical frameworks. Group guides or organizers will have a central role to play toward this end, and their performances will constitute an original form of stage setting. Over the course of the experience, they will have to mobilize adversity's imaginary aspects, as well as a certain number of epic episodes that the participants will have to overcome. This co-production can also impact on consumers' relationships to the product or service offering. Examples include Internet community development systems that are dedicated to the reconstitution of experiences; to facilitating the expression of travel narratives; or to mobilizing consumers' interests in managed events and in testimonial opportunities, which can in turn lead to self-narrative. It is, in any event, difficult to standardize one's control over an experience. This requires a great deal of effort at the qualitative level, particularly with respect to relations between the service providers' on-site representatives and the customer. Marketing such services means more than merely choosing destinations, organizing quality logistics, and publishing adapted communications.

DISCUSSION QUESTIONS

- Why are young persons so attracted by risky consumption behaviors?
- What characterizes a risky consumption experience?
- What are the different facets of the actantial schema and what is its purpose?
- Why are older consumers less inclined to include extraordinary consumption experiences in their self-narratives?
- What problems do marketing practitioners have to face when trying to control the consumption experience?

REFERENCES

Arnould, E.J. and Price, L.L. (1993) "River Magic: Extraordinary Experience and The Extended Service Encounter." *Journal of Consumer Research* 20(June): 24–45.

Augé, M. (2003) *Pour quoi vivons-nous?* Paris: Fayard.

107

Bruner, J. (2002) *Pourquoi nous racontons-nous des histoires?* Paris: Retz.

Celsi, R.L., Rose, R.L. and Leigh, T.W. (1993) "An Exploration of High-Risk Leisure Consumption through Skydiving." *Journal of Consumer Research* 20(June): 1–23.

Escalas, J.E. and Bettman, J.M. (2000) "Using Narratives to Discern Self-identity Related Consumer Goals and Motivations." In: Ratneshwar, S., Mick, D.G. and Huffman, C. (eds) *The Why of Consumption, Contemporary Perspectives on Consumer Motives, Goals, and Desires.* London: Routledge, 237–258.

Filser, M. (2002) "Le marketing de la production d'expérience: Statut théorique et implications managériales." *Décisions Marketing* 28(Oct–Dec): 13–22.

Firat, A.F. and Venkatesh, A. (1995) "Liberatory Postmodernism and the Reenchantment of Consumption." *Journal of Consumer Research* 22(Dec): 239–267.

Foucault, M. (2001) *L'herméneutique du sujet.* Paris: Gallimard-Seuil.

Greimas, A.J. (1986) *Sémantique structurale.* Paris: PUF.

Holbrook, M.B. and Hirschman, E.C. (1982) "The Experiential Aspects of Consumption: Consumer Fantasies, Feelings, and Fun." *Journal of Consumer Research* 9(Sept): 132–140.

Le Breton, D. (2000) *Passions du risque.* Paris: Métailié.

Propp, V.J.A. (1970) *Morphologie du conte.* Paris: Gallimard.

Ricoeur, P. (1990) *Soi-même comme un autre.* Paris: Seuil.

Shankar, A., Elliott, R. and Goulding, C. (2001) "Understanding Consumption: Contributions from a Narrative Perspective." *Journal of Marketing Management* 17:429–453.

Turner, V. (1982) *From Ritual to Theatre, The Human Seriousness of Play.* New York: PAJ Publications.

Chapter 8

The drivers of hedonic consumption experience

A semiotic analysis of rock concerts[1]

Chiara Santoro and Gabriele Troilo

KEY POINTS

- A hedonic consumption experience is a specific kind of consumption experience.
- A hedonic experience arouses emotional, sensorial, imaginal, and cognitive consumer's responses.
- Live performances are peculiar hedonic experiences because of audience participation and artist–audience interaction.
- Every performance can be considered as a system of signs that can arouse emotions, sensations, imagination, and perceptions in different ways.
- In a rock concert, the system of signs combines purely technical aspects of the performance with the role of the artists and the atmosphere.

In developed countries, hedonic experiences play an important role in consumers' lives. Products and services of so-called "creative industries" (music, movies, television and radio broadcasting, publishing, visual and performing arts, leisure, entertainment, fashion, design, etc.) represent a large share of consumption activities and account for a considerable proportion of individual and family expenditure.

A rich line of research dating back into the 1980s has pinpointed the main differences between hedonic consumption and a more utilitarian use of goods and services (Hirschman and Holbrook, 1982; Holbrook and Hirschman, 1982; Unger and Kernan, 1983). "Hedonic consumption designates those facets of consumer behavior that relate to the multi-sensory, fantasy and emotive aspects of one's experience with products" (Hirschman and Holbrook, 1982, p. 92). Although this means that any product or service may convey a hedonic experience, it is widely agreed that those of the creative industries (given the strong emotional involvement that they are able to arouse) best fit the features described in the definition.

What drives consumers toward hedonic products and services is the search for a hedonic response, i.e., a combined response from the emotions, senses, imagination, and intellect (Lacher and Mizerski, 1994). Consumers expect those categories of products and services to create an absorbing experience (Swanson, 1978), arousing their emotions, stimulating a physical reaction, soliciting their memories and fantasies, and triggering their cognitive development. The concept of absorbing experience, which derives from sociology, is very close to the concept of flow experience (Csikszentmihalyi, 1997) developed in psychology. The immersion in a certain context is the access to the consumption experience: even for artistic products, the understanding of the different elements composing a certain context can help in creating different experience.

In this chapter, we focus on one hedonic product, rock music, and, more specifically, on one of the ways it can be experienced: a concert. As for recorded music, previous studies have shown that four features – tempo, rhythm, dynamics, and phrasing – affect consumer experience (Holbrook and Bertges, 1981). When we look at live performances, other features come into play and can facilitate the immersion in a certain event. The artist(s), the venue, the behavior of other concert-goers may all play a fundamental role in creating an absorbing experience.

Of course, rock concerts have a fairly standard connotation in the eyes of concert-goers. However, beyond the technical aspects of the performance (play list, musical arrangements, etc. – all components of content), a rock concert can be the source of completely different experiences for each consumer, depending on the contribution provided by the context of such an event. This has prompted us to look at the role of artists and their interaction with the public, as well as at the atmosphere of a rock concert.

A good way to explore the capacity of a rock concert to create an absorbing experience – or a flow experience – is to consider the performance as a system of signs to be deconstructed and reconstructed, and show the various ways in which these signs can be assembled. The outcome of different combinations of signs is a completely new experience, even though the musical genre is unchanged. Consequently, the methodological background we use in this study is semiotics, which has made a widely recognized contribution to the analysis of consumer behavior (e.g., Mick, 1986).

The essay is structured as follows. First, we present an interpretative model of a rock concert based on a semiotic approach. Subsequently, we analyze an especially interesting case: the Italian rocker Ligabue, who, on his 2003 Italian tour, used two completely different concert formats, so combining the denotative and connotative signs of his performance in very different ways.

A CONCERT AS A SYSTEM OF SIGNS

As is true of all cultural phenomena, a rock concert can be seen as an event made up of a specific sign system produced by a transmitter (concert organizers and artists) and decodified by a receiver (the audience). In the traditional definition, a sign is a fundamental unit that is used to represent something else, i.e., a relationship that links a signifier to the signified (Eco, 1975).

In order for there to be a "sign relationship," someone has to be able to make the connection between signifier and signified. So, the sign is not a thing, but a social and cultural relationship. The process of producing and disseminating sense (semiosis) comes into play only when someone (an interpreter) links a unit, which then becomes expression, with a unit that functions as content in an anthropological frame of reference that serves as an interpretant of the sign relationship.

So, what role can the artists and the atmosphere play as signifiers?

Artists

More than a musical performance, a concert is a moment in which an event, the appearance of the artist, takes place. This physical presence is beyond normality and places the audience in a dimension totally separate and apart from daily life. Therefore, a concert is a planned event involving the physical presence of artists and their contact with the public.

The significance of this presence might seem trivial, something to be taken for granted, yet it actually forms the basis for the system of interaction between artists and their public. To understand this role more fully, we can refer to the useful concept of "aura," which Benjamin (1936) defines as the "unique appearance or semblance of distance." For a given event, three aspects of the word "aura" are relevant: the object or auratic product is unique (and unrepeatable); the situation in which it occurs is unique (not only the auratic object, but also its appearance are unique); and, lastly, the auratic object resides in a context beyond daily experience. Clearly, a concert meets these three requirements. It is a unique event that occurs in a context beyond everyday life and, as such, is a once-only, planned appearance of what is normally "distant" from the observer.

The presence of the artist is, then, the principal auratic element of a concert. Artists "appear" to the audience during the event, momentarily (and unrepeatably) reducing the physical, cognitive, and emotional distance between themselves and the public.

During the concert, the artists' aura is expressed through their body language.

The first component of this sign system is the physical position taken up by the leader with respect to the others. It is the leader who emanates the strongest aura during the event, so he/she takes the most visible position, with respect to both the public and the other musicians. Consequently, the leader is always in a central position (this is true for both soloists and group singers) and tends to stand upstage nearer to the public.

The leadership position is also reinforced by a system of behaviors, in particular the order in which the musicians make their entrance. Only after all the other members of the group have taken the stage does the leader come on and the concert actually begins.

The second component of the sign system of body language is gestures, a set of factors that determine the degree of interaction with the public. First of all, gestural interaction occurs if the public has the opportunity to play an active part in the show. This opportunity (which can be more or less explicit) mainly depends on the atmosphere and the formality of the location. Artists can inspire audience participation by dialogue, verbal encouragement, and, most importantly, gesticulation. The effectiveness of gestures and body language is essentially based on the leadership of the artist. The more the public recognizes this leadership, the more the gestural expression turns into a process of emulation between the artist and the audience. Concert-goers tend to copy what artists do, especially when encouraged to do so. The dialogue that develops is almost involuntarily physical.

However, communication by means of gestures and body language greatly depends on whether the audience is seated or standing during the concert. Naturally, people are freer to express themselves physically if they are on their feet. Dancing, moving around, applauding, and cheering on their idol are expressions of the sign system of the body language within a concert context.

Atmosphere

Atmosphere serves primarily to bring out the artists' aura in the eyes of concert-goers and, ideally, to reinforce this aura in their minds. A pop performance today is seen as a "rite in which not the music, not the song, but the performer is the centre of attention" (Sibilla, 2003, p. 164). The current concept of performance originated in the 1950s when Elvis Presley made his debut. He sparked a radical change in the history of live music, as his body became an integral part of the performance, and the staging of music began.

From Elvis on, the body became a primary sign of aura within the concert context, taking on a role similar to that of a sovereign (significantly, Elvis was known as The King) who possesses an aura of power and was a cult figure in absolutist European courts (Boni, 2002). Consequently, the value of body language materializes explicitly through the public's search for proximity. The chance to see artists up close or even to touch them has experiential value in and of itself. It is no coincidence, for example, that contests often offer as prizes the chance to spend time with a pop idol. Similarly, the value of an autograph resides in the proof of physical contact between a fan and an artist.

A series of components makes up the sign system of artists' body language at a concert. Key elements are the stage and the use of lighting.

The stage features that contribute to the semiosis of a rock concert include:

- size compared with the space reserved for the audience; the public's average viewing distance and their angle of vision also depend on this factor;
- shape, which is essential in accentuating the central role of the leader and allowing him/her to get close to the public;
- materials used and their visual (light is absorbed differently by shiny or opaque surfaces), acoustic (the same is true of sound), and tactile (wood, velvet, and fabric tend to create a feeling of warmth, while metal and glass have the opposite effect) impacts;
- colors, which can be cool or warm, making the atmosphere more formal or more "friendly;"
- staging and theming: various props can be placed on the stage to create a specific "reference reality." A theme can tie into the kind of music being performed, the musicians' preference or how the album will be promoted. The more extravagant the staging, the more intense the observer's sensorial stimulation, which translates into a higher level of excitement.

Beyond the technical features of the stage, the distance from which the audience witnesses the performance is equally vital to the process of signification, as this determines how contact between the two leading actors in the concert will play out. Aspects of the physical environment that impact the artist–audience relationship during the concert are: the average viewing distance between the artist and the public, i.e., the visual path of an observer looking at the stage from the middle of the audience; the angle of the line of vision, i.e., how far above or below the stage the observer is positioned. The further away and the higher up the artist is with respect to the audience, the more the public will perceive the artist's inaccessibility and superiority. On the other hand, a shorter average viewing distance and less inclination of the observer's line of vision represent a more equal relationship between artist and audience and greater accessibility.

Concert location, therefore, has a major impact on these factors. A stage set very high up and far away from the audience will have a different effect than a low stage that is close to the public. Sometimes, the shape of the stage is revamped to allow the leader to be closer to the audience, meaning that the average viewing distance is reduced.

In addition to the stage, the second element that enhances the sign system of body language is the lighting.

The lighting serves a number of different functions within a concert context: a basic function of optimizing the audience's view of the stage; an orientative function of directing the observer's line of vision during the course of action; a choreographic function, complementing the music and creating rhythm; a symbolic function, "representing the aura," spotlighting the key onstage element in each part of the concert (the leader, a musician during a solo, etc.).

To understand how lighting can be used within the system of signs in a rock concert, the following factors are relevant:

■ Focus: lighting can be focused on the artist, on the stage, on the surrounding area, or on the audience. The audience's attention is drawn to wherever the lighting is focused. Lighting trained directly on the audience tends to prompt participation and enhance the effects of the gestures and interaction described above, whereas mainly spotlighting the artists emphasizes the "auratic aspect."

■ Number of lights: this can vary and affects the overall intensity of the concert lighting.

■ Dynamics: light can be fixed or mobile, creating movement and rhythm.

■ Direction: the lighting may be centripetal, focused on the stage, or centrifugal, directed outward; vertical, horizontal, or diagonal lighting can also add to the dramatic visual effect and the rhythm.

■ Colors, which can be warm (yellow, red, orange), cool (purple, blue, light blue), and neutral (white), can influence the audience's mood in different ways.

■ Rhythm; the tempo of the lighting, i.e., the movement of the lights and how they change color, direction, and intensity, may be fast, slow, or absent, so enhancing or modifying the rhythm of the music.

How lighting affects concert-goers depends on the specific mix of the above characteristics. In an extravagant and flashy lighting system, there is a large number and variety of very bright lights that change direction, color, and intensity rapidly, so distorting the observer's line of vision. The light continuously contrasts with darkness, while the direction is usually centrifugal and the focus shifts constantly. The effect of this visual overstimulation is to generate excitement in the audience.

An interpretive model

In an attempt to summarize these factors, we can point to certain typical combinations of elements described above that identify different sign systems and consumer experiences. On the two-dimensional graph below, the y-axis is atmosphere which, using Baudrillard's definition (1968), plots distance and warmth, while the x-axis represents consumer expectations with relaxation and excitement as its endpoints (Figure 8.1).

Atmosphere refers to factors such as the use of natural or artificial/extravagant lighting, whether it is static/dynamic, the use of special effects, and whether the audience is seated or standing. More extravagant and dynamic lighting, greater use of special effects, and greater freedom of movement for the audience will create a warmer atmosphere. If the opposite is true, there will be a feeling of distance.

Rock concerts can be divided into four categories:

1 *Active show.* At this type of event, there is a lot of interaction primarily based on gestures and body language. In this case, the use of lighting and spectacular special effects means that the experience excites the observer. Good examples are classic concerts by U2, Bruce Springsteen, or the Red Hot Chili Peppers.
2 *Passive show.* This differs from the first category in the distance between the artist and the audience. Interaction in this case is less intense, although there are some very show-like features (size, shape, staging, use of rhythmic, colored lighting, etc.). Artists

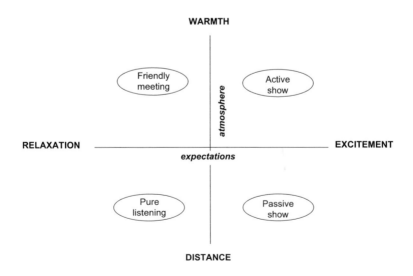

Figure 8.1 *Types of concerts and sign systems.*

use little gesticulation or body language, creating distance between themselves and the public. This type of show is typical of musicians such as Bjork or Sigur Ros, whose performances are very spectacular, but with little communication between the artists and their audiences.

3 *Friendly meeting.* This is like a get-together among friends with a good level of interaction between musicians and the public and very few show-like elements. The interaction is based more on verbal than on physical communication. Examples of friendly meetings are concerts by many singer/songwriters, such as the Italian Francesco Guccini, Tracy Chapman, or Ani Di Franco, who converse a great deal with the audience during their concerts, creating a relaxing and informal experience.

4 *Pure listening.* This occurs when there is very little interaction and the performance bears little resemblance to a show (natural lighting, no special effects). At this type of concert, the audience plays a passive role, and the distance from the artist can create a formal atmosphere. Although "pure listening" is less common in rock concerts, some examples can be found among artists who experiment with different concert formats, e.g., Nick Cave.

The concert profile is consistent with the type of artist–audience relationship and with the unique characteristics of the music being performed (Schmitt, 1999). The experience changes radically within the four quadrants (Figure 8.2). "Pure listening" has a more cognitive component ("think"), "friendly meeting" has a strong affective flavor with a good level of "relate" and "think;" "active show" mainly focuses on action and collective dynamism, while "passive show" is primarily based on sensory experience

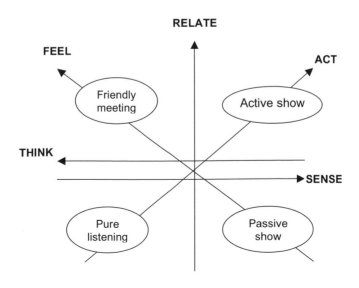

Figure 8.2 *Types of concerts and types of experiences.*

THE LIGABUE ITALIAN TOUR

An excellent example of the various sign systems that can connote the content of a rock concert is the 2003 Italian tour by Ligabue, a famous Italian rock star and today a versatile artist.

In the course of the same tour, Ligabue (who has always made his live performances a distinctive feature of his image as a rocker) presented two concerts in nearly every town where he played. Both were exactly the same length, with the same number of songs, but with two different formats, i.e., two different sign systems. This gave his fans the chance to enjoy two completely different experiences. In addition to the traditional active, electric show, Ligabue added a format he had never used before – an acoustic-type ("unplugged"), friendly meeting concert held in a theater. As a result, the artist had the opportunity to appeal to a new audience not normally attracted to an active show.

The Ligabue case study was carried out using a combination of methodologies: a semiotic desk analysis of the two formats, participant observation at the two versions of the concert, and analysis of the debate on the two formats among the Ligabue fans on the official fan club website. Our intention was to determine whether the two sign systems were recognized and what kind of experiences emerged.

Ligabue's first album was released in 1990 and met with enormous success and sales of half a million copies. The Neverending Tour (around 300 dates) ran from 1990 to 1993 with the debut band, Clandestino. However, the first stage of the artist's career ended when he split with this band.

Ligabue and his new group (with almost the same line-up as today) debuted with *Buon Compleanno Elvis!* in 1995, an album that sold a million copies and won the artist several awards. After the tour following the release of this album, a compilation of live performances was produced that sold 800,000 copies. In 1997, a six-concert tour was organized in large public spaces (typically stadiums), which was conceived as a moment of celebration for the artist.

After more than a decade, Ligabue's career has reached the stage of maturity. Recording projects now alternate with movie productions. In 1998, Ligabue directed a film based on a book he himself had written. He also wrote and recorded the film soundtrack (300,000 copies sold). The artist's second film came out in 2001. All Ligabue's albums have sold at least 500,000 copies, which undoubtedly makes him one of the best-loved rockers in Italy.

The tour described below ran from November 2002 to April 2003, enjoying resounding success and widespread audience participation.

The acoustic concert

As this format (Figure 8.3) was completely new to the artist, the first contribution to semiosis came in the period leading up to the performances during the communication campaign.

The signs used in this phase can be identified in the advertising material distributed in the places where concerts were held.

Figure 8.3 *The Ligabue acoustic concert.*

On the poster which advertises the acoustic concert, the name of the artist is immediately linked with the specification "at the theater" (*in teatro*). The members of the band and the instruments they play are listed in the center of the poster. This is done to underscore the technical aspect of the concert. It is also interesting to note that the key feature of the picture is the light, cutting diagonally across the scene and focusing on Ligabue, the leader, who is center-stage with respect to the band. The light ties the artist into the surrounding setting, shortening the distance between him and the public. The audience is shown applauding at the end of the concert. The shot is laid out with the theater itself and the public occupying most of the space. This strongly emphasizes the location, which is an essential part of the event. The audience, gathered around the stage, shows warm appreciation of the artist, and this is further emphasized by the use of warm colors.

The key messages in the communication campaign are therefore: the novelty of the project; the innovative technical aspect of the concert and how this related to artistic needs (further underscored by part of the text of the poster dedicated to the band); the importance of location, highlighted by the spatial layout of the photograph; interaction with the audience, accentuated by lighting, which shortens the distance in the photo and the semi-circular shape of the theater; the feeling of success the image conveys, which reduces the risk that may be perceived by potential concert-goers in view of the novel project.

In terms of the positioning of the musicians and the audience, the concert held in the MazdaPalace in Milan was a very revealing example. This building (a large sports arena) was radically modified to be consistent with the semiosis of a theater concert. The interior was revamped to form a shell shape with tiered seating. In this way, the observer's average viewing distance was shorter than it would have been with the audience and stage at the same level, while the line of vision was slanted downward.

Seating for the public was divided into three areas. In the first section near the stage, there were wooden seats with red inserts and red carpeting. The second section, further back, had red seats. In the furthest back third section, the original sports arena seats were kept.

The rectangular stage was enormous with a dark theater curtain. Onstage, the artists were positioned in two rows (Figure 8.4), with the band downstage and only Ligabue upstage next to a guest artist. This positioning immediately identified the leadership of Ligabue, while in the eyes of the audience, the guest was seen as a co-star.

The MazdaPalace was transformed by changing the original colors and materials. The colors were mostly dark (a backdrop and theater curtain which divided the interior into two) and warm (red seats and carpet, wood color). The original materials were covered to leave room for wood, velvet, and the fabric of the theater curtain and backdrop. Otherwise, there were wicker chairs and rugs, which can be considered stage furnishings. In fact, there was no staging or theming whatsoever at the acoustic concert. The furnishings, materials, and colors evoked a home-like setting, similar to a living room. To some extent, this ties into the very meaning of the theater within the community. The theater is actually an expanded version of the aristocratic sitting room and served the same purpose in social terms. In this case, however, the "living room" where the concert was held was not an elitist setting. A bare stage, the casual dress of the performers, and, above all (as we will see below), interaction with the audience all enhanced the feeling of warmth generated by the location.

The type of lighting used during the acoustic concert (case vignette 8.1) was natural, i.e., in harmony with the observer's view. Indeed, the lighting created no sensorial overstimulation, nor did it produce any particular rhythm. The lighting system was integrated with the location, emphasizing the tactile dimension. The overall effect served primarily to underline Ligabue's leadership (auratic function) and, second, to create continuity between the stage and the audience through the absence of stark light/dark contrasts.

Figure 8.4 Positioning of the artists on-stage.

CASE VIGNETTE 8.1: THE ROLE OF THE LIGHTING IN THE ACOUSTIC CONCERT

The characteristics of the lighting were as follows:

Focus: a white beam of light trained mostly on the stage and the leading artist, running along the observer's line of vision; when a solo was being played, this light shifted to the other musicians, in particular the guest star; generally speaking, the lighting, along with the layout of the stage, accentuated the leadership of the artist.

Number of lights: for the most part, very few lights, placed mainly at the back and above the stage, were used; only the spotlight was positioned externally with respect to the musicians.

Intensity: the brightest light was the white beam focused on the leader; the rest of the lighting was relatively muted due to the diffusion effect caused by the surroundings and materials utilized.

Dynamics: the lighting was quite static.

Direction: the lighting was almost exclusively vertical (focused on the back-stage) and centripetal (running parallel to the observer's line of vision); the overall effect was a flat scene with no depth, further accentuating the static positioning of the musicians.

Color: the use of mostly warm (yellow, red, orange) or neutral (white) colors enhanced the sense of warmth.

Rhythm: the speed of changes in rhythm, direction, and color was very limited; transitions from one type of lighting to another were relatively discreet.

In terms of interaction with the public, the singer often spoke to his audience, so interaction was essentially verbal communication. The friendly artist–audience dialogue was intended to build rapport with the public. However, audience participation occurred only when encouraged by the artist, never spontaneously.

Another factor was that the artists, like the audience, were seated. This physical position inevitably limited the opportunities for gesticulation, but at the same time made the artist more accessible.

In summary, then, Ligabue solicited audience participation through verbal communication, and focused attention on the technical aspects of the performance rather than on staging the music. The format was that of the friendly meeting rather than the more traditional active show.

The electric concert

As mentioned before, the electric concert (Figure 8.5) is the usual context for Ligabue's fans. Even if, over the years, the artist's shows have undoubtedly changed in terms of repertoire, staging, and theming, the common thread has remained the location (in sports arenas or stadiums) and musical arrangements very similar to standard album versions.

The public was already familiar with Ligabue's electric concerts, as the musician has enjoyed a long career of live performances that have taken him all over Italy. In addition, the release of the live double album in 1997 certainly enhanced public awareness of this kind of show.

Consequently, the communication objectives at concert venues simply involved publicizing when and where shows would be held and providing ticket information. There was no need to explain what the concert was all about, and so there was no attempt to characterize or differentiate the show. For this reason, promotional material consisted of relatively simple posters with minimal text and only the name of the artist and the word "Live." The focal point of the picture was the artist/leader who is center-stage and takes up most of the space on the poster.

The poster shows the concert with the artist in movement. In the background, the fans (who are lower than the stage) are cheering. There is a sharp contrast between light (on the right-hand side, like a flash) and shadow. On the left, there is the cover of Ligabue's latest album.

Various elements are highlighted in this poster: the leadership of the artist (the only musician mentioned in the text or seen in the photograph); the body language; the means of communication between the artist and the public and an essential aspect of the audience experience; the tie-in with the album (provided by the picture of the cover of the latest album).

Figure 8.5 The Ligabue electric concert.

The communication process of the electric concert was, therefore, relatively simple, because the public already knew both the artist and the type of show he would perform. The aim was to reinforce the sign system the artist had always used in communicating with his fans.

The concerts were mainly held in sports arenas. The stage was pentagonal, with one apex pointing toward the audience positioned in front of the stage, parallel with the perimeter, but at a lower level (Figure 8.6). Their line of vision tended to be frontal and inclined upward. This was true especially for the people in the rows furthest back. A big screen, positioned above center-stage, partially compensated for the difficulty in seeing the stage.

The artist was center-stage, further upstage than the other musicians. The shape of the stage enabled him to be closer to the audience, and so more visible. The rest of the band was positioned as normally at a rock concert. Besides Ligabue, the most visible musicians were the two guitarists. The soloist, in particular, would often move up toward the audience during solos, although without taking on the role of co-star.

The stage setting of the electric concert was relatively plain, with the dark colors of the stage and the metallic color of the structure. There were no objects on the stage except for the musical instruments.

Staging was left entirely to lighting and special effects. The structure of the lighting system was very complex (case vignette 8.2), with a large number of lights positioned along the entire perimeter and above the stage, as well as in the surrounding area. In this way, the entire stage area was lit up, capturing the public's attention. There was a variety of light sources as, in addition to projectors that emitted focused beams of light, less intense lights were also often used to create color effects.

Figure 8.6 The stage setup for the electric concert.

CASE VIGNETTE 8.2: THE ROLE OF THE LIGHTING IN THE ELECTRIC CONCERT

The lighting features were as follows:

Focus: the entire stage area, with the lights along the edge of the stage visually separating the stage from the audience; the leading artist was spotlighted more often than the others, usually with diagonal beams of light; during solos, lighting would shift over to the guitar soloist, underscoring his or her importance during individual numbers.

Number of lights: very many and varied.

Intensity: the most common effect was the contrast between the brightness of the stage lights and the darkness of the audience area, which added to the perception of a visual break between the stage and the audience.

Dynamics: while a few lights were fixed, most were mobile, creating an overall feeling of movement.

Direction: the lighting was mostly diagonal, giving the observer a sense of the size and depth of the stage, and so accentuating the movements of the musicians; in addition, the lights along the perimeter of the stage created a centrifugal effect, creating the impression of an opening in the stage toward the audience.

Color: various different cool, warm, and neutral colors were used; the floor lights surrounding the stage area often produced color combinations, generally to highlight certain moments during the show, such as when the concert began (purple) or, in particular, when especially popular songs were being played (red); bright colors were used throughout the show; occasionally, contrasting or even complementary colors were used at the same time.

Rhythm: throughout the concert, the changes in the color, direction, and intensity of the lighting were rapid.

Besides the lighting, other means of sensory stimulation were also present. For example, the large screen positioned over center-stage served primarily to show the musicians. This gave the public seated further back a better view. Second, the listening enjoyment of songs was enhanced with various images, often interspersed with bits of text. As a result, the audience effectively watched live video-clips of various songs expressed in a language to which they had already been exposed through music television (especially MTV).

The lighting and the big screen intensified the staging of the concert through continuous visual and audio stimulation. This resulted in an exceptional level of excitement among the audience, whose attention was riveted to what was happening onstage.

Interaction with the public occurred through gestures and body language rather than by verbal communication. First of all, the artists engaged the audience in the way they performed the songs. Gestures were a key element, underscoring, once again, the singer's leadership. Second, body language was used as an explicit invitation to the public to partici-pate in the show. The musicians' movements on the stage were clearly visible to the audience (thanks to the big screen) and, as a result, were systematically copied. This "follow my lead" established a continuous dialogue between the band and the public. The sign system used by the band to encourage participation was based totally on action. The audience was invited to jump, clap, cheer, and applaud. In turn, the fans expressed their enjoyment not only by applause, but also through body language, i.e., jumping, pointing to the stage, singing, and improvised dancing.

Beyond this type of audience involvement, interaction among members of the public was also very apparent, thanks to the strong collective flavor of the event. Obviously, concert organizers had little control over this aspect, but it was nonetheless fundamental. Before the concert began, the big screen was used to spotlight this audience interaction, and shots of the fans showed their collective spirit and elicited their enthusiasm.

CONCLUSION

This case study has brought to light the effect on consumer experience of different semiotic processes at a rock concert. Analysis of the debates on the Ligabue fan club website confirms that the two types of concerts were experienced in completely different ways.

The "friendly meeting" theater concert featured a warm, intimate setting with a minimal average viewing distance and negative visual inclination. The consumer setting was relaxed, with natural lighting. Both the public and the musicians were seated, and interaction was mostly verbal and informal.

In contrast, the electric "active show" had a more dramatic atmosphere, on account of the sensorial overstimulation created by the lighting and special effects. There was a great deal of audience participation in the form of gestures and body language and, again, there was no sense of formality. Generally, the distance between the public and the artist was greater in the sports arena than in the theater (in part as a result of the positive visual inclination), but was never too great.

The study reveals that the primary experience of the acoustic concert was a high level of involvement regarding the novelty of the project. Second, the audience paid careful at-tention to the technical aspects of the music. Most comments made reference to the ar-rangements and the talent of the musicians. Listening enjoyment was clearly enhanced by the atmosphere, which gave rise to a feeling of calmness and intimacy. Assigned seating contributed significantly to these emotions.

The electric concert experience proved to be almost the exact opposite. This event, which featured a number of elements that excited the public, tended to offer a standard consumer experience in terms of the technical aspects of the music. What mattered most to the audience was the physicality and the presence of the artist. Consequently, the kind of emotions described by this group of concert-goers essentially centered on excitement, fun, and energy.

The case study confirms and extends the findings of previous research on hedonic consumption in general and musical consumption in particular. As for the many different hedonic experiences analyzed in previous research (e.g., Arnould and Price, 1993; Celsi *et al.*, 1993), the experience of a rock concert is also based on responses from the senses, emotions, and imagination. Moreover, our study shows that the combination of several signs helps to shape consumer experience in different ways. The aura of the artist, the artist–audience interaction, and the atmosphere all play a fundamental role in facilitating the immersion of the customer in the context and in creating absorbing experiences.

The four types of rock concert described above show that varied context can be designed to arouse different experiences, i.e., different emotional, sensorial, and imaginal responses. While the friendly meeting and the pure listening concerts call for calmer emotions, the active and passive shows are more exuberant. Moreover, the activities during the various types of concert also shape the consumer response in different ways. While the friendly meeting and the active show solicit a warm atmosphere and good interaction with the audience, the pure listening and the passive show are constructed on a greater distance between artists and the public, so reducing the level of interaction. However, depending on consumer expectations, the level of satisfaction with the concert can, nevertheless, be extremely high.

In conclusion, rock concerts and the formats for live performances can be built in various ways (all technical aspects being equal) using differing semiotic processes based on the particular roles of the artists and the atmosphere, and resulting in extremely diverse hedonic consumption experiences.

DISCUSSION QUESTIONS

- What are the components of a hedonic consumption experience?
- Why are products and services with a significant creative content more capable of facilitating immersion and of creating an absorbing – or flow – experience?
- What are the principal components of the system of signs at a live performance in general?
- What impact do they have on the consumer experience?
- What types of rock concerts can be constructed using different systems of signs?

NOTE

1   The authors are grateful to Jarno Iotti for the pictures in this chapter.

REFERENCES

Arnould, E.J. and Price, L.L. (1993) "River Magic: Extraordinary Experience and Extended Service Encounter." *Journal of Consumer Research* 20(June): 24–45.

Baudrillard, J. (1968) *Le système des objets*. Paris: Gallimard.

Benjamin, W. (1936) "The Work of Art in the Age of Mechanical Representation." In: Eiland, H. and Jennings, M. (eds) *Walter Benjamin: Selected Writings, Volume 3, 1935-1938*. Harvard, MA: Harvard University Press, 2002.

Boni, F. (2002) *Il corpo mediale del leader*. Rome: Meltemi.

Celsi, R.L., Rose, R.L. and Leigh, T.W. (1993) "An Exploration of High-Risk Leisure Consumption through Skydiving." *Journal of Consumer Research* 20(June) 1–23.

Csikszentmihalyi, M. (1997) *Finding Flow. The Psychology of Engagement with Everyday Life*. New York: Basic Books.

Eco, U. (1975) *Trattato di semiotica generale*. Milan: Bompiani.

Hirschman, E.C. and Holbrook, M.B. (1982) "Hedonic Consumption: Emerging Concepts, Methods, Propositions." *Journal of Marketing* 46(Summer): 92–101.

Holbrook, M.B. and Bertges, S.A. (1981) "Perceptual Veridicality in Esthetic Communication: A Model, General Procedure and Illustration." *Communication Research* 8(Oct): 387–424.

Holbrook, M.B. and Hirschman, E.C. (1982) "The Experiential Aspects of Consumption: Consumer Fantasies, Feelings, and Fun." *Journal of Consumer Research* 9(Sept): 132–140.

Lacher, K.T. and Mizerski R. (1994) "An Exploratory Study of the Responses and Relationships involved in the Evaluation of, and in the Intention to Purchase New Rock Music." *Journal of Consumer Research* 19(Sept): 366–380.

Mick, G.D. (1986) "Consumer Research and Semiotics: Exploring the Morphology of Signs, Symbols, and Significance." *Journal of Consumer Research* 13(Sept): 196–213.

Schmitt, B. (1999) "Experiential Marketing." *Journal of Marketing Management* 15: 53–67.

Sibilla, G. (2003) *I linguaggi della musica pop*. Milan: Bompiani.

Swanson, G.E. (1978) "Travels through Innerspace: Family Structure and Openness to Absorbing Experiences." *American Journal of Sociology* 83(4): 890–919.

Unger, L.S. and Kernan, J.B. (1983) "On the Meaning of Leisure: An Investigation of Some Determinants of Subjective Experience." *Journal of Consumer Research* 9(Mar): 381–392.

Chapter 9

Fashion as the ultimate experiential object

The case of Issey Miyake's A-POC brand

Patrick Hetzel

KEY POINTS

- The product, because of its intrinsic and symbolic aspects, is likely to play an important role in offering consumers a real consumption experience.
- Experiential products convey some very specific semiological contents.
- The experiential approach generally implies a specific relationship between consumer and brand, a role play that can extend as far as the co-construction of a product offering.
- Experiential marketing constitutes a relatively complex form of marketing.
- In marketing experiences, marketers must remain both modest and cautious when preparing their marketing strategies. Not everything can be controlled.

Most proponents of experiential approaches to marketing use the distribution sector to make their point, despite the important role that a product, because of its intrinsic and symbolic aspects, is likely to play in offering consumers a real consumption experience. The present chapter starts with a product category that we consider particularly emblematic in the experiential domain: clothing and fashion wear. We will be focusing more specifically on the "A-POC" (A Piece of Cloth) brand developed by the designer Issey Miyake. There is something unique about A-POC, specifically its way of developing relationships with its customers. The brand's discourse is very sophisticated and redolent with extremely intellectual tones. At the same time, it is not accessible to each and every one, possessing a rich image but only within a small and very well-defined group. Not everyone is familiar with A-POC. Issey Miyake created this new brand with the sole idea in mind of transforming his buyers into fashion designers. It constitutes a very original collection based on a simple principle: the different items of clothing are woven so that they can be cut without the fabric fraying.

The present chapter begins by recapping the history of the brand and describing its operative concepts. We then ask questions about experiential marketing before trying to contextualize the themes driving the efforts being made in this discipline to create connections. Finally, we show how experiential marketing provides an opportunity to renew the meaning of the brand–consumer relationship.

THE ISSEY MIYAKE BRAND: THE A-POC CONCEPT

Born in Hiroshima in 1935, Issey Miyake studied graphic design before beginning his career working for haute couture houses such as Guy Laroche and Hubert de Givenchy in Paris. His final apprenticeship was with Geoffrey Been in New York. In 1970, Miyake decided to return to Japan to create the Miyake design studio. Even though many of his designs clearly bore traces of the silhouettes and materials found in traditional Japanese clothing, Issey Miyake's idea was to create a whole new style that would be both multi- and metacultural in nature. He has tried throughout his career to attain "creative truths." In fact, this is what Miyake's customers love about his work. The man is a true intellectual and has worked hard to develop new foundations underpinning the way consumers relate to his brand.

Issey Miyake is probably best known for his "Pleats Please" brand, a line of clothing he launched in 1990. The wardrobes of some of Miyake's biggest female fans are generally filled with products from this specific house brand, which they are very proud to wear as they usually have a guaranteed effect: everyone in their entourage will comment upon their very unique dress sense and make highly sympathetic and admiring remarks about how original it is. What this shows is that Miyake's brand played a major role in helping his female consumers to develop their sense of identity. To top it off, true connoisseurs are usually the only people capable of appreciating how expensive and unique these items are. Everyone knows that Chanel or Gucci costs an arm and a leg, but things are much more subtle with Miyake's collections, which relate to materials and forms in a highly idiosyncratic manner. Light effects still constitute an integral part of Miyake's work.

The "Pleats Please" collection is both elegant and relaxed, which is exactly what people who buy Miyake products seek. In some cases, where greater attention has been paid to an item's geometric shape, the ensuing form features a sort of organic complexity. Clearly, Miyake has been developing products for cultured people with a highly developed sense of fashion and esthetics. His products are not easily and immediately accessible. They convey a very specific semiological content. Issey Miyake's new "A-POC" (A Piece of Cloth) brand was an attempt to transform buyers into fashion designers. This very original collection is based on a simple principle: the different items of clothing are woven so that they can be cut without the fabric fraying.

During the autumn/winter 1999 shows, Miyake presented the principles underlying his new collection in public. Standing on the catwalk with a model dressed from head to toe in "A-POC," he took a pair of scissors and hypnotized the audience by showing how a silhouette can be entirely transformed with these products to make it into something unique. The fashion press created a great buzz around Miyake's spectacular actions. The show was a strong expression of the values underlying the designer's creative philosophy, with

127

its constant contrasting of individual and universal values. A few weeks later (in February 2000), Issey Miyake opened his first "A-POC" store in Tokyo, followed by a second one in Paris in September of that year. The Paris boutique was located in the city's Marais district, a choice translating the designer's explicit desire to attract a progressive, intellectual clientele, one capable of properly appreciating work that clearly broke with the traditional Carré d'Or top fashion houses' more conservative values system. The A-POC outlet was perched on a street corner in the heart of a pedestrian neighborhood. When entering the boutique, the first thing one noticed would be the sharp contrast between the intense white light inside and the darker colors outside. The street-side storefront had windows painted in a milky white that made it impossible to see what was going on inside. This reinforced the sense of privacy, isolating the "happy few" insiders (Miyake's tribe) from any outsiders.

The inaugural evening found the boutique full of fans who were real brand connoisseurs and generally very much liked belonging to a small inner circle that had its own specific code of esthetics and rituals of "adoration" for this designer. Some clients knew everything about Issey Miyake and his life, collections, and philosophy. The event would be an excellent opportunity to get close to him and experience something unique. Issey Miyake stood in the middle of the boutique, introducing guests to the Bouroullec brothers, who had been the premises' architects and were considered to be highly creative and very trendy members of their profession. Ronan Bouroullec spoke a few words:

> Here we have tried to use the A-POC concept to re-create the atmosphere of a place where people can work and create things. In other words, as per Issey Miyake's wishes, we have tried to build a tailor's workshop with a fluid atmosphere. After all, the A-POC concept owes it to itself to evolve constantly. The store's operational codes should help to position it within a greater transformational movement.

Issey Miyake then added:

> My dear friends! All you need is a pair of scissors. With this new brand, I wanted to create a new link, a new kind of relationship between you and my creative output. When imagining this new collection, I was thinking about the kind of relationship we have. Who is really the designer here? You or me? We now know that the answer is you AND me. I have tried to embody the fact that we are all designers and wearers of fashion, both at the same time. I hope that this collection will help to bring my work off its pedestal whilst imbuing it with new meaning. What we have here is a deconstruction process that should be able to translate into a new reconstruction. Instead of having a one-way street, I very much wanted to get you more involved so that you can reappropriate my clothes, including creatively. By using scissors as we did, we have launched a co-design process. This will also help me to learn from you and I hope to have a chance to see my clothes worn in many different forms that I myself might never have imagined. That's the magic I hope to be able to conjure up around A-POC.

CASE VIGNETTE 9.1: JOSYANE, A TRUE FAN OF THE ISSEY MIYAKE BRAND

Josyane is a 35-year-old manager at a communications agency located in the heart of Paris's "Golden Triangle." She isn't married and lives in the city's trendy Marais district. Every morning, on the way to the office, she passes in front of the Christian Dior and Thierry Mugler shop windows and often thinks the same thing about these brands, which is they are very conventional and far too "easy to interpret." Josyane is a middle-class "bohemian" and prefers "cooler" brands. Her colleagues see her as a "fashion victim" as she is always looking for brands featuring a sophisticated discourse with very strong intellectual overtones. Moreover, although she is looking for a strong image, she doesn't want one that the whole world is familiar with, just a small circle of people in the know. Josyane was invited to the A-POC boutique's inaugural ceremony and is very enthusiastic about what she saw and heard there. She is also very proud of the fact that her more than ten years of loyalty to this fashion designer's brand means that she belongs to a small tribe of persons whose original practices have helped to create new clothing styles. When Josyane goes home at night, she says to herself, "I'm so happy to have this secret garden, this unique relationship with Issey Miyake. It gives me a lot of pleasure, even in my day-to-day existence, and helps me to escape the modern mass consumption society that suffocates us all." Josyane is very convinced that hers is a unique experience and feels that her experiential reality is strongly linked to her relationship with the brand. The brand identity sustains her in much the same way that her own identity bolsters the identity of the brand she loves so much.

EXPERIENTIAL MARKETING: A NEW PARADIGM?

The focus above was on a specific case of marketing that is perfectly illustrated by the A-POC brand, but this was mainly because we are of the opinion that this form of marketing (at least for a certain number of marketers, be they practitioners or researchers) offers a new way of looking not only at the relationship a firm entertains with its customers but also at how it "represents" its customers to itself. Clearly, it is always a bit reductionist to consider things from a binary perspective alone and to categorically contrast experiential and traditional marketing – especially as it is very possible that this contrast might disappear were we to reason in terms of relational practices over time (Badot, 2001). Still, what has arisen with experiential marketing (mainly alongside "behaviorist" visions in which the customer is seen as someone to be stimulated so that a response can be obtained) are a number of practices that remain very present not only among certain practitioners but also among many theoreticians. In any event, experiential marketing has accentuated a new vision of how companies view their customers. The latter are no longer purely thought of as existing at "the end of the chain" but as fully fledged actors with whom the company will try to develop a relationship in which both parties act as the "co-builders" of what is going to occur.

Literature on this brand–consumer connection has grown greatly in recent years (Heilbrunn, 1995; Fournier, 1998). From our perspective, this involves a steady slide toward an experiential paradigm as what we have here is a formalization of the relational modalities between two entities (the brand and the consumer). In a certain number of cases, this relationship is to be assimilated with the kind of connection that can exist between two "beings," insofar as it can become a veritable passion. Some consumers are no longer able to cope without their favorite brands. Of course, these brand–consumer connections should not mask another reality, which is the possibility for consumers to live through experiential realities where one of the main elements is precisely embeddedness in a community, i.e., an instance where consumption and brands constitute forms of interaction with other actors. Thus, in a certain number of cases, the marketer can replace the individual with another reference, such as the group or tribe (Cova and Remy, 2001).

CONNECTION CREATION THEMES IN EXPERIENTIAL MARKETING

Some theoreticians in the hotly debated arena of marketing theory have asked whether it is the company or the consumer that has a greater need of this fuller relationship, concluding that preoccupations of this sort are often more managerial than consumerist in nature. The following section starts out with the implicit hypothesis that creating a connection should be of greater importance to us (hence to the marketer as well), more because this could indicate the existence of an interactive process linking companies and consumers, and less because it constitutes a simple outcome. What mainly guides us here are levers capable of achieving a certain level of relational intensity between the two stakeholders (the consumer and the company). We can identify six major themes pertaining to this connection, or to its forms of creation: complicity; customized contacts; ethics; the search for an identity; the presence of something spectacular; and proximity. We will not be specifically elaborating on all of these themes here, although a few examples will be given to explain the specific directions that such practices can take in the field of experiential marketing.

Complicity is often used as a way of "getting close" to the consumer. One illustration is *Elle*, the women's magazine. To "get close" to their women readers, the company's management pursued an enunciative strategy whereby readers steadily became the magazine's "editorial team," expressing themselves in their letters to the editor. Over the years, *Elle*'s readership became its point of focus, with the real editors sometimes even agreeing to "play second fiddle" to their customers.

Customized contacts help to reconcile the imperatives of mass production with consumers' legitimate desire for personalization. Actors often talk about setting up a "customization" process in which certain techniques will be used to develop a relatively unique relationship with one's consumer. Here, the aim is to reduce the "distance" between a company and its potential clients. One example is the Skechers brand, which tried to front-run street fashion by "infiltrating" all types of urban culture, joining specific tribes, and imitating people's daily patterns. Not only did the brand go all across the world looking for new trends and ideas, but each new model was also cleverly sent out to opinion-makers who could help to diffuse it by word of mouth. Skechers did everything it could to develop customized contacts with potential clients at two levels:

- At a very reduced and closed level, designers and marketers would be in direct contact with people we can describe as innovative and wielding a great deal of influence in the fashion world. This included not only stars, but also young people belonging to other professional or cultural tribes. These targets would be offered the latest novelty products in exclusivity, before the articles went on sale in the brand's 25,000 points-of-sale across the world.

- At a wider level, a customized contact was developed using a wide array of new information and communication technology (ICT) resources. Not only were there a number of chat rooms or forum discussion groups to talk about the brand (venues moderated by company representatives 24/7) but, as the brand had developed an Internet-based approach to its marketplace, customers leaving their e-mail address and some personal information would receive personal attention, with the company sending messages relevant to their areas of interest, or on their birthday, or concerning specific actions or company news that could be of interest to them.

In the ethical arena, we find brands such as Patagonia, Ben & Jerry's or The Body Shop. Considering customers as responsible, environmentally concerned individuals is also one way for a company to "look at others in a certain way," i.e., to see people as targets for its goods. This way of looking at customers conveys meaning. Ultimately, one of the things that consumers in this situation are sanctioning through their purchasing acts is their use of a "reflection" process to interpret how they themselves have been construed by the company. If someone is construed as being socially responsible and not irresponsible, this can become the basis for building up a company–consumer connection. It is also a way of using a product offering's strong semiological content to develop an experiential approach (Heilbrunn, 2005).

Companies are also increasingly being scrutinized by associations and non-governmental organizations (NGOs), or their behaviors are being dissected by consumer groups. Once, firms were alone in eyeing up consumers – now the opposite holds true. A good example is the career of Ralph Nader, one of the better known representatives of the consumerist movement, who will support only "ethical" products and organizes boycotts of brands that adopt practices considered to be unethical.

CASE VIGNETTE 9.2: CONSUMERS ARE FAR FROM NAIVE ABOUT MARKETING PRACTICES BUT . . .

Few experiential marketing texts concentrate on the ethical issues underlying the relationships that companies build with their customers (Holbrook, 1997). Yet these issues are clearly crucial. If the experiential marketing approach lacked this ethical dimension, companies would be at great risk, as the results they could achieve may be the exact opposite of what they were looking for when they first tried to establish a relationship with their clients. Consumers are not at all naive about marketing practices. At the same time, they ask no more than to be able to remain loyal to a brand. Of course, this must be worth it for them, with the brand being sincere in the approach it follows. One relatively eloquent example is the adventure in experiential marketing conducted in Japan by the Shiseido cosmetics brand. To improve customer relations, Shiseido surveyed customers to identify their positive and negative perceptions of its brand. The general feedback was that, despite Shiseido's excellent image, problems did exist. Women customers would go to big department stores to buy brand products, but sales staff at these outlets were paid a commission on top of their basic salary. This often gave customers an impression of purchasing greater quantities of good-quality Shiseido products than they really wanted to. As they clearly could not lose face in public, nothing was said at the time, but they would feel a great deal of dissatisfaction afterwards. Shiseido's marketing department tried to make optimal use of this information to improve its product offer system. It decided to modify its distribution strategy in Japan by developing a new kind of relationship with its customers.

New Shiseido outlets were opened up in most of Japan's major cities. Unlike most of the chain's existing stores, however, the new ones served solely as advice and brand enhancement centers, places where women could come to put on makeup and receive advice, but not make any purchases. Customers in these new locations had to settle for samples, making their purchases subsequently online using the brand's website. By acting in this way, Shiseido was making a strong statement to its customers that their relationship to the brand was not only commercial in nature. By combining the advisory center and "e-commerce" concepts, Shiseido changed the way it related to its client base, making the commercial side of this relationship less oppressive and omnipresent and trying to create a more balanced company–customer connection. This exemplifies the fact that, as long as a customer base is being offered an ideological system that corresponds to its aspirations, it will remain loyal to a company, its values, and what it represents (Hetzel, 1997). In our opinion, the success of Shiseido's strategy in Japan can be explained by its being rooted in an approach in which a great deal of respect is shown for the company's customers. There is little doubt that respect for others is a key component in the field of ethics, and that this is extremely important in marketing in general and in experiential marketing in particular.

AN OPPORTUNITY TO RENEW THE MEANING OF THE BRAND–CONSUMER RELATIONSHIP

Consumer experience investigation methods (. . .) that mainly stress respondents' personal experiences could or should be a way for companies to envisage greater intimacy with their consumers. The starting point for genuine relational marketing lies in listening to one's customers. However, this close contact to customers must not be perceived as a violation of their privacy. Experiential marketing encourages (but also counts on) the establishment of lasting trust-based relationships. In other words, companies must do their utmost at a practical level to try and get into their customers' skins.

(Boulaire, 2003, p. 47)

Clearly, genuine experiential marketing must be grounded in a new view of commercialism. Customers understand that companies have economic imperatives but do not like it when

CASE VIGNETTE 9.3: BRANDS' SPECIFIC ROLE IN THE CONSTRUCTION OF AN EXPERIENTIAL CONNECTION

To prove this, it suffices to look at the continued success of Ben & Jerry's ice cream. Four key ideas drive the general policy being followed by this brand:

- develop original products that customers cannot find in other ice cream parlors;
- consider aims other than profit alone;
- become a socially responsible company;
- get involved in "charitable" actions.

The brand's success is food for thought. Its initiatives are taken very seriously on the other side of the Atlantic, where the company has become a strong force for progress (7.5 percent of pretax earnings are given by its foundation to charities, environmental protection causes, or general interest projects). The success of Ben & Jerry's stems at least as much from its ethical activist commitments as it does from the company's very real knowhow, particularly its ability to mix fresh fruit into its thick ice cream. Ben & Jerry's sources its coffee from a Mexican cooperative called Aztec Harvests; its blueberries from Maine's Passaquamody Native American Indian tribe; and the brownies it uses are manufactured by Greyston, an association that battles social marginalization. Some product sales serve to support greenhouse gas reduction actions, protect the Amazon rainforest, etc. The company regularly takes part in social inclusion operations targeting youths from disadvantaged neighborhoods and asks its franchisees to recruit vulnerable individuals. Furthermore, customers are strongly solicited to give their opinions and can make suggestions about the company's products, decisions, etc., with consumer representatives even sitting on its board. For example, customer ideas led to the launch of Ben & Jerry's "Peace Perfume" and "Cherry Garcia" flavors, the latter in homage to Jerry Garcia, the sadly missed leader of one of the Woodstock generation's favorite rock bands.

Clearly, there is nothing superficial about the experiential construct at Ben & Jerry's. This is a very deep-seated approach rooted in a highly ethical conception of the company–consumer relationship. Moreover, there is little doubt that this trend is still in its early days. If we believe that the future is bright for this way of doing business, it is because it is a modus operandi grounded in consumer involvement, meaning that it brings together consumption and action. Some observers already use the expression "buycott" to counterbalance "boycott." The idea here is that consumers want to take an active role in the determination of their own destinies and, above all, that they are trying to get more involved in certain purchasing acts, ones that in the past could be trivialized and not very engaging. This is a form of re-enchanting oneself with day-to-day living through the creation of new meaning (Ritzer, 1999). Experiential marketing will have either an ethical future or no future at all.

commercial logic tries to masquerade as a relational component, when the only real aim is profit maximization. This gives customers the impression that they are being lied to, and they cannot help but react negatively. Inversely, every time customers realize that a sincere and truthful marketing approach is being used, one based on a balanced relationship between all parties, they generally react favorably.

CONCLUSION

In conclusion, there is little doubt that the experiential marketing concept is not set once and for all. In this author's opinion, experiential approaches occupy a much more central role than they did in the past. Clearly, a distinction should be made between marketer practices and marketing theory. Yet, from our perspective, "experiential circumstances" have significantly modified the research programs of certain analysts working in the marketing community, with greater importance now being ascribed to systemic approaches toward the phenomena under study. Moreover, attempts have been made to leverage the theoretical bases of neighboring disciplines such as linguistics (notably semiotics to understand the mechanisms underlying the emergence of meaning), sociology, anthropology, and economics (especially industrial economics and the economics of conventions). All one has to do is peruse the contents of marketing research magazines to realize that complexity has progressively replaced more mechanical visions of one's relationship to the marketplace. Of course, this assertion should also be nuanced, and much as researchers have done, we too have witnessed the use of a diversity of approaches. Moreover, it would be naive to conclude that practitioners are in any way different in this respect. It is true that some of them want more than ever to dominate the marketplace and control people's experiential realities. Yet a number of firms have also made considerable efforts to "co-construct" with their customers a partner relationship based on great mutual respect. Marketing contains within itself an ideological dimension that can sometimes be incantational, but it would be a shame to throw the baby out with the bath water. In any event, experiential marketing can help to resituate individuals at the system's center and, for the business world, it is surely worth experimenting with an all-encompassing project of this sort. Regardless of what experiential marketing's detractors may say [viewing it as yet another attempt at manipulation by actors in a position of strength (here the company) to the detriment of those who are weak (supposedly the customer)], the reality is that people can sometimes be very wrong about which party is really in a position of weakness. Now, in the early years of the twenty-first century, customers appear to have the final say in more than a few numbers of cases — as illustrated tangibly by the prevalence of consumer boycotts.

DISCUSSION QUESTIONS

- What are the bases for the unique relationship between a fashion brand and its customers?
- To what extent can the brand–consumer connection become a form of human interaction?
- What are the six major themes pertaining to this connection?
- What is the link between brand experiences and fandom?
- How should experiential marketing approaches treat consumers?

REFERENCES

Badot, O. (2001) "The 'Consumer Value' of Costco as a Test of Holbrook's Typology." 8th Interdisciplinary Conference on Research in Consumption Studies, Paris, La Sorbonne (28–29 July), 30–55.

Boulaire, C. (2003) "Marketing relationnel: la carte d'anniversaire revisitée." *Recherche et Applications en Marketing* 18(1): 43–63.

Cova, B. and Remy, E. (2001) "Comment et où classer la valeur de lien en marketing?" Proceedings of the 17th AFM Conference, Deauville, May.

Fournier, S. (1998) "Consumers and their Brands: Developing Relationship Theory in Consumer Research." *Journal of Consumer Research* 24(4): 343–373.

Heilbrunn, B. (1995) "My Brand the Hero? A Semiotic Analysis of the Consumer–Brand Relationship." Proceedings of the EMAC Conference, Essec, Cergy-Pontoise, 451–470.

Heilbrunn, B. (2005) "L'utopie est dans le Big Mac!!!" In : Boutaud, J.-J. (ed.) *L'imaginaire de la table*. Paris: L'Harmattan, 257–281.

Hetzel, P. (1997) "When Hyperreality, Reality, Fiction and Non-Reality are Brought Together: A Fragmented Vision of the Mall of America through Personal Interpretation." In: Englis, B. and Olofsson, A. (eds) *European Advances in Consumer Research*, 3. Provo, UT: Association for Consumer Research.

Holbrook, M.B. (1997) "Romanticism, Introspection and the Roots of Experiential Consumption: Morris the Epicurean." *Consumption, Market and Culture* 1(2): 97–164.

Ritzer, G. (1999) *Enchanting a Disenchanted World, Revolutionizing the Means of Consumption*. Thousand Oaks, CA: Pine Forge Press.

Part IV

Company-driven experiences

Chapter 10

Converging industries through experience

Lessons from edutainment

Stefano Podestà and Michela Addis

KEY POINTS

- The consumption experience is multidimensional.
- Edutainment is the integration of entertainment and education to facilitate learning.
- The consumption experience is one of the drivers in the convergence of entertainment and education.
- The design and management of the consumption experience should follow clear managerial guidelines.
- Differentiated strategies based on the consumption experience appear to be the future of competition: they should be segmented as a function of the customers' level of expertise.

Education and entertainment are two of the four realms of experience defined by Pine and Gilmore (1999), but may be the objective of the experience itself. In particular, the literature has extensively analyzed entertainment experiences as important examples of hedonic consumption, while education has been viewed as that part of the economy belonging to "high culture" (generally differentiated from popular culture, which is consumed in the pursuit of functional benefits).

Despite these specific characteristics, the two areas share the importance of the individual's immersion into the experience. Only if the contact with the environment in which the experience occurs (or, better, with all the elements of the environment) is close and direct will the individual be able to assimilate the entertainment or educational input and appreciate the experience to the full, so gaining maximum value. This depends in part on the fact that both entertainment and educational experiences are part of the broader world of the services, in which, typically and traditionally, the physical context plays a critical role in determining consumer attitudes and behavior. On the other hand, however, the crucial importance of the context depends on a number of peculiarities of entertainment and education. Indeed, in these two cases, the borderline between the element with which the consumer interacts and the context in which the interaction takes place is so indistinct that the two concepts almost become one. In these types of experience, it is difficult for the consumer to identify precisely when the experience begins and when it ends (is the experience of a concert just the duration of the performance, or does it begin as the members of the audience prepare at home to attend the concert and end with their memories?). Similarly, it is difficult to distinguish the importance of the social environment of an experience in forming the individual context (is the presence of other colleagues at a scientific seminar just a secondary variable, or does it, too, generate value for the learner?). Or again, what is the role played by staff in an individual's interaction with an experience (do the staff at a theme park merely help the visitors, or do consumers see them as actors in their own right?)?

These difficulties in defining an entertainment and an educational experience are the result of the central position of the emotions, even predetermined emotions, and the intense involvement of the individual in the course of the experience.

Therefore, the individual's immersion in these experiences is critical both for researchers who want to understand the significance and for those interested in the managerial implications and opportunities to exploit to the full the economic returns from the underlying investments. If, on the one hand, entertainment has recently been indicated as one of the most significant areas of western economies (Wolf, 1999), on the other, business schools, for example, are interested in discovering how to use new technologies to design and deliver online courses which overcome the traditional barriers to training (time and space) with direct and immediate interaction.

It is precisely the more recent economic trends that have proposed the convergence of entertainment and education as a new area of value both for the consumer and for the economic players, institutions, and companies involved. The ultimate aim is that the learning experience is enriched if the learner is immersed in an entertainment experience. However, in order to understand the logic and identify the best levers, we must focus our attention on the ways in which these two traditionally distant economic fields can be integrated.

THE DEBATE ON EDUTAINMENT

The term edutainment is a neologism to describe an educational experience which is at the same time entertaining. Consequently, edutainment also defines the convergence between two traditionally distinct areas of the economy, entertainment and education. Initially, the term referred to CD-ROMs bridging education and entertainment, which were expected to develop strongly. Recently, however, the scope of edutainment has increased to cover any experience that is in part educational and in part entertaining.

Although the concept of edutainment refers exclusively to the convergence between education, i.e., learning, and entertainment, it is mainly used to define cases in which this convergence is driven by technology. Despite the apparent simplicity of the definition, a more in-depth analysis of the concept is anything but easy for at least two reasons.

First, it is difficult to define the scope of edutainment, because the terms education and entertainment are themselves not completely clear. On the one hand, the meaning attributed to education is strictly dependent on the social context of which it is part. Generally, education is used in the sense developed in pedagogics, i.e., all individual or collective activities and initiatives that contribute in various ways to the formation of an individual's intellectual and moral personality. The objectives pursued in the structuring of the personality and the means to realize these objectives may vary in time and space, as they are determined historically and are part of social life. This definition includes schools as well as institutions outside a country's official educational system which contribute to its development, e.g., musical, theatrical, etc. On the other hand, the dynamism of entertainment does not help the identification of those products that fall into this category. Entertainment is, therefore, understood as fun and amusement, a pleasurable activity without any educational implication, symbolized in America, above all, by the Walt Disney Company and Time Warner (King, 1993). Generally speaking, entertainment products are for leisure, so include toys and sports goods, video recorders, televisions and consumer electronics, books, magazines, and newspapers, casinos and betting agencies, theme parks, and amusement arcades. Overall, the sector is showing strong growth and is expected to be a future dynamo of advanced economies (Wolf, 1999; Askegaard, 2000).

Second, the topic has stimulated a lively debate regarding not only its definition, but also, albeit to a lesser extent, its value. There are at least two schools of thought.

The first is that derived from traditional pedagogics, which sees entertainment and education almost as opposites. In this case, true learning assumes hard endeavor on the part of the student, which would be difficult to reconcile with entertainment. This position also appears to find fertile ground in the sociological interpretation of experience, which has recently warned of the impact on social and individual development of new trends in western society. The everyday nature of experience is questioning its significance, impoverishing and ultimately refuting the experience itself. Western societies are becoming the breeding ground of simulation (Jedlowski, 1999). The individual has lost contact with objective reality and lives in the midst of a multitude of contexts which are all valid and simultaneously accessible, and all, at the same time, the fruit of simulations. As present-day society is built on fiction and simulation, it offers indirect experiences, in which the individual is unable, or maybe unwilling, to learn how reality really is. Learning and the knowledge derived therefrom are reduced to a minimum and even nullified. Moreover, experience has become a media event.

The second position on edutainment and its effects is that which emphasizes the absence of any dividing line between education and entertainment. From a less elitist point of view, for education to be effective, the experience must be pleasurable, going as far as to nullify any distinction between entertainment and education (McLuhan, 1960). The theoretical basis of this view is *experiential learning theory*, i.e., an approach to education that emerged in the 1960s. However, the origins of the theory can be traced back to Dewey, Lewin, and Piaget (Kolb, 1984). Very briefly, *experiential learning theory* can be defined as

> a sequence of events with one or more identified learning objectives, requiring active involvement by participants at one or more points in the sequence. That is, lessons are

> presented, illustrated, highlighted, and supported through the involvement of the par-
> ticipants. The central tenet of experiential learning is that one learns best by doing.
>
> (Walter and Marks, 1981, p. 1)

The foundation of this theory is, then, the fundamental role of direct experience, exploration, and action in learning: "at the heart of all experiential learning theory is the basic belief
that effective learning occurs when students are actively involved with an experience and
then reflect on that experience" (Frontczak and Kelley, 2000, p. 3).

The convergence between education and entertainment is primarily driven by multi-
media technologies, i.e., new interactive systems based primarily on CD-ROMs and the
Internet, which create virtual reality, or real-time three-dimensional interactive graphic systems (Kinney, 1995). In virtual reality, people are able to interact with digital environments
in real time while using their senses; they become active participants in the environment.
New technologies possess two important features: interactivity, which is the ability to respond to users' input (Shih, 1998); and the "virtual" creation of the content of the message
transmitted to the consumer, together with delivery to a virtual environment that is more
realistic, vivid, and immersive. There is much controversy on this subject (Sullivan, 1998).
In particular, Green (2001) suggests that immersive virtual reality systems aim to stimulate
the immersion of the consumer in a digital or cyberspace which is generated by information. Possibly thanks to virtual reality, the concept of immersion is at the base of the area
of clinical psychology that studies the human mind in cyberspace (Robillard *et al.*, 2003).
The convergence of entertainment and education as a result of the increasing number of
technological applications in the areas of art and culture gives rise to a pressing need for
in-depth analysis of how such applications impact what these institutions offer from the
client's perspective.

THE ROSE CENTER: AN INNOVATIVE EXAMPLE OF EDUTAINMENT

The Rose Center for Earth and Space, which opened on 19 February 2000, is the latest
branch of the American Museum of Natural History (AMNH) in New York, the second
largest museum in the world. The AMNH aims to show and explain life and, in so doing,
to promote new and adventurous discoveries. Educational goals are its primary focus. For
this reason, it also puts a great deal of effort into research. The Rose Center is completely
devoted to the mysteries of the cosmos. The Hayden Planetarium sky theater has been rebuilt inside the Rose Center and is its centerpiece. The new version of the planetarium is
completely different from any other in the world.

CASE VIGNETTE 10.1: THE ARCHITECTURAL PROJECT OF THE ROSE CENTER

The building is able to attract the astronomer as well as people approaching science for the first time. The project, realized by Polshek Partnership Architects, received the Best of 1999 Award from the *New York Construction News*.

The chief architectural element of the new Hayden Planetarium is The Great Sphere. This sphere is built into a glass cube. From an architectural point of view, the Rose Center is considered the finest example of a glass-walled construction ever built in the United States. Nearly the entire surface (90.2 percent) is transparent, and it reveals the internal structure of the building, as an act of symbolic demystification of the science within, sending an explicit invitation to the world outside to enter, and encouraging greater involvement of the general public.

A broad staircase leads visitors down from the balcony on the first floor of the building where the Cullman Hall is located. From there, they can take a glass elevator, which affords a view of the exhibition floor from various angles, up to an attic. They then enter the antechamber of the planetarium in almost total darkness and watch an introductory video on the Rose Center narrated by Tom Hanks on small television screens. A bridge, also made of glass, links this space with the sphere, the inside of which is divided horizontally into two hemispheres.

The top half hosts the new version of the Hayden Planetarium, the core of the Rose Center. In this case too, the architectural project is brimming with allusions to scientific principles: outside the building, visitors are outside the universe; inside the building, they enter and perceive the universe and their perspective changes. The aim is to make visitors alter their viewpoint, make them aware that the universe works according to a set of physical principles, and that everything is relative.

The theater in the Hayden Planetarium is named the Space Theater and is the world's most technologically innovative installation with the most advanced visual technology, including the Zeiss Star, a customized, state-of-the-art star projector, and the Digital Dome Projection System. The Zeiss Star projector is the result of adaptations of the company's most advanced projector, the Mark VIII, requested by Jim Sweitzer, an astrophysicist and director of special projects for the planetarium, and Neil Tyson, the director of the centre.

These modifications were so radical that the museum's projector is the first of a new series: Mark IX. Thanks to this technological support, visitors to the Space Theater are presented with a spectacular virtual universe that recreates the galaxy. They watch the Space Show, the most technologically advanced in the world, with clear, realistic, three-dimensional images and sound delivered through fifty loudspeakers. The theater holds 429 spectators and, with the circular design and hemisphere-shaped screen, each seat is literally the best in the house. The shows are narrated by well-known personalities, e.g., Tom Hanks and Harrison Ford, and the texts are written by astronomers and astrophysicists of international fame. All of this is possible thanks to three-dimensional images, highly advanced digital technology and computerized graphics, the most advanced star projector ever made, and the most scientifically accurate astronomical data available.

In the first week, the inaugural show was seen by 30,000 people.

Visitors are also given a "cosmic passport," as a souvenir of the excitement of this trip.

Thanks to its cutting-edge technology, the planetarium is the most powerful virtual reality simulator in the world and uses the most complete stellar database. Before its opening, 10,000 advance tickets for the tour of the virtual universe show had already been sold. The Rose Center makes ample use of technology to fulfill the mission of its host institution. The Rose Center for Earth and Space was designed to give broad scope to technological and architectural variables, which are a central element of the building and the exhibitions. Indeed, the Rose Center offers the world's most advanced, powerful, and highest resolution virtual reality simulator. The Rose Center is one of the most ambitious non-profit projects ever undertaken in Manhattan, with a final cost exceeding $210 million. The structure of the Rose Center is particularly complex.

The innovativeness of the project has provoked no small amount of controversy. In fact, the inauguration of the center attracted the attention of the American media and public, and has frequently been cited as a break with the past and traditional museums, particularly as it is part of one of the American institutions most tied to its history. Furthermore, the inauguration stimulated lively debate in the United States between those emphasizing its educational benefits and those attacking its spectacular nature.

For this reason, the center represents an extremely interesting case of customer-centered reformulation of a service offered to the public by means of technological applications.

CASE VIGNETTE 10.2: THE INFORMATION AND COMMUNICATION TECHNOLOGY APPLICATIONS AT THE ROSE CENTER

Today, computerized modeling is one of the methods of scientific investigation, along with mathematical theory and experimentation/observation. To reconstruct the Milky Way galaxy inside the Space Theater, the most recent astronomical data from the most important databases in the world were used in an effort to create a three-dimensional atlas of the universe.

The technology used can project images of the universe as it appears from any point on the globe. The National Aeronautics and Space Administration (NASA), the European Space Agency (ESA), the American Museum of Natural History, the principal supercomputing centers of the National Science Foundation, the National Center for Supercomputing Applications, and the San Diego Super Computer (SDSC) participated in the project.

The advantages offered by the maps and virtual observations are the full exploitation and integration of the enormous quantity of data available to astronomers (measured today in terms of terabytes, or thousands of billions of bytes) and the possibility to manipulate and compare data and observations in time and space.

The same care with which the galaxy was reconstructed was also used to display the information to visitors. The new planetarium utilizes revolutionary technological instruments, such as the powerful multipipe supercomputer, Silicon Graphics® Onyx2™ InfiniteReality2™ (booth 1201/1401), the most advanced visualization platform on the market, the Virtual Reality Theater (booth 2057), the custom-made, one-of-a-kind Zeiss Mark IX Star Projector, the world's most advanced and sophisticated star projector, the Digital Dome System, which allows visitors to fly through a spectacular and scientifically accurate recreation of the universe, and the C-Galaxy™, a real-time computer graphics image generation solution for interactive visualization.

Together, the technologies make the Hayden Planetarium the largest and most powerful virtual reality simulator in the world, and visitors can enjoy a three-dimensional, virtual astronomical journey.

The internal space of the Rose Center is set up in a way that breaks with tradition and makes use of the most modern communications instruments from performance arts to three-dimensional computerized models and sophisticated audiovisual systems. The final effect is to bring the material on exhibition to life, making science interesting and attractive to an extremely diversified public of different ages, education, and background.

Many opinion leaders consider the Rose Center to be the most spectacular project ever undertaken by the institution, part of a recent, widespread expansion in American museums. It is a fascinating case, as the planetarium is one of the biggest investments ever in the education industry. Despite its reputation for being among the more traditional institutions, the AMNH project has literally upended the sector's conventions. Some say that it is no longer a planetarium, and a new word is needed to identify this kind of reality, such as "future theater" or "cyberdome." In a highly innovative way, the entire structure has been designed and created to help visitors learn about and appreciate astrophysics through a meaningful – and unforgettable – experience.

The museum's new positioning is based on a real visitor orientation strategy which considers the visitor as the customer, the starting point of its marketing approach. Every component of the services offered, including virtual reality, is utilized to create the experience of the visit. This approach leads to the convergence between education and entertainment, and between high art and popular art.

The center addresses the most abstract concepts in modern science, from the structure of the universe to that of subatomic particles. It is the home of the Hayden Planetarium, named after the philanthropic banker who paid for this original building, completed in 1935, which has been replaced by the new structure.

Although the project was drawn up in strictly architectural terms, it was based from the outset on collaboration between people playing different roles and with different skills: managers of the museum, astrophysicists, architects, exhibition designers.

The new Center for Astrophysics, begun on 5 January 1997, had to find a way to bring together two objectives which are typically tradeoffs: reaching out and capturing the interest of the general public, while upholding the educational mission of the AMNH, thus guaranteeing the quality and scientific accuracy of the knowledge transmitted.

CASE VIGNETTE 10.3: THE EXHIBITION DISPLAYS AT THE ROSE CENTER

Displays in the center were planned by Ralph Appelbaum and around twenty members of his staff, including architects, researchers, scientists, and model designers.

For the Rose Center project, Appelbaum directed work on the Big Bang Theater, the Scaling Walk, the Cosmic Pathway, and the Hall of the Universe. The total cost of these displays was approximately $30 million.

The bottom half of the Great Sphere hosts the Big Bang Theater, which aims to take visitors back to the beginning of time and space. To this end, it uses a multisensory recreation of the Big Bang, according to the theory of the same name that holds that this event marked the birth of the universe. The show is narrated by Jodie Foster.

To help visitors understand the tangible sense of the scale and relative dimensions of the universe, as well as humankind's place in it, smaller spheres representing cosmic and human objects are scattered around the Great Sphere. By comparing the size of the Great Sphere with the others suspended at varying heights in the space within the cube, people can clearly see the relative size of all things, from the furthest planet to an atom of hydrogen. For example, relative to a ten-inch globe representing the Earth, the Great Sphere would be the sun.

The Scaling Walk leads visitors to a spiral ramp, the Cosmic Pathway. The gently sloping, 360-foot-long walkway starts at the equatorial line and circumscribes the Hayden Planetarium one and a half times. Here, visitors relive the evolution of the universe starting from the Big Bang, 13 billion years ago. With the help of artefacts (including presolar granules extracted from a meteorite, which date back to a time before the solar system was formed), interactive computers, and explanatory panels, the Pathway is a unique representation of the history of the universe and of the cosmic scale of things.

The Pathway leads to the areas that connect the new center with the old museum building.

Continuing down the Cosmic Pathway, visitors come to the Hall of the Universe, a new permanent hall on the ground floor of the Rose Center just below the Great Sphere. This hall hosts an exhibition of modern astrophysics utilizing advanced technological applications and cosmic artefacts. The continual functioning of this equipment over time is guaranteed by video data, interactive computers, and computerized animation that is constantly updated. The most significant example is the AstroBulletin, a set of twenty video wall panels that show up-to-the-minute images from space and give the latest space news, including ongoing missions. In this room, there are also eight stations that allow visitors to discover what their weight would be on Jupiter, the Sun, Saturn, a neutron star, Halley's comet, and a giant red star.

Cullman Hall affords a view of the entire structure. The various elements described here seem like fragments of an exploratory mission in which visitors have participated. Standing under the sphere in the center of the hall, you have the impression of facing an enormous asteroid which has fallen to earth from space. This association is one that the architects sought to create by using a computer-generated image present in the museum that represents the destructive impact of a meteorite on Manhattan.

This description of the center's structure and its exhibits clearly highlights the key role of technology.

LESSONS FROM THE ROSE CENTER: SOME GUIDELINES ON EDUTAINMENT

The analysis of the Rose Center for Earth and Space highlights the constituent elements and the features of one of the most interesting and innovative installations in the world. Looking again at the three case vignettes, various critical factors in the success of the design and realization of the project are clear.

Close integration between the architecture, the technological applications, and the astrophysics content

This is a feature of the entire Rose Center project and is therefore as evident in the final result as in the organizational process pursued to realize the result. On the one hand, the architecture aims to create an environment in which visitors are not passive spectators, but active participants. The environment contributes to the development of the experience enjoyed. On the other hand, the use of technology seeks to integrate the exhibition modes. The attention paid to the presentation of just a small number of objects explicitly tries to create, rather than simply recount, the concepts of astrophysics. There is greater interactivity offering new opportunities. One interesting conclusion that can be drawn from the importance given to technology and the limited number of exhibits is that, with the exception of a few cases, the Rose Center does not house objects for conservation, but works above all to increase and disseminate knowledge. What is very clear from the case vignettes is that the two sides of the investment must be strictly interrelated.

Indeed, although some variables can be traced back to education (the emphasis on research, employment of staff with PhDs, exhibition of old and rare scientific tools) and others to entertainment (computer workstations, video-clips, audio recordings, the technologically advanced equipment and facilities in the Space Theater), in other cases, the distinction is not so clear. This is true, for example, of the development and use of the world's largest stellar database (with important contributions from NASA, ESA, and the museum's scientists) as the basis for a virtual theater designed and built with the help of SIGGRAPH99, one of the most experienced software houses in the field of entertainment. The theater is used for educational and entertainment purposes, as well as for scientific research. Regarding the former, there are, in particular, the shows, for which the music and all the details have been carefully created. With respect to the latter, seminars and scientific meetings are held in the theater and use its equipment. In other words, it is difficult to distinguish between entertainment and education, and it becomes very evident that the Rose Center is a composite reality in which education and entertainment are intertwined and produce an intense experience of edutainment.

An innovative project, updating the scientific data and developing an entertainment component

Another very important aspect of the case is its innovativeness. The Rose Center wanted to change the rules of the game. The shared cultural project was combined with a significant investment to realize something new that would be seen as a reference point not only for the present, but also for future generations. From this point of view, it is obvious that the innovativeness of the project architecture, technologies, and displays attracted the interest of the media and the general public, so guiding and mediating the success of the institution.

Case vignette 10.2 reveals that one of the drivers of the investments by management is the scientific data. The director of the center has paid close attention to the public availability of and access to the data. All the exhibits in the Rose Center, even those that seek to involve visitors through entertainment, are based on the most up-to-date scientific information. Thus, even where astrophysics is simplified in order to facilitate the involvement of the general public, it remains completely reliable precisely because it is based on continuously updated scientific data, which serve as the reference database for the discipline.

The Rose Center was at the heart of an intense debate as a result of the considerable investments made to involve the general public in an entertaining way. Over and above any value judgments, this is clearly an element of the experience offered by the center and, in particular, of the Hayden Planetarium and the shows that it hosts.

Differentiation of experience on the basis of the skills of the reference target

A very evident strategy in case vignettes 10.1 and 10.2 is the differentiation of the experiences offered, which are clearly defined in the finest detail. In building an up-to-date, scientific center with a complex and elaborate structure, management has aimed to create different experiences for different targets. On the one hand, the astronomers, astrophysicists, and other members of the scientific community have an important facility for study and scientific advance, including through the social contacts made possible via the center. On the other hand, the general public, who would be little inclined to study astronomy in depth, can enjoy an experience designed to stimulate the interest and curiosity that are prerequisites of the passion necessary to address this discipline. The variable used to differentiate the service offered and to segment the Rose Center's target audience is, then, the level of expertise. For those with little experience, the objective is to generate interest and, to fulfill this objective, a strategy explicitly emphasizing entertainment has been developed. As the level of expertise increases, the entertainment component falls, while the level of detailed analysis of the skills generated rises.

It is by means of these three lessons that the association between education and entertainment becomes a balance which can increase the advantages of the experience. Management's attention to interactivity and the pleasure of the experience does not aim to cannibalize the educational role of the institution. At the Rose Center, the most advanced technologies and the techniques taken from entertainment seem to be at the service of education. The center uses different elements in its technologies, architecture, and displays to involve the multisensory experiences of its visitors. Case vignette 10.3 clearly reveals the considerable effort by management and the players involved in the project to integrate the various elements coherently. The history of the design and realization of the project illustrates that the American Museum of Natural History has paid close attention to the planning and management of the services offered and to the integration between the visitor and the knowledge that the museum wishes to disseminate. In particular, the application of new technologies to education enriches and transforms the visitors' experience. Especially regarding museums, the visitors' perception of an innovative experience can be totally different from that of a traditional museum visit. It is by virtue of the association between technology, architecture, and the exhibition mode, as well as their coherence with the astrophysics content, that this consumption experience is strengthened.

The Rose Center case thus becomes an icon of the phenomenon called "implosion," i.e., "the disintegration or disappearance of borders such that previously differentiated units collapse into each other" (Ritzer, 2005, p. 116). This means that the difference between services offered, a key principle of the modern age, becomes increasingly unstable, creating, again in the words of the sociologist, a situation of dedifferentiation, i.e., difficulty in differentiating objects and places, because everything is subject to implosion.

It has already been shown, albeit in specific and well-defined fields of learning, that the variety of tools used improves individual learning, as the variety of learning styles can be addressed. This does not mean that visitors will become astrophysicists, nor is this the management's objective. The center simply wants to arouse curiosity for further study in the future. This should overcome the argument about the presumed numbing of individuals' ability to reason caused by the use of technological applications. Indeed, one report has warned of the danger that the knowledge acquired via the new technologies is so prepacked that it requires no effort in terms of personal elaboration or interpretation (Kinney, 1995). If this thesis can be considered reasonable, at least potentially, nevertheless it must also be recognized that one of the possible advantages of innovative applications is the integration and combination of traditionally distinct and unrelated disciplines. Tradition and innovation therefore complement rather than replace each other.

THE ROLE OF THE CONSUMPTION EXPERIENCE IN THE REDEFINITION OF THE BOUNDARIES BETWEEN INDUSTRIES AND THE RULES OF COMPETITION

The Rose Center case clearly shows that the consumption experience is a very powerful factor in the convergence between sectors. Convergence is not based exclusively on technological applications. The exhibition mode and the architectural structure in general play a very important role in making the experience both pleasurable and useful. What these types of investment have in common is that they all have an impact on the interactive and participative dimension of the experience. Interaction is, therefore, the core of the experience. Consequently, anything that stimulates interaction increases the value of the experience itself.

If, then, interaction is the core of experience, its direct and immediate consequence, i.e., immersion, is the value perceived by consumers, through which they obtain other, important, long-term benefits. In the present case, the immersion of the individual facilitated by the stimulation of entertainment becomes the vehicle by which learning (or at least interest in future investigation) is maximized. By means of the elements described, the educational message is enriched with new aspects that not only provide greater detail and information, so enhancing the reach of education, but also exploit consumers' multisensory faculties, rendering the involvement more profound.

Given this increase in the reach of individual experience, new opportunities arise for companies and economic bodies. If the design of an experience is a powerful driver in involving consumers more extensively and more deeply, then companies have new scope to differentiate themselves from their competitors. This means seeking a market position that is determined as much by emotional as by rational considerations, and breaking with the classical distinctions by sector.

The present case shows how the traditional divisions by sector become invalid, especially when applied to the study of contemporary and innovative phenomena. The so-called experiential differentiation strategy involves defining a product that not only satisfies functional and social needs, but also offers emotional benefits. Moreover, if this is a result that can be pursued with success in education (which, as we have seen, is generally considered to be opposed to entertainment), then the same strategy can be profitably, and probably more easily, adopted in many other sectors closer to entertainment. Thus, it is very clear that experiential differentiation can constitute a valid strategy for institutions and companies seeking to reposition in the market and revitalize their product range.

Obviously, the realization of a strategy that potentially offers important advantages requires careful attention, above all in addressing innovation and project complexity.

The former concerns policy to select, manage, and exploit the skills to be used in the planning and realization of the consumption experience. Although this has always been a critical issue, it is even more so with regard to experiential differentiation. There are two difficulties. On the one hand, skills come from various businesses, which may even be far from the company's or institution's core activities, and are therefore unfamiliar to management. Marketing managers cannot oversee these skills, because they lack the cognitive tools to assess them effectively. On the other hand, these skills acquire value not by themselves, but by integration, making leverage even more problematic.

The second major difficulty in experiential differentiation strategies is the active participation of the customer. Precisely because interaction is the main source of value for the customer from the experience, it is critical for the market success of the experience. This critical aspect is further combined with the impossibility for management to control each single component of the experience and each single interaction with the individual. Giving consumers power even in their involvement in the creation of an experience means adopting an innovative marketing policy (with the derived advantages in terms of competitive position), but also leads to a situation in which management loses the responsibility, at least in part, for the success of the experience. If consumers contribute actively and decisively (and beyond management's control) to the creation of the experience, then the replicability and the control of the process become critical elements in the realization and commercial exploitation of this experience.

Consequently, experiential differentiation, which is based on convergence between sectors, could be the competitive strategy of the future. On the one hand, it offers significant advantages but, on the other, it also requires innovative project planning and administration skills, in which management must be suitably prepared.

It is clear that the starting point must be a shared project and shared objectives within the organization.

DISCUSSION QUESTIONS

- Why does the consumption experience have an impact on competition between companies?
- Which product factors must be controlled in seeking differentiation based on consumption experience?
- What problems does the innovation of an experiential formula present over time?
- Why does the realization of consumption experiences require strong integration of different skills?
- With which operational activities and mechanisms can the varied skills needed to create an intersectorial consumption experience be integrated?

REFERENCES

Askegaard, S. (2000) "Marketing, the Performing Arts and Social Change: Beyond the Legitimacy Crisis." *Consumption, Markets and Culture* 3(1): 1–26.

Frontczak, N.T. and Kelley, C.A. (2000) "Special Issue on Experiential Learning in Marketing Education." *Journal of Marketing Education* 22(1): 3–4.

Green, N. (2001) "How Everyday Life Became Virtual. Mundane Work at the Juncture of Production and Consumption." *Journal of Consumer Culture* 1(1): 73–92.

Jedlowski, P. (1999) "Le trasformazioni dell'esperienza." In: Leccardi, C. (ed.) *Limiti della modernità. Trasformazioni del mondo e della conoscenza*. Rome: Carocci, 147–178.

King, M.J. (1993) "The American Theme Park: A Curious Amalgam." In: Browne, R.B. and Ambrosetti, R.J. (eds) *Continuities in Popular Culture: The Present in the Past and the Past in the Present and Future*. Bowling Green, OH: Bowling Green State University Popular Press, 49–60.

Kinney, T. (1995) *Entertainment Technology and Tomorrow's Information Services*. Medford, NJ: Information Today for the American Society for Information Science.

Kolb, D.A. (1984) *Experiential Learning. Experience as The Source of Learning and Development*. Englewood Cliffs, NJ: Prentice Hall.

McLuhan, M. (1960) *Classrooms Without Walls*. Boston: Beacon Press.

Pine, B.J. and Gilmore, J. (1999) *The Experience Economy: Work is Theatre and Every Business a Stage*. Boston: Harvard Business School.

Ritzer, G. (2005) *Enchanting a Disenchanted World. Revolutionizing the Means of Consumption*, 2nd edn. Thousand Oaks, CA: Pine Forge Press.

Robillard, G., Bouchard S., Fournier T. and Renaud P. (2003) "Anxiety and Presence during VR Immersion: A Comparative Study of the Relations of Phobic and Non-phobic Participants in Therapeutic Virtual Environments Derived from Computer Games." *Cyberpsychology and Behavior* 6(5): 467–476.

Shih, C.F. (1998) "Conceptualizing Consumer Experiences in Cyberspace." *European Journal of Marketing* 32(7/8): 655–663.

Sullivan, R. (1998) "The Object in Question. Museums Caught in the Net." In: Wolf, M.T., Ensor, P. and Thomas, M.A. (eds) *Information Imagineering. Meeting at the Interface*. Chicago: American Library Association, 147–154.

Walter, G.A. and Marks, S.E. (1981) *Experiential Learning and Change. Theory Design and Practice*. New York: John Wiley.

Wolf, M.J. (1999) *The Entertainment Economy. How Mega-Media Forces Are Transforming Our Lives*. New York: Times Books.

Chapter 11

How value-based brands create valuable experience

The case of sports brands

Vanni Codeluppi

KEY POINTS

- Today, brands develop strategies that are focused on experience in order to involve an expert consumer who is ever more difficult to reach.
- In order to function better, brands construct specific cultural images that are based on social values.
- Brands tend to enter into the most private experience of an individual, that of values, and can influence this space.
- Television, which sells sports events spectators to firms, is one of the factors that contribute most to the transformation of sport from the point of view of consumption.
- The main sporting brands present worlds with values that involve the consumers and contribute to making sport ever more consumption oriented.

During the twentieth century, sport underwent a radical transformation with regard to consumers. The large global brands have gradually taken over and, with them, their accompanying commercial logic. This is true for all brands, but refers above all to the brands of products in the sports sector. These tend ever more to build communication worlds that are fascinating for consumers and to translate these worlds in various ways on to the physical and experiential plane with events, tournaments, fitness centers, sales points, etc. This also has consequences at a social level, in as much as the widespread appeal exercised by the worlds of sporting brands contributes in a significant manner to the creation of a gradual process of "sportification" of society.

If this has happened, it is because sport represents a universal language able to attract a high level of involvement in all cultures. It is therefore particularly useful for the communication of brands with a need to be "global" (Aaker and Joachimsthaler, 2000). But this has also happened because the brands themselves have begun to develop particularly sophisticated communication strategies focused on the concept of experience. Indeed, this has become the main goal, as it allows an expert consumer to become involved and because it is ever more difficult to reach. We will therefore use the concept of experience as our starting point in reconstructing the "experience" strategies used by the main global brands and the processes of change in sports brands.

THE GROWING IMPORTANCE OF THE CONCEPT OF EXPERIENCE

Among the aspects that are most characteristic of the evolutionary phase of western social systems, the development of an esthetic of sensation which seeks to stimulate the body using the immediateness of its primary processes (aroused by desire), the communicative capabilities of sounds and images (all that is not conversational), and the possibilities provided by immersion of a previously detached subject into an experience must be considered to be particularly important (Featherstone, 1991). This aspect is certainly not new to social culture. It can be found, for example, in the excitement, uncontrolled emotion, and direct physical pleasure experienced in the "chaos" of carnivals, popular festivals, and fairs that took place in the Middle Ages. At the time, however, these experiences were limited to the working classes and to certain times, and only later spread to the middle classes. It was above all the new places of consumption (in the nineteenth century, the voyages, department stores, and universal exhibitions; in the twentieth century, the shopping centers, airports, and theme parks) that offered this experience of cultural disorder which, in the past, had belonged to the carnivals, popular festivals, and fairs (Codeluppi, 2000). Actually, we are not really talking about the same experience, as the process of civilizing imposed physical and emotional control on the middle classes. What these classes felt was only an "ordered disorder" (Featherstone, 1991).

However, the fact remains that, in recent decades, individuals have sought ever more intensely the sensations and emotions produced by experiences. What we want to buy today is an experience and not merely a product. Consequently, even firms, having passed from product to brand, are now progressively focusing on a new concept of marketing which is called "esthetic" (Schmitt and Simonson, 1997) and "experience" (Schmitt, 1999). They are increasingly trying to make consumers feel physical and emotional sensations during their experiences with products and brands. These sensations are stimulated by all the forms of communication, by the product design, but, above all, they flourish in new places of consumption.

The importance of the atmosphere created in the sales environment as a means of influencing buying behavior had already been underlined in the 1970s (Kotler, 1973–74). It was, however, necessary to arrive at the current situation of communication saturation at all levels of society to take more decisive action and give greater visibility to the subjects who communicate. This is why today there is great emphasis in the places of consumption on the exploitation of a certain theme, or rather on "theming," a technique of self-representation that focuses on a particular conceptual category which should already be known to users and should therefore generate a high level of involvement. Any geographical, mythical, historical, current, or future place can be used for theming, providing it is sufficiently attractive. Above all, however, the chosen theme must be presented in such a way as to create an experience or, rather, something that changes people in a certain way so that they are no longer the same after having tried it. Any experience, be it weak or strong, will be integrated into a person's knowledge as "personal baggage," which will be remembered over time.

IMAGES OF BRAND AND VALUES

All the major global brands today use the communication tools at their disposal to build a specific, but extremely intriguing and seductive, world around their products. This world is autonomous and refers only to itself. It is for the most part immaterial, but represents for the consumer a precise reality that can be tried out, something extremely concrete. At the same time, it has been known for some time that the media can operate socially by "duplicating reality," i.e., by placing next to reality another reality that is just as "true" for individuals, even if it is a purely virtual place. Similarly, the new communication reality produced by brands seems to be transformed through the media into a real and concrete object. This is because we are talking about a reality that has been given richness and communicative density, but also because this reality tends to establish a continual relationship with the consumer through various communication channels (advertising, direct marketing, marketing events, Internet, point-of-sale communication, etc.). Reality has an ever more concrete representation through those spectacular consumer spaces that are built by many global brands (Codeluppi, 2000).

The communication worlds of brands have been called the "possible worlds of the brand" (Semprini, 1996). These possible worlds are mainly:

- fictional, but can sometimes appear to be particularly close to day-to-day reality and therefore use a realistic language;
- internally coherent, with respect to their past history and the expectations of the target market with regard to the represented world;
- highly differentiated from the similar worlds of competing brands;
- selective of their specific audience.

Semprini has further maintained that, despite their high level of definition, these possible worlds of the brand remain virtual worlds that can be made concrete only with the fundamental contribution of the eventual target. Therefore, "the brand does not construct the possible world alone. It is the consumers who by subscribing to the imaginary construction set up by the brand attribute a 'real' existence to this world" (Semprini, 1996, p. 141).

However, the concept of a possible world is limited with respect to the richness and communicative power of today's most important brands. What these brands really define is a true and proper cultural image. This is an image that naturally cannot be constructed *ex novo*, but develops by appropriating a portion of the wider social imagination. The brands first pick a specific value and then use the different forms of traditional communication (advertising, promotions, etc.), the design of the visual–verbal elements of identity (name, logo, and other codes of the brand), the product design and that of the points-of-sale, co-branding initiatives with other brands, active Internet sites, and company employees (Schmitt, 1999) to build around this value an entirely communication-based reality that appears to have an equally specific identity. In contemporary society saturated by communication in all its forms, and where products are increasingly similar to each other and therefore less attractive to consumers, it is not enough to communicate the existence of a product or information about the benefits that a product can offer. It is imperative to impose one's presence by communicating a specific identity.

Furthermore, brands cannot limit themselves to giving their own name to a certain line of products, they must propose models of behavior, a lifestyle, an esthetic, and even social and moral values. Without the foundation of a social value, the image of the brand is weaker. It is, on the other hand, now clear that a brand that proposes values sets itself up as an extremely influential interlocutor, able to demonstrate the principles that should inspire and direct behavior. Consumer identification with the brand therefore becomes particularly profound.

The brand is not able to create new values, it can only reinforce those that already exist, and consequently seeks to acquire one of these values (case vignette 11.1). The result is that the firm is transformed into a powerful social actor that tends to invade the private space of individuals and penetrate ever more deeply into their lives (Holt, 2005). What really happens in a situation such as today's crisis in the system of past certainties (values, traditions) is that "we live in a society where common ideals and political resolve have been largely replaced by shared meanings revolving around brand names and advertising images" (Lewis and Bridger, 2000, p. 13). We need to ask whether this does not lead to consequences for individuals and society as a whole. It is clear that that which in the past was developed within a collective elaboration of social culture is increasingly delegated to firms. This becomes particularly serious if values are seen as a basic element that should guide the cultural dynamics of any society. It is no coincidence that today "brands have the potential to become the new centers of community" (Atkin, 2004, p. 200).

CASE VIGNETTE 11.1: "JUST DO IT"

Nike's advertising slogan "Just do it" probably derives from the world of running where the firm made its first impact. As the product range gradually expanded, however, Nike developed this concept of individual challenge, seeking to respond to the typically US desire of people who want to feel free from the institutional aspect of sport, i.e., sport dominated by Olympic federations and teams, as in the European sporting tradition. Gradually, this individualistic conception of sport has placed Nike at the opposite end of the spectrum to Baron de Coubertin's classic conception of sport as a competition for moral benefit ("The important thing is not the winning but the taking part"). In Nike's advertising messages, what counts is winning at all costs. Even if they originate in running, the values that Nike evokes are universal. They are applied to all types of sport, but also to all profiles, from Michael Jordan to the Sunday sportsman. And this ethic can cross the boundaries of sport and be applied in all areas of life (Riou, 1999, p. 81). "Just do it" therefore underlines the effort and the action with which any individual can win a personal challenge and reach a goal This slogan also works because, semantically, its meaning is not precisely defined. It is sufficiently ambiguous to be interpreted differently by different people.

Consequently, a large number of Nike contracts are given to sports personalities such as Ilie Nastase, John McEnroe, André Agassi, or Charles Barkley, all with strong and independent personalities representing individualistic values, the difference of the individual with regard to the social system. Above all, however, the brand values have been incarnated by basketball star Michael Jordan. Beyond the extraordinary sporting results of the athlete, the merit of this choice should be attributed to the firm's decision to make Jordan the focal point of its marketing and communication strategy. Nike has concentrated its attention and investments on various high-quality adverts in which Jordan is shown as a "superman" who literally flies into the air to make a basket. His nickname, "air," derived from his great jumping skills, has been effectively translated to the visual level, as the image showing him airborne has become the graphic brand of the Air Jordan product range. This is now a famous icon, a brand image as important as the famous swoosh.

Certainly, not all brands use social values to communicate, but the number is growing. Moreover, it should be remembered that, in the sports sector, the presence of brands that adopt a "value-based" strategy is extremely important.

THE NEW CONSUMER-ORIENTED NATURE OF SPORT

From the late 1980s onwards, sport in the west moved toward being more spectator orientated and industrial, a break with its traditional popular and amateur nature. Sporting events are now more geared toward being seen by paying spectators and are therefore being defined with a view to being played in purpose-built arenas (tracks, stadiums). At the same time, athletes have also become professionals who receive appropriate compensation.

This process has affected all sports. For example, professional football started in England in 1885. A little later, confirming the increasing industrialization of sport, many large firms created football teams: Fiat (Juventus), Philips (PSV Eindhoven), Bayer (Bayer Leverkusen), Peugeot (Sochaux), and Guichard (Saint Etienne). Teams were already managed industrially and professionally, even if they officially respected the amateur rules. The timing of the recognition of professionalism in football in fact varied between countries: 1924 in Austria, 1929 in Italy, 1932 in France, and 1963 in Germany. In 1903, the journalists of the magazine *L'Auto*, which later become *L'Équipe*, organized the first Tour de France cycling race, initiating a similar process of economic exploitation in this sport. Some sporting disciplines have resisted transformation more than others, but sooner or later they have succumbed. Tennis, for example, refused to admit professional players into its prestigious international competitions until 1968. The International Athletics Federation (IAAF) only began to accept the new reality in 1983. However, amateurism was already an illusion in the 1950s and 1960s, as the most important firms gave the best athletes fees to use their products. The phenomenon exploded at the 1968 Mexico City Olympics, where the Adidas and Puma brands were involved in a dispute relating to the fees paid to athletes to wear their shoes (Vanderbilt, 1998).

During the 1980s, businessmen such as Silvio Berlusconi in Italy and Bernard Tapie in France completely transformed the management of football teams, integrating them into a wider business and financial strategy. The teams from the big cities (Manchester United, Real Madrid, Bayern Munich) became global brands, less tied to a specific geographical area, often quoted on the Stock Exchange (and therefore conditioned by the price of the shares), and able to generate profits not through the sale of match tickets, which were in constant decline, but, above all, from television rights and merchandising. Obviously, this was true only for the élite teams, while those from small cities are generally not able to keep up and begin to constitute a burden. The replacement of the old European Cup with the Champions League was an attempt to reinforce the big clubs, because it is the television spectacle rather than the live match which is fundamental. Television has been one of the prime factors in making sport more professional and ever more linked to the industrial and consumer system. Television networks make substantial investments to buy the transmission rights for the main events from sporting clubs. They know that they can sell the advertising slots linked to these events at a high price, because the matches attract many viewers who are not simply spectators, but fans who are emotionally involved in their "home team" and, it is hoped, equally involved when they watch the advertising.

CASE VIGNETTE 11.2: THE OLYMPICS OF BRANDS

The Olympics demonstrate in the most obvious way the gradual commercialization of sport. Already in the nineteenth century, bourgeois culture had begun to promote the value of professionalism and an "industrial" conception of sport, a conception directly derived from the Industrial Revolution and its conception of the body as a machine. It is not, therefore, surprising that the modern Olympics, which began in 1896, have been influenced by this conception. For example, the Paris Games in 1900 took place in the large arena usually used for universal exhibitions (Vigarello, 2002).

During the course of the twentieth century, however, the Olympics also moved toward a greater focus on spectacle, again changing the nature of the games from the point of view of consumption. What in the past was the incarnation of the moral purity of amateur sport has become an extraordinarily efficient promotion tool for global brands. The ten main sponsors of the 1996 Atlanta Olympics together invested $1.5 billion, a fact symbolized in the Olympic Village itself where "six McDonald's restaurants served 7500 free meals a day, while a Burger King hot-air balloon simultaneously dominated the sky above" (Miles, 1998, p. 130). This process has been pursued further at subsequent Olympics. At Athens 2004, for example, television shots were so calibrated that they always included at least one "top sponsor" brand, while even the bodies of the athletes became seductive "consumer objects." They are now good-looking, erotic images rather than sporting examples. One of the most popular television sports is now women's beach volleyball, an insignificant sport until a few years ago, but now considered sexy because of the extremely skimpy outfits worn by the players.

Today, the Olympics are essentially a made-for-television event. Only one in 100,000 people who watch the games see them in person. For most people, the Olympics are strictly a TV experience. Thus, the ability of television to hold the audience's attention is critical for the brands. However, the increasing inclusion of brands can spoil the consumer experience:

> I love watching the Olympics and have spent a very lazy weekend doing little else but . . . my one big problem is the commercial side of the games. I am amazed that people are being told they are not allowed to wear their own choice of clothes, use camcorders/cameras, drink their own water, use certain umbrellas, eat certain types of food unless it is provided by one of the sponsoring companies. This attitude is disgusting and is ruining the games and no wonder there are so few tickets sold.
>
> (Rob, York, UK)

Sporting events further stimulate consumption by placing the brand or an advertising slogan right at the center of the action, where the hearts and minds of the spectators are concentrated (case vignette 11.2). When watching a Formula 1 or motorcycling Grand Prix, the spectator sees a number of adverts, but also the brands on the drivers' helmet or overalls, on the racing car, on the side of the track, on the buildings by the track, and sometimes even on the track itself. Even the colors of the cars have become those of the sponsors. For example, Ferrari, the most prestigious team in the world, has given up its famous red and taken on the shades of red of its main sponsor, Marlboro. Also, at football matches, the sponsors appear everywhere: on the players' shirts, on the side of the pitch, behind players being interviewed, etc.

It should also be remembered that sport on television is not seen directly, but through a medium that inevitably alters the spectacle. Indeed, "the screen does not allow us to see better, but creates a new way of seeing. It immerses the television viewer directly inside the myth, within a story constructed outside the game, made for the viewer, exciting and seductive" (Vigarello, 2002, p. 161). What is presented on television differs from what is seen at the stadium. The television director of necessity makes various changes to the competition, breaking up the unity of the game by "zooming in," repeating and slowing down the most spectacular scenes. Television shows the face of the competitor close up (above all in motor sports), it increases the viewpoints, even taking in things that are not directly relevant to the action; it emphasizes scenes that do not have a competitive importance but are valuable for the media. Sport on television is a narrative and so more spectacular. The television director accelerates the tendency to narrative of various sports, demanding that they adapt to the rhythms of television, which are the frenetic rhythms of advertising.

The increasingly consumer-oriented nature of sport is also clear from the role played by important athletes, whose fame is the base of the whole sporting system today. They are seen as gods like the cinema celebrities and are able to ask enormous salaries without any feelings of affection for the team for which they play. In any case, they receive only part of their earnings from the team, with greater amounts coming from advertising endorsements. For footballers such as Beckham, Zidane, and Ronaldo, these activities represent more than 50 percent of their earnings. Furthermore, thanks to the "Bosman law," all European footballers have become freely exchangeable "goods," meaning that the teams have fewer local players from their own country.

It is therefore not surprising that the big stars of sport lead their public lives more off the pitch than on it. The growing number of romantic ties between sportsmen and actresses, the steady flow of news about their private lives, their appearances at events such as fashion shows or on television programs, and the portrayal of famous sports stars and "sporting fiction" in adverts for the main brands all create a dimension outside the sport that tends to absorb the sporting environment and create abstract icons which are easily consumed throughout the world. A perfect example of this phenomenon is the English footballer David Beckham: blond and handsome, married to Victoria Adams, ex-member of the pop group Spice Girls, and comparable to a rock star in the way he is treated by the media.

THE IMAGES OF SPORTS BRANDS

In recent years, a particularly fascinating, symbolic merchandising universe has arisen for sports shoes. This universe is now appearing in ordinary clothing as well and is a part of the trend toward informal and casual dressing. This is surprising if we remember that, a little over a century ago, canvas shoes were considered poor footwear and were usually associated with thieves and criminals. With the process of vulcanization patented by Charles Goodyear in 1839, rubber could be used for footwear and, in the 1860s, the English aristocrats were the first to wear very simple canvas, rubber-soled shoes to play grass sports. These later led to the first shoes for playing tennis, and many firms began industrial production of sports shoes. In the United States, the market for sports shoes expanded rapidly after World War I because the Americans began to play more sport and pay attention to their physical well-being (Vanderbilt, 1998).

Meanwhile, on the other side of the Atlantic, the Dassler family created the Dassler Schufabrik in Germany in 1926. Their shoes were worn by many athletes at the 1928 and 1932 Olympics and, above all, by the American runner/jumper Jesse Owens (winner of four gold medals) at the 1936 Games in Berlin. The two brothers, Adi and Rudi Dassler, split up in 1948, founding Adidas and Puma respectively. Adidas gradually emerged as the market leader thanks to its ability in creating innovative products, such as spiked shoes, football boots with studs screwed into the soles, etc. It was only in the early 1970s, however, that the company managed to become the global market leader, distributing its immediately recognizable products (thanks to the three parallel stripes) everywhere. During this same period, Nike was founded in Beaverton, Oregon, by Phil Knight and Bill Bowerman.

During the 1980s and 1990s, demand in the sports shoes and clothing market grew enormously. This success was linked to the appearance on the mid-1970s social scene of the so-called "me generation" or the "baby boom" generation. These were people who grew up in the 1960s, an era in which the value of informality was highly appreciated, but who were, above all, very egocentric and mainly focused on developing their physique. As a result, great attention was paid to physical well-being and health. In particular, jogging developed, and Nike knew how to take advantage of this phenomenon. While Adidas continued to look to professional runners, Nike focused its strategies decisively on amateurs and, by the end of the 1970s, half the running shoes sold were branded Nike.

The Beaverton firm emerged primarily thanks to its advertising ability, which leads the world. One reason may be that Nike has stopped seeking to show the quality of its products in its adverts. It simply presents values and cultural models. However, behind their apparent diversity, these adverts use the same irreverent language and express the same concept: the individual's need for a challenge, the lack of interest in others, the test of physical and mental limits (as the advertising slogan "Just do it" states).

In Europe as well, Nike has been successful thanks to a particularly aggressive and engaging advertising language, which has been particularly appreciated by young people who identify with this brand, partly because it comes from the United States, a fashionable nation and the home of jogging, but mainly because it focuses on irreverence. Adidas, in contrast, has normally used less strong language and focused on belonging: these are the shoes that your father and grandfather wore (Aaker and Joachimsthaler, 2000).

In recent years, however, Adidas has relaunched its image, so that it now competes directly with Nike. It has done this by using the same type of advertising language as its competitor, innovative and engaging, but to communicate almost the opposite value-based world. While Nike has exploited an egoistic view of individual challenge, Adidas has proposed a model hinged on professionalism and competence, which in certain ways can be considered "altruistic," as it shows famous athletes performing good actions. The result is that Adidas has succeeded in becoming an important brand again (case vignette 11.3).

CASE VIGNETTE 11.3: ADIDAS STORES CONVEY VALUES

May 2005. Niketown (Sherry, 1998) may have a competitor: the 29,500-square-foot Adidas Sport Performance Store stocks shoes and accessories for soccer, baseball, basketball, tennis, running, and football. For the fashion conscious, there's the complete Stella McCartney line and customizable sneakers. This New York store is the largest sport performance store in the world. The Adidas Sport Performance Store is a long-term retail concept, created by Adidas' own retail design team in order to sustain a unique and stimulating Adidas experience. Designed as more than a sports store, it will further demonstrate Adidas' passion for sport by offering clinics and seminars in the store on an ongoing basis. Including New York, Adidas currently has nineteen of the new concept stores worldwide.

"Our Adidas Sport Performance Stores are an important communication platform for us — here we can showcase the breadth and depth of our brand offering in a unique setting" said Paul McGuire, Head of Retail Development, Adidas America. "Adidas makes products for more sports than any other brand and this is our opportunity to demonstrate that. We want people to think of the Adidas Sport Performance Store as more than just a store, but a destination for athletes."

The store design is minimalist in concept — all the walls and furniture are black or white, which allows the product to be the focal point for the customer. The materials, shapes, and fixtures throughout the store are inspired by components found in sport, but are still practical and functional, based on specific product presentation needs: hanging product bars resemble weightlifting bars; hooks on the wall allow products to be draped over them, as if someone casually hung them there after a long workout; and instead of traditional shoe racks, shoes are displayed on running starter blocks.

Finally, it is to be noted that, in order to address the consumers' needs in a targeted and focused way, Adidas takes a two-track approach to experiential context. The Sport Performance Stores offer consumers high-performance product and leading-edge technologies, while Sport Heritage Stores feature the Originals product, a true fusion of sport authenticity and global street style.

Like Adidas, other brands have worked in recent years to increase their social and market importance. In particular, Puma has succeeded in introducing into the world of sport a new set of images based on irony and enjoyment. Here, sport is associated with values that are very far from the traditional ideas of competition and success, but can equally fascinate and seduce consumers.

As we have seen, all sports brands represent behavioral models which enter into and spread throughout society. Indeed, it is thanks to these models that the brands are successful. These are, then, "value-based brands" or, rather, brands that act in a social context by which they are certainly influenced and which they, in turn, influence through the use of the social values that they have appropriated. This does not, however, imply that consumers passively accept the value-based worlds that are proposed to them by sports brands. What in fact happens (as for the forms of communication produced by any brand) is that consumers recodify the brand messages based on experience and on the symbolic functions undertaken by the product. The images proposed by sports brands therefore play an important social role today. However, it is only with the key contribution of consumers that these images are transformed into an effective consumption experience.

DISCUSSION QUESTIONS

- Why are brands turning out to be value-based brands?
- Why do we need to understand brands at a societal level?
- What are the roles of television and athletes in sustaining the brand experience?
- Why could the increasing inclusion of brands spoil the consumer experience with sport events?
- What is the contribution of the brand store to the brand experience?

REFERENCES

Aaker, D.A. and Joachimsthaler, E. (2000) *Brand Leadership*. New York: The Free Press.

Atkin, D. (2004) *The Culting of Brands: When Customers Become True Believers*. New York: Portfolio.

Codeluppi, V. (2000) *Lo spettacolo della merce. I luoghi del consumo dai passages a Disney World*. Milan: Bompiani.

Featherstone, M. (1991) *Consumer Culture and Postmodernism*. London: Sage.

Holt, D.B. (2005) "How Societies Desire Brands: Using Cultural Theory to Explain Brand Symbolism." In: Mick, D.G. and Ratneshwar, S. (eds) *Inside Consumption: Frontiers of Research on Consumer Motives*. London: Routledge, 273–291.

Kotler, P. (1973–74) "Atmospherics as a Marketing Tool." *Journal of Retailing* 48(Winter): 48–56.

Lewis, D. and Bridger D. (2000) *The Soul of the New Consumer*. London: Nicholas Brealey Publishing.

Miles, S. (1998) *Consumerism as a Way of Life*. London: Sage.

Riou, N. (1999) *Pub fiction. Société postmoderne et nouvelles tendances publicitaires.* Paris: Éditions d'Organisation.

Schmitt, B. (1999) *Experiential Marketing: How to Get Customers to Sense, Feel, Think, Act, and Relate to Your Company and Brand.* New York: The Free Press.

Schmitt, B. and Simonson, A. (1997) *Marketing Esthetics: The Strategic Management of Brands, Identity and Image.* New York: The Free Press.

Semprini, A. (1996) *La marca.* Milan: Lupetti.

Sherry, J.F. (1998) "The Soul of the Company Store: Nike Town Chicago and the Emplaced Brandscape." In: Sherry, J.F. (ed.) *Servicescapes: The Concept of Place in Contemporary Markets.* Lincolnwood: IL: NTC Business Books, 109–150.

Vanderbilt, T. (1998) *The Sneaker Book: Anatomy of an Industry and an Icon.* New York: The New Press.

Vigarello, G. (2002) *Du jeu ancien au show sportif: la naissance d'un mythe.* Paris: Seuil.

Chapter 12

Re-enchantment of retailing
Toward utopian islands[1]
Olivier Badot and Marc Filser

KEY POINTS

- Marketing strategies should include a consumption re-enchantment concept.
- This re-enchantment can revolve around spectacular, but also ordinary, phenomena ("street corner re-enchantment").
- Surprisingly, discounters can be positioned as experience providers.
- Flagship stores have been positioning themselves in the space between experiential marketing and brand management.
- Commercial spaces should be designed via a hybridization of varying experiential dimensions.

What is the first tourist destination in Canada? Niagara Falls? No longer! Today, the number one tourist destination in Canada is the largest and most amazing shopping center in the world, West Edmonton Mall, in the Province of Alberta, which attracts 22 million visitors a year, has more than 800 boutiques, eleven department stores and variety stores, one supermarket, two car dealerships, a Multiplex movie theater with thirty-two screens, etc. . . . mixed with the largest indoor amusement park, a professional skating rink, an artificial tropical beach, underwater submarine experience, an artificial lagoon (with sealions, sharks, alligators, penguins, and 200 species of fish), an eighteen-hole miniature golf course, a casino, a replica of Bourbon Street (New Orleans), as well as a replica of Christopher Columbus' *Santa Maria*, a wide variety of hotels (the Fantasyland Hotel features numerous theme rooms), a chapel, 132 restaurants, many souvenir shops, sixteen doctors, a coin and stamps editor, etc.

Actually, the most visible strategies developed by western retail corporations for the last twenty years – international expansion and multichannel combination (recently upgraded with e-commerce) – seem to have occulted a third highly differentiating and valuable strategy: the re-enchantment of commercial areas and shopping processes. The success of Aveda (a Guru cosmetics chain based on aromatherapy and Ayurveda rituals), Bass Pro Shop (where shoppers have a fishing experience inside a 200,000-square-foot store) or Victoria's

Secret (which projects the shopper in a highly sensual environment and turns every ordinary woman into a "femme fatale") is likely due to their differentiation strategy based on "fun shopping," also known as "retailtainment" or "shoptainment," a strategy that makes visitors and buyers live unique and re-enchanted experiences.

In this framework, this chapter aims: (1) to propose a state of the theory and practice for the concept of "re-enchantment of retailing;" (2) to suggest a widening of the concept of "re-enchantment of retailing" addressing at this point in time the issue of the positioning of re-enchantment; (3) to suggest the conditions for sustainable re-enchantment in a strategic and managerial perspective; and (4) to sketch the mall of the future as a "utopian island" based on a new definition of the public sites.

RE-ENCHANTMENT OF RETAILING: A STATE OF THEORY AND PRACTICE

Re-enchanting of consumption has been a common theme in the marketing and sociological literature since the mid-1990s (Firat and Venkatesh, 1995). Re-enchantment of consumption can be defined as a set of practices initiated by both manufacturers and consumers to incorporate non-functional sources of value in goods and services, and turn them into sources of hedonic, symbolic, and interpersonal value. Following this conceptualization, re-enchantment of retailing would then be viewed as a set of practices initiated by retailers and customers that activate non-functional sources of value during a store visit. It is to be noted that, despite the recognition of the multiple dimensions of retail value, retailing executives and academic researchers tend to focus on a single dimension in positioning retailing formats: at one end of the continuum, the store would be mostly perceived as a mere source of supplies, a point of purchase, and shopping value would be mostly derived from the functional efficiency of the store environment (finding the right item, at the lowest price, with minimum effort and time investment). At the other end of the continuum, the store has turned into a source of entertainment, competing with movie multiplexes and theme parks; visiting the store is a constant source of stimulations and hedonic gratifications, with the purchasing of products or services as only a side-benefit. The implementation of re-enchantment strategies in retailing focuses primarily on this second orientation. What is usually called "re-enchantment of retailing" is essentially extraordinary re-enchantment, as can be found in such settings as megamalls or extremely spectacular flagship stores or themed restaurants, i.e., "means of consumption" (Ritzer, 1999). This is a major shift from the theory of the re-enchantment of consumption that recognizes the importance of "ordinary" re-enchantment of everyday life, and the active role of the customer in the creation of the re-enchanted experience. Let us try to develop a framework in which to conceptualize retail re-enchantment with the same terms as the re-enchantment of consumption.

Let us first consider the visit to a store as an experience, i.e., an interaction between the customer and the store, that creates a set of utilities tied into forming store value: a functional value (the evaluation of the capability of the store to fulfill the functional expectations of the customer in terms of product availability, price, and time spent), and an immersion value (the evaluation of the hedonic, symbolic, and social benefits provided by the visit to the store). Every shopping experience can be positioned on a continuum between mostly "functional" and mostly "immersive" shopping experiences. This continuum will provide the first dimension of our descriptive model.

The second dimension will describe the contrast between ordinary and extraordinary re-enchantment. Ordinary re-enchantment is the creation of value through a combination of minimal sources of personal gratification; more specifically, through the active behavior of the consumer which is conceptualized as "everyday re-enchantment." Extraordinary re-enchantment, on the other hand, is mostly the output of a combination of resources designed by the retailer to create a spectacular shopping experience, "moments of magic" (Gottdiener, 1998), through the manipulation of stimulating and complex environmental sources (such as megamalls or flagship stores such as Nike Town).

The implementation of re-enchantment strategies by retailers focuses primarily on the immersive–extraordinary combination (Table 12.1). Visiting the retail settings competes with other purely leisurely activities, such as a visit to a theme park or a cruise in the Caribbean. To be successful, this strategy requires two conditions:

- the experience has to be very extraordinary, i.e., provide a unique combination of stimulations, usually linked with a very costly and lasting investment in order to maintain the mystic and lure of the retail outlet;
- the trading area of the outlet has to be extremely large (consider, for instance, the choice of Minneapolis for the location of Mall of America, to attract every potential visitor in the United States, or the vicinity of Disneyland Paris and the Val d'Europe shopping mall). Consequently, every national market may sustain a limited number of such outlets if the primary objective is to make money with the outlet. Otherwise, the outlet must be conceived as a way of promoting the image of the brand, in the tradition

Table 12.1 *A typology of forms for retail re-enchantment*

	Ordinary experiences	Extraordinary experiences
Functional store value	Bargain at a discount store	Theatricalization of store assortment
	Economic value	Hedonic value
	Stimulation, positive surprise	Esthetic stimulation
	Example: special price promotions in a hard discount store	Example: factory outlet, thematic animation in a hypermarket
"Immersive" store value	Social routines at a street corner store	Hyper-reality
	Stimulation through the visit of the marketplace	Hyper- and esthetic stimulation
	Social interactions	Social interactions
	Multisensory stimulation	Escapism, flow
	Example: market square	Example: megamall, flagship store

of the "flagship stores" created by the pioneers of department store chains at the end of the nineteenth century (Williams, 1982).

A parallel may be drawn with the old "wheel of retailing" theory. According to this theory, innovating retail formats rely on a unique combination of attributes to develop a cost advantage over their competitors and provide a significant price differential to customers (intertype competition). If the new format is successful, imitators enter the market, and intratype competition becomes the driving force behind retail strategies. According to the wheel principle, competitors try to maintain their position by incorporating new benefits in their offerings: more comfortable amenities, broader assortment, and new services. This upgrading of offerings leads to an increase in margins, and higher prices, creating an opportunity for less expensive and more price-sensitive formats in the marketplace. The wheel model has proven relatively reliable in the long run, explaining the impact of upgrading originally low-priced formats. Turning back to our model of re-enchantment, we may observe that upgrading a format most often relies on attempts to provide extraordinary experiences in a nondescript shopping environment. And following the theory of neo-institutionalism, as all competitors tend to implement the same strategy, no lasting competitive advantage can be derived. A managerial orientation can be derived from this analysis: rather than upgrading their offerings in an effort to provide potentially unwanted extraordinary retail experiences, retailers may benefit from an increased focus on their core functional positioning.

Finally, managers should keep in mind an important aspect of the proposed model of retail re-enchantment. The academic literature in marketing places a major focus on the creation of valuable experiences for the customer through the manipulation of all the components of the retailing mix. The literature in the sociology of consumption, on the other hand, considers that most consumption experiences are constructed, or at least co-constructed, by the customer, through a process of appropriation, most notably in retailing environments. This difference in perspective suggests that re-enchantment is pushed not only by the supply side of the strategy, but also by the retailer, who must leave enough autonomy to the customer to build his/her own experience through the manipulation of stimuli in the shopping environment. For instance, the ability to explore a largely unorganized supply of products, to switch from one store to another, and the challenge created by the search for the unexpected bargain are all identified as key factors attracting customers to factory outlets.

Re-enchantment has been narrowly linked with an experiential marketing strategy, and viewed as the output of a massive investment on the part of the retailer in specific marketing assets. Considering the contributions of important research fields such as consumer behavior and the sociology of consumption, we suggest broadening the experiential perspective to incorporate low-key experiences, specifically those experiences co-constructed by the customers themselves.

CONSPICUOUS VS. "STREET CORNER" RE-ENCHANTMENT

In both professional and academic literature, as well as through common sense, re-enchantment deals very often with some extraordinary experiences: the way it is implemented has to

169

be original, priceless, memorable, unforgettable . . . and the sites considered as examples of such strategies are huge and spectacular: Disneyland, Nike Town, Mall of America, etc. Re-enchantment is a way to "turn ordinary products into extraordinary experiences" to para-phrase the subtitle of the book *Priceless* by LaSalle and Britton (2003). This "conspicuous" orientation (in Veblen tradition) is both a risk for retail managers and limited in scope.

The risk is to overposition the retail concept; by relying more on a uniquely original store design than on the whole retailing mix (and to increase the risk of obsolescence and of cognitive dissonance); by using the design of a flagship store as a template for all subsequent expansion, etc. Recent failures or critical cases (e.g., Dive!, Steven Spielberg's restaurant chain; Planet Hollywood) prove how re-enchanting stores or restaurants cannot rely only on partial and spectacular attributes and ignore the basic principles of marketing (environmen-tal constraints, nature of the competition, marketing strategy, positioning, targeting, mix). Furthermore, less value is created today by products providing patrons with clues expressing a social status than by experiences increasing the level of esteem of their peers and family (Holbrook, 1999). Even the upper classes are now highly influenced by the symbols of everyday life, and by the street and work culture (Von Dutch, Hummer, Caterpillar, etc.), in other words, by the "street corner society," a kind of reverse process of the Simmel trickle-down theory.

In terms of insights, this one-track orientation of re-enchantment does not allow, for example, an explanation for the success of hard discount retailing in industrialized markets (Aldi, Costco, Giant Tiger and . . ., to a certain extent, Wal-Mart). The tremendous success of this format, most notably in food retailing, but increasingly in other product categories, usually exhibits two attributes: low prices and an efficient use of time, the result of a limited assortment. The widening of the concept of re-enchantment suggests a less intuitive benefit provided by this format: hard discount stores may provide a psychological benefit to the cus-tomer by offsetting the risk of buying a useless product on impulse and the risk of paying too high a price. The design of these stores (palettes, stacks, racks, cardboard cases, low lighting, etc.) and their positioning create a sense of pure functionality that can be gratifying for the customer through the "romancing of low prices" . . . re-enchantment by treasure hunting.

Based on the previous comments, we can position these varying potential re-enchant-ment strategies along two axes (Figure 12.1). On the one hand, there is the contingent/non-contingent axis that positions on its contingent side those managerial strategies that give strong consideration to the pressures found in both external and internal environments, while positioning on its other, non-contingent, side those strategies that are based more on an entrepreneur's creative gesture than on management performance. On the other hand, there is the conspicuous/street corner axis that positions on its conspicuous sides those strategies that emphasize the spectacular and the extraordinary, while positioning on its other, street corner, side those strategies that are rooted in the microevents constituting our daily lives. The four strategies are the following:

- Strategy 1 (non-contingent and conspicuous): re-enchantment is an entrepreneurial act to promote the brand (e.g., Nike) or the site (e.g., Mall of America) more or less independently from the demand needs or desires. In line with amusement parks

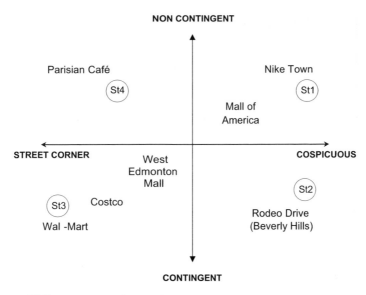

Figure 12.1 *Positioning of re-enchantment strategies.*

strategies, the objective is to attract the highest number of visitors by the extraordinary originality of the commercial proposition (assortment, design, events, etc.) and to make them buy impulse (and high-price) products as a result of the euphoria of the experience. Here, attraction marketing and transformation marketing dominate over loyalty marketing.

■ Strategy 2 (contingent and conspicuous): here, re-enchantment is fully contingent on the characteristics of the demand – which in this case is composed of the aristocratic class (evolving in its natural environment) and the middle class, which projects itself in upper-class lifestyles. The more conspicuous the experience, the more consistent is the strategy.

■ Strategy 3 (contingent and street corner): the shopping experience is more or less hidden within a day-to-day environment that does not appear at first glance to be re-enchanted. The subtle and progressive invitation for the buyer to participate in a treasure hunt process, as is practiced by West Edmonton Mall, Costco, or Wal-Mart, drives him/her to engage in a shopping experience that is based on discovery, entertainment, escapism, and esthetic (Pine and Gilmore, 1998). The more the experience seems affordable, the more the shopper is appealed to participate and the longer s/he stays. The more surprising, innovative, and complex the experience, the more the customer will revisit the store, with a feeling of a "never completed experience." Loyalty is facilitated. These examples of "street corner re-enchantment" confirm a widening of the framework (Carù and Cova, 2003) from the dominant concept of "extraordinary experience" (high re-enchantment) to one of "ordinary well-being" (street corner re-enchantment).

■ Situation 4 (non-contingent and street corner): here, the operator enacts the re-enchantment almost blindly, as would be the case in a small Parisian café, where there is no room to maneuver.

CASE VIGNETTE 12.1: SHOPPING AT WAL-MART, A CASE OF STREET CORNER RE-ENCHANTMENT

As the all-category killer and leading retail company – with a 2004 revenue of $US285 billion with continual increases in profit and sales – Wal-Mart's success is most often referenced in terms of the performance of its management model and, particularly, its back-office management systems (supply chain management, optimized procurement, information systems, data mining, etc.). Amazingly, very few analysts cite other reasons to justify Wal-Mart's success, for example the marketing concept, the imagery of its stores, or the shopping experience.

If the shopping experience at Wal-Mart is clearly understated, it is because it deals with a very "low-profile imagery" emblematic of both everyday life (neighborhood, popular culture, etc.) and a warehouse mentality far from the exaltation of re-enchantment. The prestigious and spectacular codes of department stores have been replaced by the symbols of garage, workshop, basement, etc., which promote "trick and treats" as commercial value (Miller, 1988).

The Wal-Mart success seems to be based on four experiences that are tied together and acted out by the shoppers and narrated by the stores:

1   *The household composition*: the Wal-Mart assortment narrates the household composition by the accumulation of simple and colored commodities (dry food, basic clothes, and cosmetics, etc.), common products for decoration (plastic flowers, home ornaments, knick-knacks, etc.), and accessories for leisure and hobbies (sports, fishing, handicraft, bricolage, gardening, car tuning, etc.). The shopper access to the store also signifies a kind of life cycle going through various stages: seduction (cosmetics and jewel products come first), household (furniture, electronic appliances, decoration, leisure), kids (clothes, toys), pets (food and accessories), and sickness (drugstore). All these products not only stress the stages of life, they serve to promote a calendar of events (Christmas, Valentine's Day, Mother's Day, summer time, Halloween, etc.). Clues of the house environment are widespread everywhere in the stores: messy atmosphere of the children's room, display and decoration of the bedroom, flyers to promote stationery for family and religious events, frequent repetition of the word "home" on products and merchandising items. This is what Gary Raines, manager of the Bentonville store, has concluded: "If you treat customers like your family, in most

towns, they become your family, certainly your friends" (Slater, 2003, p. 115).

2   *The prevalence of popular on seriousness*: this experience is based on a symbolic system romancing the prevalence of popular and casual culture in a too serious and too professional world (extreme paradox isn't?). As Sam Walton pleaded, Wal-Mart stores must reflect affordability, family, small and . . . fun. This experience is implemented by delivering: (a) a festive and friendly atmosphere in the stores; (b) the oversimplification of messages (see for example the two shopping carts displayed at the front door presenting a price comparison between Wal-Mart products and those of the closest competitor): and (c) a kind of "organized mess" (stock shortage, badly fixed labeling, torn promotional materials, etc.), which projects a low-price image consistent with the banner positioning.

3   *The promotion of ordinary people*: this third experience is tied to the previous ones. Shoppers as well as front-office persons who are less performance and efficiency oriented interact in a more friendly and empathic manner, and are viewed more as "local heroes." The symbolic reference here is one of a street corner grocery store in Bentonville, mythical city and matrix of Wal-Mart culture. Some clues to this experience are not far from the tribal marketing principles: photographs of clients with salespeople displayed in the stores, recurrent use of the word "we," actual customers and members of staff performing in TV commercials, etc.

4   *The oversimplified symbolization of Wal-Mart's economic advantages*: Wal-Mart uses easy-to-understand and visible symbols to express four components of its competitive advantage: (a) economies of scale (symbolized by stacks of products and the famous slogan "We sell for less everyday," which convince the clients that the price of each stock-keeping unit is the lowest in the marketplace); (b) disintermediation (the warehouse design made of racks and wooden palettes gives an impression of a short channel, a channel with less intermediaries, thus supplying cheaper products); (c) minimization of costs (like German hard discount retailers, Wal-Mart doesn't communicate on service, never promotes product quality, and delivers a friendly but "not so clean" atmosphere in its stores, in order to signify that cost killing has been integrated into the pricing policy); and (d) hunting for bargains (the use of a "clearance rhetoric," bulk displays as well as the numerous labels and promotional posters produce an additional image of a good deal).

All the minimalist rhetoric developed by Wal-Mart not only supports the marketing positioning and the price image of the banner, but it also contributes to the creation of a mythology relating to a sort of "street corner re-enchantment" (Arnold *et al.*, 2001).

CONDITIONS FOR A SUSTAINABLE RE-ENCHANTMENT

Three key ingredients for the success of themed retailing formats that lead to retail re-enchantment have been identified (Kozinets *et al.*, 2002): they need a customer base responsive to a combination of shopping and entertainment stimuli; the positioning of the store must be congruent with the sources of re-enchantment provided; and the ultimate objective of the strategy is to develop relationship marketing, i.e., to strengthen the relationship with the customer. Considering these conditions, one may ask which retailers will find a long-term benefit in such a strategy. This leads to three major questions.

Who is the target of the re-enchantment strategy?

The emphasis of most analyses of retail re-enchantment on the supply side of the strategy is contradictory with the importance of the role played by the retail customer for its success. The first part of this chapter showed the critical importance of customer expectations and perceptions in the construction of the retail experience. Several conditions have to be met before a retailer launches a broad-scale re-enchantment strategy:

- How congruent is the planned re-enchantment process with the present positioning of the store? If the retailer is perceived as a low-end discounter, it will hardly be able to transform itself to become a major source of escapism and hedonic hyper-reality. The example of the French Carrefour hypermarkets is an illustration of this hurdle; this chain is traditionally perceived by most customers as a convenient and relatively inexpensive place for one-stop shopping. When Carrefour implemented a themed environment in the non-food sections, its price image deteriorated, and meeting expected sales objectives was difficult.
- Are there enough customers to reach the break-even point of the stores? Too many retailers only keep traffic in mind when they are planning retail re-enchantment. A spectacular retail concept may draw customers, but it will be profitable only if the conversion rate of the visitors is high enough to reach break-even sales, or if re-enchantment is implemented only in a few key flagship stores, and is mostly used as a way of improving the image of the other stores.
- Are the planned locations of the re-enchanted sites congruent with their trading area? Géant (a French retailer) tested an experimental sophisticated format in a new hypermarket in Roubaix: the economic structure of the trading area of the store was incongruent with such qualitative offerings.

These criteria may seem trivial, but a review of major failures of retail re-enchantment strategies underscores their importance.

How is the re-enchantment strategy implemented?

Like any planned positioning, re-enchantment will increase the performance of the stores if it is implemented correctly. Managerial literature constantly stresses the critical importance that the smallest details can have on the success of positioning strategies, thus relying on store importance and the theatricalization of the assortment (Underhill, 2000). The congruence between the planned re-enchantment process, the corporate culture of the retailer, and the perceptions of personnel in the stores is critical. A key ingredient of the success of the Nature & Découvertes chain in France or Build-a-Bear Workshop in North America is the training of personnel, who play a key role in the creation of the customer experience. Minute details will play a still more critical role in the creation of ordinary shopping experiences, in which interactions between customer, store, and staff will be key ingredients in the valuation process.

A re-enchanted store will need to monitor the perceptions of its customers and the efficiency of the implementation of its strategic orientations. Traditional benchmarks for customer satisfaction would probably not be relevant, as they tend to capture only the most functionalist dimensions of the store. Indicators derived from the taxonomy of values (Holbrook, 1999) might be more useful, for instance to embrace the hedonic, esthetic, and symbolic components of the shopping experience (extrinsic vs. intrinsic, individual vs. interpersonal, active vs. reactive). Indicators might even be borrowed from hospitality marketing. In their analysis of the experience economy, Pine and Gilmore (1998) have already mentioned this option. Tools measuring the perceived value of a hospitality experience might improve the monitoring process of a re-enchantment strategy.

How sustainable is the re-enchantment strategy of the retailer?

Two alternative views have to be considered to address the question of the sustainability of the re-enchantment strategy:

■   Creating re-enchantment can be part of a promotional strategy. A brand (either producer or retailer) aims to position itself using a combination of mostly symbolic attributes. This positioning can be communicated through theatricalization of the attributes of the brand in a retail setting. Nike Town is a prototypical example of such a strategy, where the stores are designed not as much to sell products as they are to tell a narrative about the brand and its values. Historical flagship department stores played a somewhat similar role: they were points of purchase, but they were mostly designed as vectors of the positioning of the chain, valuing the image of the locations of the chain in much less spectacular settings. Flagships such as Printemps and Galeries Lafayette in the Haussmann district of Paris are important stores in terms of both sales and the creation of image for all the provincial branches of these chains. It may even be suggested that, in some cases, flagship stores can be primarily perceived as pure sources of satisfaction for the ego of the retailer him/herself. In this perspective, re-enchantment is more a part of the promotional strategy and may be sustained as long as the profitability of the investment in the store medium is higher than the investments in more traditional mass media. Interestingly enough, product brands recognize the potential communicating power of stores and include them in their own promotional strategy (Pine and Gilmore, 1998).

175

■ Creating re-enchantment can be the core of a pure retailing strategy. The store design targets a customer segment that values a combination of retailing and entertainment, and purchasing in this store is an experience the customer is ready to pay for. We have already discussed the problems an established retailer will face to convert traditional functional retailing into experiential retailing. Similarly, few experiments combining retailing and entertainment have turned profitable. However, retailing is considered by social planners as a key ingredient to re-enchant public spaces: to revitalize decaying downtown areas, to provide entertainment to the high volume of visitors in ventral stations or motorway service areas – even to enrich the cultural experience in museums through gift shops and cafeterias . . .. We need to address this question in radically new terms: What is the role of retailing in the contemporary culture? What innovative retailing formats can be designed to capitalize on emerging trends?

MALLS OF THE FUTURE: TOWARD UTOPIAN ISLANDS AND A NEW DEFINITION OF PUBLIC SITES

Contrary to what Max Weber believed, the rationalization of our society has not led to the end of the religious and to disenchantment but, rather, the utopian has reappeared in the form of a symbolic supermarket, a metaphor where everyone circulates and fills up his shopping cart according to his/her needs and desires. The marketplace in general, and malls in particular, are becoming a theater where consumers can create their own world and fantasize and deliver their parts in a play; retailers provide the staging, props, lighting, etc. In order to give meaning to one's life, individuals seek sacred, everyday objects and places (Belk *et al.*, 1989), which represent important turning points in western religious history (DeChant, 2002). If, according to the analysts of the "puzzling religions," through the centuries, beliefs have been sucked up by the preoccupation with the other world, within the contemporary universe, this obsessive concern for the great beyond seems destined to disappear. Today, religion is of interest only if it "brings good," even if it can manifestly be experienced by each individual in different aspects of his/her life on earth. As such, malls are safe, habitable, and serve as a substitute for the medieval church.

West Edmonton Mall, for instance, brings together numerous stimulations and strange methods setting its visitors in a state of identity construction/questioning, thus fully participating in one's psychic life through a succession of symbolization of world experiences. As well, visitors participate in the partial failures of both these symbolizations which permit the simultaneous construction of his/her inner life and the links binding one to people and things. Utopia at the West Edmonton Mall consists then of an immanent phenomenon aiming to harmonize an individual's collective attitudes and behaviors with seeking to integrate them within the socioeconomic order by founding a common culture (DeChant, 2002). Today, this function is filled, in the west, by consumption that would structure lifestyles, shape an independent culture, and signal the sacred dimensions of existence. By the way, more and more customers are becoming "evangelists" – religious believers roaming the backstreets of the world spreading the world with their faith – who share and spread, not love, but products and banners (such as Build-a-Bear Workshop or Krispy Kreme).

With so many boutiques, stores, restaurants, with schools, housing resorts, offices, streets, avenues, amusement areas . . ., with so numerous entertaining and projective experiences . . ., with so many employees, visitors, shoppers, etc., these new malls tend to materialize a new kind of bright future . . . in "utopian islands," a format close to the "cave planets" imagined in the 1970s by the French futurologists (Gaudin, 1993). According to them, around the 2040s, the human being will live in "cave planets," huge and radiant resorts in space, covered with crystal glass, always lit by sunshine, and with a perfectly controlled internal climate (to control the horticultural environment and weather, for example). Inside, the vegetation and landscaping evoke the earth's atmosphere but with a much higher level of well-being, leisure, tourism, ecological independence, and democratic governance. However, they predict a great competition will exist on earth because of the emergence of a gap between those earthlings (who live a more difficult and complex existence) and those inhabitants of the "cave planets," who are experimenting with such a different and innovative way of life.

This metaphor seems to be a prophetic framework for sketching not only malls (McLaran and Brown, 2005) but, more generally, public sites of the future. Thus, we can foresee the shopping malls of the future as overcolored and funny "urban islands" in urban archipelagos, providing the consumers with safe, autonomous (power and air plants, phone networks, etc.), and esthetic substitutes for the everyday life conditions. These "islands" would be oriented to a prophylactic society of hedonic and spiritual value as well as leisure and friendliness, full of simulacra, where the ideas of fear and death will be absent (Figure 12.2).

All this shows to what extent the current evolutions of various public sites (shopping areas, amusement parks, cultural and sacred sites such as museum and churches, or tourist locations) tend to lead to a common hybrid pattern close to the previous utopian projections. This new pattern of public sites addresses a mythology aligned with the postmodern imaginaries highly irrigated by an ethic of esthetic.

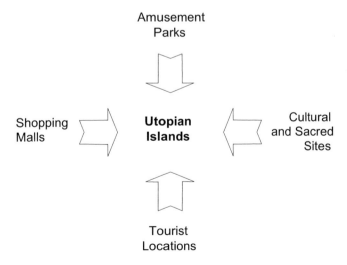

Figure 12.2 "Utopian Islands" as a hybrid pattern of public sites.

CASE VIGNETTE 12.2: MADRID XANADU, THE EXAMPLE OF A UTOPIAN ISLAND

Lying southwest of Madrid, the Madrid Xanadu mall, which was built in 2003 along *retailtainment* lines, is quite different from other shopping and leisure centers. Its architecture, spatial layout, and artistic decors were designed in such a way as to assure consumers a true experience. Visitors here are captivated by an unusual environment involving a perfect marriage between shopping and fun. This is the only place in the world where consumers can stroll past 150 shops yet find family entertainment activities such as go-karting as well as nightclubs, merry-go-rounds, and even ski slopes! Indeed, one way Xanadu gives its visitors a sense of the exotic is by offering them (through a simple entrance such as they would find at a movie theater in a restaurant and fast food district) an Alpine ski experience with all of the associated sensations: cold, snow, ski-tow, chair lifts, slopes, etc. In short, Xanadu appears to be a good (albeit incomplete) illustration of the utopian islands model. These are places characterized by the hybridization of shopping centers, tourist spots, amusement parks, and holy sites:

- With its 150 shops, large department store (Corte Ingles), restaurants, and fast food stands, Xanadu is one of Madrid's leading customer locations.
- Xanadu is a real tourist spot and actually constitutes Spain's leading ski resort south of Madrid (the country's main mountains being located to the north of the city). Like its northern rivals, it attracts visitors in both summer and winter. More precisely, it is visited in wintertime by skiers from south of Madrid and in summertime by everyone. A ski resort experience is created all year long in an atmosphere replete with chalet dining hall (with a grate even in the middle of summer), equipment rentals (anoraks, snow boots, gloves, etc.), sensorial stimulations (light, temperature, etc.), and experienced skiers traipsing around carrying skis on their shoulders.
- Xanadu is also an amusement park. It may be primarily positioned (in external and internal design terms) as a standard shopping center cum ski resort, but it is also an amusement park that attracts children (with its luna-park, re-enchanted day nurseries, children-oriented thematized events, and many Disney Village-style restaurants).
- Xanadu resembles a holy site (even if this dimension is less obvious than the three mentioned above). There are religious connotations to Xanadu's architecture (Figure 12.3). Developed by a well-known US company (the Mills Corporation) that has already promoted a slew of shopping centers in North America, this cultural variable (Spain's age-old Catholic tradition) probably offers the best explanation for the sacred overtones of the

Figure 12.3 *Xanadu Madrid.*

architectural choices that have been made at Xanadu. Moreover, the mall's design and management have been carried out in partnership with a Spanish firm called Parcelatoria Gonzalo Chacon S.A.

DISCUSSION QUESTIONS

■ What distinguishes re-enchantment with a product/service offer from experiential marketing?

■ Does experiential marketing necessarily have to be spectacular in nature?

■ Describe the elements of the mix that can be used to help people have a hard discount experience.

■ Which brakes and levers can a retailer use to implement an experiential strategy?

■ Based on the utopian island construct, draw a mall for the year 2025.

NOTE

1 The authors are indebted to Paul McElhone, Executive Director of the Canadian Institute for Retailing and Services of the School of Business (University of Alberta, Edmonton) for his help with the formalization of this text.

REFERENCES

Arnold, S.J., Kozinets, R.V. and Handelman, J.M. (2001) "Hometown Ideology and Retailer Legitimation: The Institutional Semiotics of Wal-Mart Flyers." *Journal of Retailing* 77(2): 243–271.

Belk, R.W., Wallendorf, M. and Sherry, J.F. (1989) "The Sacred and the Profane in Consumer Behavior: Theodicy on the Odyssey." *Journal of Consumer Research* 16(June): 1–38.

Carù, A. and Cova, B. (2003) "Revisiting Consumption Experience. A More Humble but Complete View of the Concept." *Marketing Theory* 3(2): 267–286.

DeChant, D. (2002) *The Sacred Santa. Religious Dimensions of Consumer Culture.* Cleveland: The Pilgrim Press.

Firat, A.F. and Venkatesh, A. (1995) "Liberatory Postmodernism and the Reenchantment of Consumption." *Journal of Consumer Research* 22(Dec): 239–267.

Gaudin, T. (1993) *2100, Récit du prochain siècle.* Paris: Payot.

Gottdiener, M. (1998) "The Semiotics of Consumer Spaces: The Growing Importance of Themed Environments." In: Sherry, J.F. (ed.) *Servicescapes: The Concept of Place in Contemporary Markets.* Lincolnwood, IL: NTC Business Books, 29–54.

Holbrook, M.B. (1999) *Consumer Value. A Framework for Analysis and Research.* London: Routledge.

Kozinets, R.V., Sherry, J.F., Deberry-Spence, B., Duhachek, A., Nuttavuthisit, K. and Storm, D. (2002) "Themed Flagship Brand Stores in the New Millennium: Theory, Practice, Prospects." *Journal of Retailing* 78(1): 17–29.

LaSalle, D. and Britton, T.A. (2003) *Priceless, Turning Ordinary Products into Extraordinary Experiences.* Boston, MA: Harvard Business School Press.

McLaran, P. and Brown, S. (2005) "The Center Cannot Hold: Consuming the Utopian Marketplace." *Journal of Consumer Research* 32(2): 311–323.

Miller, D. (1988) *A Theory of Shopping.* Ithaca, NY: Cornell University Press.

Pine J.B. and Gilmore, J.H. (1998) "Welcome to the Experience Economy." *Harvard Business Review* July–Aug: 97–105.

Ritzer, G. (1999) *Enchanting a Disenchanted World, Revolutionizing the Means of Consumption.* Thousand Oaks, CA: Pine Forge Press.

Slater, R. (2003) *The Wal-Mart Decade*. New York: Portfolio.

Underhill, P. (2000) *Why We Buy. The Science of Shopping*. New York: Simon and Schuster.

Williams, R.H. (1982) *Dream Worlds: Mass Consumption in Late Nineteenth-Century France*. Berkeley: University of California Press.

Conclusion

Part V

Conclusion

Chapter 13

Consuming experience
Retrospects and prospects
Eric J. Arnould

KEY POINTS

- Marketspace is defined by the interaction of marketers who offer and consumers who extract value in use from marketers' value propositions.
- Experiences may be redefined in terms of a fourfold performance space.
- Experiences are both substantively and communicatively staged.
- Consumers extract value from experiences through narrative frames and devices.
- The experiential framework calls into question the continued scientific value of the consumption and consumer constructs.

ORIENTING THOUGHTS

A period of opportune crisis appears to be unfolding across the marketing field, with scholars from many countries proposing fundamental paradigmatic-level reorientations of either local or more general applicability. Critical marketing, Mediterranean marketing, consumer culture theory, multisensory marketing, and the evolving service-dominant logic are among the labels applied to these theorizing tendencies. Important among them is the experiential marketing framework.

The experiential marketing framework claims adherents across national boundaries, across methodological orientations, and among practitioners and consultants (Pine and Gilmore, 1999; Schmitt, 1999), as well as theoreticians. Further, it appears to incorporate a number of elements from a relatively long period of conceptualization into a potentially fruitful way of approaching today's rapidly evolving marketspaces.

What all of these tendencies, of which the experiential marketing prospective is one of the most fruitful, have in common is an assertion of the co-creative role of what have traditionally been called consumers in the production of commercial outcomes. As Vargo and Lusch (2004) now argue, marketers mobilize operand (tangible things such as products and servicescapes) and operant (intangible things such as core competences and brand images) resources to deliver offerings into marketspace. And, indeed, that is all that marketers can do. They cannot induce satisfaction, loyalty, or perceived value in the targets of their marketing efforts. In fact, Vargo and Lusch argue that the marketing process is completed only if and when consumers mobilize their own operant and operand resources to avail themselves of the services that firms' market offerings propose, and extract value-in-use from these services. For example, sports brands provide a potential range of services to consumers: ranging from improved performance or safety to identification with the image of the celebrity sports spokesperson whose persona is associated with the brand (McCracken, 1989; Codeluppi, Chapter 11 in this volume). Through performances ranging from skillful execution of a basketball jump shot to being seen in the right place, at the right time, and with the right relevant others, the consumer extracts the value-in-use delivered by this service. We have diagrammed this conception (Arnould *et al.*, 2006) in which co-production is the experiential marketspace (Figure 13.1).

The point of this is that consumer experience may be thought of as the outcome of the value extraction processes in which consumer engage, a proposition amply demonstrated across the cases reported in this volume. In the remainder of this brief contribution, I want to highlight what I think of as some organizing concepts for a fully developed consumer-centric notion of experience and bring in a few elements that may enrich future discussions this book will surely animate. In this regard, I want to discuss the performance metaphor, two important performative modalities, press the issue of how it is that consumers appropriate commercial experience, and then, finally, end with a conceptual question, does the experiential metaphor mean that we have reached the end of the useful life of the consumer construct?

THE PERFORMANCE METAPHOR

I would like to suggest the enduring and still relatively underused value of the performance metaphor in discussions of experiential marketing. The performance metaphor has emerged

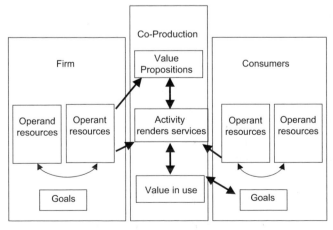

Figure 13.1 *Firm and consumer resource interaction.*

to organize, understand, and explain the significance of a broad range of cultural forms, including consumer behaviors. In fact, foreshadowing Vargo and Lusch (2004), Deighton (1992) argues that performance or purposive action is a necessary condition that gives rise to all consumption experience. In other words, consumers behave as if they were audiences responding to or participating in performances with products, services, retail environments, and commercially staged experiences. A consumption performance assumes a plot-like form; importantly, therefore, it has a narrative dimension, involving anticipation, tension, and resolution; it has a rhetorical purpose and enlists participants in the action. All performance takes places in space and over time.

Drawing on a diverse literature, Deighton developed a still useful typology of consumer performances differentiated by the extent to which consumers play a passive consumer or active co-constructive prosumerist role in the performance, and whether the performance takes place in a naturalistic, realistic setting, or an artificial, fantastic setting (Figure 13.2).

Skill performance is the staged display of competence in a naturalistic setting for the benefit of a passive observer, as exemplified in the professional service provision of lawyers and accountants for instance. In this volume, the charming description of Italian youth discovering the commensal pleasures of cooking pasta for guests (see Dalli and Romani, Chapter 5 in this volume) documents the process of developing a skill performance. This depiction implies that marketers might usefully develop communications with young Italians anxious to acquire or improve their skills in pasta-based meal production.

Thrill performance refers to the active participation by the consumer in naturalistic

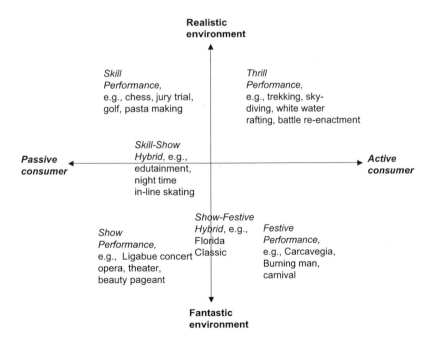

Figure 13.2 Classifying consumer performances (adapted from Deighton 1992; Stamps and Arnould 1998).

activity in which the staging, while present, is not intrusive. Ladwein (Chapter 7 in this volume) discussed an example of a thrill performance, adventure trekking.

A show performance has elements of spectacle: extravagant display, separation of audience and performers, and rhetorical amplification of moral values (DeBord, 1994/1977; Firat and Venkatesh, 1995). Show performances incorporate rich, complex visual images and environments that convey cultural meanings that consumers/participants understand. Further, interest lies not with the outcome, but in the process. The action that unfolds at the utopian retail islands described by Badot and Filser (Chapter 12 in this volume) and Ligabue's rock concerts described by Santoro and Troilo (Chapter 8 in this volume) are two diverse examples of show performances. The Live 8 global concert series for African aid in 2005 provides an excellent illustration as well.

In festival performances, events unfold in a fairly ritualistic and predictable manner within relatively narrow limits, retaining the artificiality of staging characteristic of show performances. Nevertheless, festival-like events allow for more interchange in the roles of audience and performer, and exhibit multiple, rather than singular, foci of action and attention. Ligabue's unplugged performances, as described by Santoro and Troilo (Chapter 8 in this volume), are perhaps an example. However, the most striking examples in this volume are found in Chapter 2 by Sherry, Kozinets, and Borghini, where descriptions of a variety of fire-based ritual festivals in North America and Italy draw attention to the role of prosumption ritual and sacrifice. Indeed, all of the festive performance rituals they discuss – Burning Man, Carcavegia, the Ducati motorcycle, and custom automobile – involve fire (external and internal fires respectively). Insofar as many theorists argue that ritual, and especially sacrifice, is at the origin of culture itself (Miller, 1998), the fascination of such festive performances is not hard to understand. Hence, when consumers are investing in such rituals, they are no longer acting as consumers, those who consume resources that others are providing. In fact, they are acting as protagonists, producers of narrative, historical, and cultural resources, as indeed Sherry *et al.* intimate (Chapter 2 in this volume).

This fourfold classification admits of hybrid forms, as Stamps and Arnould (1998) discuss in describing the Florida Classic show-festive performance. The night-time skating activities of the Parisian inline skaters described by Cova and Cova (2001) could similarly be reinterpreted as hybrid skill–show performances. In this volume, we might well conceive of edutainment discussed by Podestà and Addis in Chapter 10 as a hybrid performative form combining elements of skill and show performances.

The point of classificatory schemes such as Deighton's is twofold. First, it helps us sort out the myriad forms of experiential consumption into meaningful groups. Second, it suggests the kinds of interventions that marketers may undertake to increase the value people derive from commercial experiences. Thus, in experiences in which consumers take an active role, marketers must play a background, supportive role, as apparently have some of the skating companies in Cova and Cova's (2001) example. If they attempt to overproduce, direct, or control experiences, participants will reject them. Stamps and Arnould (1998) refer to a major gaffe in this regard by a local retail mall. In contrast, where consumers take a more passive role, marketers may deliver both more operant and operand resources into the marketspace as in edutainment and in the utopian retail islands described by Badot and Filser (Chapter 12 in this volume).

TWO PERFORMATIVE MODALITIES

I would like to turn my attention for a moment to two performance modalities that contribute to the formation of consumer experiences, but which remain somewhat implicit in the chapters in this volume. We can think of commercial landscapes or marketspaces as contingent, interlocking outcomes of the deployment of managerial strategies and consumer resources and inputs. As argued elsewhere (Arnould *et al.*, 1998), commercial landscapes are produced through both substantive and communicative staging, and we can find high or low levels of substantive staging combined with either high or low levels of communicative staging, thus producing another fourfold classificatory model. Substantive staging refers to the physical creation of contrived environments, a marketer-controlled operand resource. Santoro and Troilo (Chapter 8 in this volume) detail many elements of the substantive staging that provides raw material for the experiences consumers derive from Ligabue concerts. Similarly, Badot and Filser (Chapter 12 in this volume) dwell on the substantive staging of utopian malls, divining elements that are needed to create these performance spaces. Finally, Hetzel (Chapter 9 in this volume) describes the clever substantive staging of Miyake's A-POC brand in fashion shows, retail venues, and, indeed, on Miyake's Internet sites, showing how substantive staging may become a multichannel affair. Even servicescapes that emphasize authenticity ranging from zoological flight cages and safari parks to Caribbean scuba diving-oriented resorts are contrived, as Ladwein (Chapter 7 in this volume) points out in the context of trekking adventures.

The authors in this volume dwell far less than one might like on the communicative staging of consumer experiences, an operant resource. Communicative staging refers to ways in which the environment is presented and interpreted by commercial service providers or by consumer adepts and experts who become implicit or explicit confederates of marketers. Communicative staging involves the transmission of experiential meanings, both those directly related to the delivery of commercial offerings and those transcending the instrumental context. Communicative staging moves meanings from commercial landscapes through service providers to customer, between customers, and, potentially at least, from customers to providers. Communicative staging is patterned through the who, what, how, and when of communication. And it requires the active participation of both service providers and clients; and as suggested in the Santoro and Troilo and Sherry, Kozinets, and Borghini chapters (Chapters 8 and 2 in this volume respectively), communicative staging relies for its effectiveness on a mutuality of cultural understandings.

To illustrate, servicescapes typically use at least some substantive staging, and may combine that with either high or low levels of communicative staging. For example, a restaurant serving French cuisine may decorate in a manner redolent of Provençal life; this is substantive staging. It may also print the menu in French, hire French-speaking wait staff, and feature a singer of Edith Piaf songs. This is communicative staging.

Previous research, like much of the research in this volume, has stressed the substantive staging of the consumer experiences over communicative staging. Yet, servicescapes can be dramatically affected by communicative staging. Arnould *et al.* (1998) showed that, through their actions and commentaries on the natural environment, white water river guides helped consumers sort their experiences in the "same" landscape into narratives consistent with four different, enduring myths about the American wilderness. They include the view of wild nature as: a transcendental force; a molder of human character; a restorative, healing agency; and as a refuge, whose irreplaceability and complexity makes it essential to conserve and preserve. Ladwein (Chapter 7 in this volume) similarly shows how certain pervasive narrative themes structure trekkers' experiences, although he does not detail the role of providers in helping consumers structure their experiences narratively. Similarly, Chronis *et al.* (n.d.) show how service providers help consumers reframe their experiences of the historical events that unfolded 160 years ago at the Gettysburg Civil War battlefield into stories about heroism, redemption, freedom, and patriotic unity. In future research on experiential consumption, we need far more work on the communicative staging of commercial experiences if we are to realize the full potential of the experiential marketing framework.

CONSUMER APPROPRIATION OF EXPERIENCE

A further issue of great importance is contained in the question: How do consumers derive value from experiences that they variously perform? Ladwein (Chapter 7 in this volume) makes the point that "The ongoing ambiguity that consists of both soliciting danger yet hoping that the risks are not excessive (or are at least under control) can be grasped via the notion of an 'event'." Thus, he points to the fact that it is only when consumers narratively bracket out from the relentless flow of sensory experience the realization that something is happening that events can become experiences. This is especially likely when consumers experience narrative "transportation," or what Carù and Cova (Chapter 3 in this volume) term immersion into consumption experience.

Deighton (1992) furthers the discussion of some of the ways in which consumers derive experiential value from events. He remarks that commercial providers of experiences provide settings and sanction particular kinds of actions. However, consumer performers must also construct narratives built up from the raw materials provided by commercial providers and their own actions. They do so, as a number of chapters in this volume show, by drawing on their beliefs about human motivation and emotion, upon lay psychology, upon cultural blueprints for action and interpretation such as mythic templates (Holt and Thompson, 2004; Thompson, 2004). Marketers often suggest narrative elements, as in the types of activities substantively staged at ESPN Zone (Kozinets *et al.*, 2004), or the themed restaurants that Deighton describes, but consumers actively create much of the rest. Arnould (2005) suggests that consumers deploy narrative frames that reimagine marketer's value propositions in terms of consumers' own life projects. Narrative reframing introduces active consumer agency into the firm-supplied resource by associating the consumer's self, life project, and goals with the firm-provided resources. Both Heilbrunn and Badot and Filser (Chapters 6 and 12 in this volume respectively) seem to be thinking along similar lines in inviting attention to mundane subject—object relationships, and the trajectories consumers take through retail utopias respectively. More specifically, consumers create experiences out of commercial performances by way of several specific narrative devices such as filling narrative gaps, recontextualizing, and imagining, processes detailed in Chronis *et al.*'s (n.d.) discussion of consumer narrative experiences at the Gettysburg battlefield in the USA.

To fully understand the value of experiences to consumers and how marketers could successfully co-create them with consumers, researchers still need to know a lot more about the different types of consumers' narrative frames and devices that consumers employ, the operation of transportation or immersion, the ways in which narrative frames and devices facilitate value-adding performances by firm-provided resources, and how marketer-provided resources cue consumer narrative practices that turn performances into experiences.

THE END OF THE CONSUMER?

The authors of this volume are perhaps too wise or too circumspect to say so directly, but it seems to me that adopting an experiential marketing framework calls into question the continued scientific and managerial utility of the consumer construct. For example, Carù and Cova (Chapter 3 in this volume) discreetly suggest,

> Self-determination is rooted in a vision that equates consumers with protagonists, who are traditionally considered to be operating in reaction to something. The idea here is that consumers are trying to be less passive and injecting a personal touch into their consumption experiences. Self-determination is based on the idea of consumers' active participation in an experience.

The key point here is that the "consumer" has indeed been typically conceived in marketing as a reactor, someone who responds to the rhetorical blandishments of marketing and advertising. Indeed, this notion of consumers as manipulable reactors is built not only into a lot of management literature, including some of that dealing with experiential marketing (Schmitt, 1999), but also into that literature that ostensibly critiques these practices (e.g., Packard, 1957; Miller, 1998; Schor, 1998; Ewen, 2001). Alternatively, we may follow the experiential logic that Hetzel (Chapter 9 in this volume) expresses,

> . . . experiential marketing has accentuated a new vision of how companies view their customers. The latter are no longer purely thought of as existing at "the end of the chain" but as fully-fledged actors with whom the company will try to develop a relationship wherein both parties act as the "co-builders" of what is going to occur.

If so, then we must move away from passive constructions of consumer action. This means, for instance, as Cova and Rémy (Chapter 4 in this volume) point out, that:

> A customer's "*intention to*" should be distinguished from the notion of motivation that is so often used in marketing. Motivation is linked to the individual so that a new

equilibrium can be found wherever needs are unsatisfied – whereas intention is linked to an act under the egis of an identity-laden logic, the purpose being to offer meaning.

But this is indeed a radical proposition for mainstream marketing. For it means that consumers are indeed no longer the "end of the chain" but the beginning of the chain and, further, that the marketers' goals can play only a role secondary to the intentionality of agentic persons. The hoary notion of motivation to achieve psychological balance through need satisfaction is replaced with the proactive goal-oriented notion of intention, thus opening the space for creation and, indeed, transformation through commercial experience. Dalli and Romani (Chapter 5 in this volume) develop this critique quite explicitly. And they take the next step of implicitly asking whether the experiential perspective calls into question the utility of the notion of consumption itself when marketers' offerings are secondary to the value-in-use that people derive from the services they provide, in their case the emotional, linking value (Cova, 1997) derived from the preparation of pasta:

> the role of "consumption" is clearly secondary to that of preparation, in which the conditions are created for the development of an emotional relationship, whose importance goes well beyond any material or commercial consideration. That the "product" then appears to be appreciated by the other players in the situation is completely secondary.

Now, if we take Dalli and Romani's point that consumption is now secondary to preparation or production, and "preparation," "immersion," and "transformation" are privileged outcomes of commercial experience, then how are we to reimagine the actors who instigate commercial experiences? None of the authors in this volume throws down a polemical figurative gauntlet on this point, but Cova and Rémy (Chapter 4 in this volume) imply that a new term is needed when they propose:

> we will be focusing on the experiences of *prosumers* who take it upon themselves to weave realities that are more human, genuine and political, but also less commercial, in nature.

Whether one chooses "protagonist," "consum'actor," "prosumer," or some other neologism of choice, the point of these awkward verbal gestures is that the co-creative producer of genuine, political, less commercial experiences is far removed from the passive mass market consumer of the postwar consumerist boom (Cohen, 2003). Our scientific language must hasten to catch up with her in the very near future.

DISCUSSION QUESTIONS

- Is the classic four Ps model thrown into question in the context of the new experiential marketing theorizing?
- What kinds of consumption performances do you most engage in? Which do you find most enjoyable?
- Can you identify some servicescapes that are especially well or especially poorly staged either substantively or communicatively or both?
- Think about stories of commercial experiences you tell or have heard. What makes them memorable?
- So, are you a consumer, a protagonist, consum'actor, a prosumer, or something else? What defines your relationship to the marketplace?

REFERENCES

Arnould, E.J. (2005) "Animating the Big Middle." *Journal of Retailing* 81(2): 89–96.

Arnould, E.J., Price, L.L. and Tierney, P. (1998) "Communicative Staging of the Wilderness Servicescape." *Service Industries Journal* 18(3): 90–115.

Arnould, E.J., Price, L.L. and Malshe, A. (2006) "Toward a Cultural Resource-Based Theory of the Customer." In: Lusch, R.F. and Vargo, S.L. (eds) *The New Dominant Logic in Marketing*. Armonk, NY: M.E. Sharpe.

Chronis, A., Hampton, R.D. and Arnould, E.J. (n.d.) "Gettysburg Re-Imagined: The Role of Narrative Imagination in Consumption Experience." Unpublished manuscript. Turlock, CA: California State University–Stanislaus.

Cohen, L. (2003) *A Consumers' Republic: The Politics of Mass Consumption in Postwar America*. New York: Knopf.

Cova, B. (1997) "Community and Consumption: Towards a Definition of the 'Linking Value' of Product or Services." *European Journal of Marketing* 3(3,4): 297–316.

Cova, B. and Cova, V. (2001) "Tribal Aspects of Postmodern Consumption Research: The Case of French In-Line Roller Skates." *Journal of Consumer Behaviour* 1(June), 67–76.

Debord, G. (1994/1977) *The Society of the Spectacle*. New York: Zone Books.

Deighton, J. (1992) "The Consumption of Performance." *Journal of Consumer Research* 19(Dec): 362–372.

Ewen, S. (2001) *Captains of Consciousness: Advertising and the Social Roots of the Consumer Culture*, 25th Anniversary edn. New York: Basic Books.

Firat, A.F. and Venkatesh, A. (1995) "Liberatory Postmodernism and the Reenchantment of Consumption." *Journal of Consumer Research* 22(Dec): 239–268.

Holt, D.B. and Thompson, C.J. (2004) "Man-of-Action Heroes: The Pursuit of Heroic Masculinity in Everyday Consumption." *Journal of Consumer Research* 31(Sept): 425–441.

Kozinets, R., Storm, D., Duhachek, A., Nuttavuthist, K. and DeBerry-Spence, B. (2004) "Ludic Agency and Retail Spectacle." *Journal of Consumer Research* 31(Dec): 658–672.

McCracken, G. (1989) "Who Is the Celebrity Endorser? Cultural Foundations of the Endorsement Process." *Journal of Consumer Research* 16(Dec): 310–322.

Miller, M.C. (1988) *Boxed In: The Culture of TV*. Evanston, IL: Northwestern University Press.

Packard, V.O. (1957) *The Hidden Persuaders*. New York: MacKay.

Pine, B.J. and Gilmore, J.H. (1999) *The Experience Economy: Work is Theatre and Every Business a Stage*. Boston: Harvard Business School Press.

Schmitt, B.H. (1999) *Experiential Marketing: How to Get Customers to SENSE, FEEL, THINK, ACT and RELATE to Your Company and Brands*. New York: The Free Press.

Schor, J. (1998) *The Overspent American: Upscaling, Downshifting, and the New Consumer*. New York: Basic Books.

Stamps, M.B. and Arnould, E.J. (1998) "The Florida Classic: Performing African American Community." In: Alba, J.W. and Hutchinson, W. (eds) *Advances in Consumer Research*, Vol. 25. Provo, UT: Association for Consumer Research, 578–584.

Thompson, C.J. (2004) "Marketplace Mythology and Discourses of Power." *Journal of Consumer Research* 31(June): 162–181.

Vargo, S.L. and Lusch, R.F. (2004) "Evolving to a New Dominant Logic for Marketing." *Journal of Marketing* 68(Jan): 1–17.

Index

197